W9-BLQ-451

Events That Changed
America in the
Eighteenth Century

Events That Changed America in the Eighteenth Century

edited by
John E. Findling
&
Frank W. Thackeray

THE GREENWOOD PRESS
"EVENTS THAT CHANGED AMERICA" SERIES

GREENWOOD PRESS
Westport, Connecticut • London

Library of Congress Cataloging-in-Publication Data

Events that changed America in the eighteenth century / edited by John
  E. Findling and Frank W. Thackeray.
      p.   cm.—(The Greenwood Press "Events that changed America"
  series)
    Includes bibliographical references (p.   ) and index.
    ISBN 0–313–29082–2 (alk. paper)
      1. United States—History—Colonial period, ca. 1600–1775.
    2. United States—History—Revolution, 1775–1783.   3. United States—
    History—1783–1815.   I. Findling, John E.   II. Thackeray, Frank W.
    III. Series.
    E195.E94   1998
    973—dc21   97–48573

British Library Cataloguing in Publication Data is available.

Library of Congress Catalog Card Number: 97–48573
ISBN: 0–313–29082–2

First published in 1998

Greenwood Press, 88 Post Road West, Westport, CT 06881
An imprint of Greenwood Publishing Group, Inc.

Printed in the United States of America

The paper used in this book complies with the
Permanent Paper Standard issued by the National
Information Standards Organization (Z39.48–1984).

10 9 8 7 6 5 4 3

Contents

Illustrations

Preface

This volume, which describes and evaluates the significance of ten of the most important events in the United States during the eighteenth century, is the third in a multivolume series intended to acquaint readers with the seminal events of American history. Earlier volumes, published in 1996 and 1997, highlighted events in the twentieth and nineteenth centuries, and a future volume will cover the most important events prior to the eighteenth century. There is also an ongoing series of volumes addressing the global experience.

Our collective classroom experience provided the inspiration for this project. Having encountered literally thousands of entry-level college students whose knowledge of the history of their country was sadly deficient, we determined to prepare a series of books that would concentrate on the most important events affecting those students (and others as well) in the hope that they would better understand their country and how it came to be. Furthermore, we hope these books will stimulate the reader to delve further into the events covered in each volume and to take a greater interest in history in general.

The current volume is designed to serve two purposes. First, the editors have provided an introduction that presents factual material about each event in a clear, concise, chronological order. Second, each introduction is followed by a longer, interpretive essay by a specialist exploring the ramifications of the event under consideration. Each essay concludes with an annotated bibliography of the most important works about the event. The ten chapters are followed by three appendices that provide additional information useful to the reader. Appendix A is a glossary of names, events, organizations, and terms mentioned but not fully explained in the introductions and essays. Appendix B is a timeline of key eighteenth-century events, and Appendix C traces the population growth of each of the thirteen colonies (and, after 1776, states) and several colonial towns during the eighteenth century.

The events covered in this volume were selected on the basis of our combined teaching and research activities. Of course, another pair of editors might have arrived at a somewhat different list than we did, but we believe that we have assembled a group of events that truly changed America in the eighteenth century.

As with all published works, numerous people behind the scenes deserve much of the credit for the final product. Barbara Rader, our editor at Greenwood Publishing Group, has encouraged us from the very beginning. The staff of the Photographic Division of the Library of Congress provided genial assistance to us as we selected the photographs that appear in this book. Our student research assistant, Bob Marshall, was helpful at many stages of the project. We are especially grateful to Brigette Colligan, who was always ready to type or retype whatever we asked her to. Carol Findling and Jo Ann Waterbury helped with word-processing in the final stage of the project. Various staff members of the Indiana University Southeast (IUS) computer center cheerfully unscrambled disks and turned mysterious word-processing programs into something we could work with. We benefited from funds that IUS provided to hire student research assistants and pay for other costs associated with the project. Special thanks to Roger and Amy Baylor and Kate O'Connell for making their establishment available to us, enabling us to confer about this project and discuss its many facets with our colleagues and former students in a congenial atmosphere at a time when our campus administration was not inclined to provide that sort of supportive environment. Among those who helped us in one way or another to make this a better book are John Newman, Sam Sloss, Sheila Anderson, Kim Pelle, Brook Dutko, Andrew Trout, and Deborah Bulleit. And, most important, we thank our authors, whose essays were well-conceived and thoughtful and whose patience when the project seemed to lag was much appreciated.

Finally, we wish to express our appreciation to our spouses, Carol Findling and Kathy Thackeray, and to our children, Jamey and Jenny Findling and Alex and Max Thackeray, whose patience with us and interest in our work made it all worthwhile.

John E. Findling
Frank W. Thackeray

George Whitefield, shown here in a typical preaching pose, was one of the leading lights of the Great Awakening. (Reproduced from the Collections of the Library of Congress)

The Great Awakening, c. 1730s–1760

INTRODUCTION

The Great Awakening is a term used to describe a significant outburst of enthusiastic religious feeling that swept the colonies in the 1740s and continued to exert influence on colonial culture nearly until the Revolutionary era. Its roots and substance are both rather complex and varied among the different regions of colonial America, but its consequence was far-reaching in the changes it brought to American religion.

Religion, of course, was one of the principal motivating forces for those who came to America in the seventeenth century. This was especially true in New England, where Pilgrims and then Puritans (who rapidly absorbed the Pilgrims) came in search of the freedom to worship as they pleased. Strict and zealous, the first generation of Puritans set up a theocratic society in which religion affected every aspect of one's daily life. However, as non-Puritans moved into New England and as the first generation gave way to the second and third generations of Puritans, much of the earliest zealousness wore off. The society became more secular, fewer people were becoming "Saints," that is, experiencing the mystical act of conversion that marked one as a person in a state of grace, and there was concern that the church was becoming irrelevant. An attempt to stem the drift away from the church was seen in the so-called

Halfway Covenant of 1662, in which Puritan ministers agreed to baptize the children of those people who themselves had not had the conversion experience. This kept more people in the church (and subject to its moral code) but did not really do much to increase the rate of conversions to grace. By the late eighteenth century, Puritan ministers were worrying less about conversion and more about improving society based on their moralistic beliefs.

One way in which this was done was through the implementation of public expressions of faith and conscience, in what we call a religious revival. It was a way in which the religious message could be brought to everyone, whether they attended church or not, and it was a way in which the prevailing apathy about religion could be attacked. Among the most effective of the revivalists was Solomon Stoddard, Jonathan Edwards' grandfather, who organized massive revivals (he called them "harvests") on several occasions between 1679 and 1718. After Stoddard's death in 1729, Edwards continued his work and for some twenty years was the most heralded preacher in New England. In a sense, Edwards reverted to the old Puritan doctrine of a stern and omnipotent God, combining this with the new evangelistic preaching style of revivalistic religion. He called upon his listeners to return to the faith of their fathers and spoke in often terrifying images of the absolute sovereignty of God, the depravity of man, and salvation by God's grace alone. An excellent writer and fine (though not dramatic) public speaker, he had the ability to captivate his audience by his vivid descriptions of hell and what those who were not saved would experience when they got there. One of his best sermons, given in Enfield, Connecticut, in 1741, was titled "Sinners in the Hands of An Angry God," and phrases such as these were said to have produced "breathing of distress and weeping":

> Your wickedness makes you as it were heavy as lead, and to tend downwards with great weight and pressure towards hell; and if God should let you go, you would immediately sink and swiftly descend and plunge into the bottomless gulf. . . .
>
> O Sinner! Consider the fearful danger you are in; it is a great furnace of wrath, a wide and bottomless pit, full of the fire of wrath, that you are held over in the hand of God. . . . You hang by a slender thread, with the flames of divine wrath flashing about it, and ready every moment to singe it, and burn it asunder.

In the middle colonies, New York, New Jersey, Pennsylvania, Maryland, and Delaware, the situation was considerably different. Settlers from a range of ethnic origins came to these colonies, and brought with them a number of different religious creeds that produced a far more diverse and tolerant society than existed in New England. Rather than a colonial-supported religion, legislative assemblies allowed communities to determine what religion would be subsidized by taxes, and in Pennsylvania, legislators determined that no religion should receive tax support. Into this environment came German pietism, a form of religious belief that stressed a personal relationship with God, based on a high sense of morality and emotionally expressive church services. The nature of pietism lent itself to revivalism, and in the 1720s and 1730s, Theodorus Frelinghuysen and William and Gilbert Tennent, a father-and-son team, led successful revivals in New Jersey. Compared with Edwards' message, that of Frelinghuysen and the Tennents was refreshingly optimistic.

The southern colonies, from Virginia to Georgia (not founded until 1733), were nominally Anglican in religion, and although colonial taxes supported that church, relatively few people attended services or paid attention to the moral guidelines. Moreover, slaves were barred from participating in church life. Into this atmosphere came George Whitefield in 1739. The greatest orator among the preachers of the Great Awakening, Whitefield came to America from England, where he had been a follower of John Wesley, the founder of Methodism, which at that time was a movement within the Anglican church and not a separate denomination. Whitefield was also familiar with and influenced by German pietism and its emotion-laden message. He was not a forceful-looking individual, but his voice could reach an audience of up to 20,000 in a day long before mechanical or electronic amplification. Not only could he project well, but also he had a marvelously dramatic speaking style that had a great emotional impact on his audiences. It was said that he could bring an entire crowd to tears just by the way he said "Mesopotamia." His message, which theologically was somewhere in between those of Edwards and the German pietists, was popular all over the colonies and brought him countless invitations to speak from the pulpits of local ministers from Georgia to New England. Whitefield's tours brought about the Great Awakening on a national scale.

The Great Awakening reached its fullest bloom during the decade of the 1740s, partly because of Whitefield's presence during the early part of that decade and partly because of social and economic conditions of the time. In the late 1730s, a serious diphtheria epidemic struck the colonies; perhaps as many as 20,000 people, including many children, died of the then mysterious "throat distemper." In any time period, sudden and unexplained epidemics will convince many people of their helplessness in the face of powerful natural forces, and they will seek solace in religion. The diphtheria epidemic made people pay more attention to what Whitefield and others were preaching.

In addition, the 1740s were years of relatively bad economic times in many parts of the colonies. This was a result of the War of Jenkins' Ear, which began between England and Spain in 1739 over an incident in which Spaniards had mutilated a British sea captain's ear. A more generalized European conflict, the War of the Austrian Succession, which lasted from 1740 until 1748, followed this minor affair. The war disrupted the lucrative American trade in molasses and the export of American tobacco and other commodities to Europe; this caused prices to fall in the colonies, reducing farmers' income. The agricultural depression spread to other sectors of the economy, significantly reducing what Americans imported from England and causing distress throughout the colonies. While the increased level of poverty was bad enough, another social consequence seemed even more serious to many. Many families did not have enough money or work for all their children, who then left home to find work elsewhere. Freed from their parents' (often strict) supervision, they also found illicit romance wherever they went, and the incidence of premarital sex and children born less than six months after marriage rose rapidly, a fact of life that caused great consternation among a traditionally religious people and became fodder for the evangelists.

The Great Awakening did not sweep across the colonies without arousing controversy. Traditional religious leaders soon came to perceive the evangelists as a threat to their established churches and began to take action to suppress their message. In New England, the more conservative Congregationalist (the denomination into which Puritanism had evolved) leaders came to be known as "Old Lights," and the revival leaders as "New Lights." Fearful of losing their flocks to the New Lights, the Old Lights in Connecticut used their influence with the colonial assembly to get legislation passed that barred itinerant preachers from working in the colony. Thus when Whitefield returned to Connecticut in 1744, he found that he could no longer speak in many churches. Although the effort of the Old Lights caused so much resentment that it probably hurt their cause before the New Lights managed to get the law repealed in 1750, the incident reflects the tension between the two sides.

In many towns in Connecticut, congregations split between followers of the Old Lights and those who cast their lot with the New Lights.

In New England, the New Lights split among themselves. While all of them were nominally Congregationalists, there was dispute first over the degree to which each congregation should be autonomous, and later over the issue of infant baptism and whether that sacrament should be offered to the offspring of adults who had not experienced conversion. Many people left the Congregationalist church over this issue and joined the rising Baptist church, where baptism was the most important sacrament.

In the south, and especially in Virginia, the Baptist church arose during the Great Awakening and made great progress in winning souls from the Anglican church by the 1760s. The Baptists followed the New Light Presbyterians, who had tried and failed to shake the authority of the established Anglicans in the 1740s. In the case of the Baptists, the differences were class-based rather than theological. The landed gentry in Virginia dominated the Anglican church just as it dominated all other aspects of society. The church reciprocated, in a sense, by condoning what many small landowners and working-class people considered to be a casually amoral lifestyle. Upper-class Virginians reveled in their wealth, drank excessively, gambled on horse races and other contests, and abused their slaves, sexually and in other ways. By the 1760s, itinerant Baptist preachers were giving emotional sermons to crowds of ordinary people, attacking the lifestyles of the rich and famous, condemning slavery, and encouraging a far more egalitarian society, even to the point of urging church members to call each other "brother" and "sister." Moreover, the ordinary people found comfort in the ritual of the baptism sacrament, in which large numbers of people, having heard enough emotional sermons to be "born again," were baptized together in a ceremony in which they were completely immersed in water.

The Anglican gentry soon took notice and responded. Some complaints were rather frivolous: "The Baptists in Loudoun County [are] quite destroying pleasure in the Country; for they encourage ardent Prayer, strong & constant faith, & an intire Banishment of *Gaming, Dancing*, and Sabbath-Day Diversions" (quoted in Henretta and Nobles, *Evolution and Revolution* [1987], p. 111). More seriously, bands of angry men, often led by the local sheriff, broke up Baptist revivals and beat or whipped the preacher. Nothing really worked; by the 1770s, some 20 percent of white Virginians, as well as many slaves, had become Baptists.

Although the Great Awakening was, to a large extent, based on the emotional appeal of people like Jonathan Edwards and George Whitefield, it did have an intellectual side, seen in the founding by new churches of colleges at which ministers could be trained. Thus, in 1746, the Presbyterians founded the College of New Jersey, later Princeton; in 1754, the Anglicans founded King's College in New York, later Columbia; in 1764, the Baptists established the College of Rhode Island, later Brown; in 1766, the Dutch Reformed Church founded Queen's College, later Rutgers; and in 1769, the Congregationalists organized Dartmouth College.

INTERPRETIVE ESSAY
Carl E. Kramer

During the middle of the eighteenth century, from the 1730s through the 1760s, a wave of religious revivalism swept through the British colonies in North America. This era of religious enthusiasm, later called the Great Awakening, not only marked the emergence of revivalism as a characteristic feature of American religious life, but also generated a host of conflicts which divided several existing denominational bodies, altered traditional lines of social authority, and added a new layer of religious diversity to the emerging American society.

The roots of America's religious diversity are centuries old. When Spanish and French Roman Catholics began colonizing North America during the sixteenth century, they also confronted—and attempted to convert—native populations who had their own religious traditions. During the seventeenth century, English colonizers established the Anglican church in Virginia and the Carolinas. But these were theologically troubled times in England, and English dissenters also made their presence felt in the New World. Particularly notable were the colonizing and settlement efforts of various branches of English Calvinism whose ministers preached the doctrine of predestination and sought to reform the Church of England. In 1620 radical Separatists established the Plymouth colony. Ten years later nonseparating Congregationalists, more commonly known as Puritans, created Massachusetts Bay. During the closing years of the century, Scotch-Irish Presbyterians began settling in North and South Carolina. Meanwhile, in the mid-1630s, Puritan exiles such as Roger Williams and Anne Hutchinson moved into Rhode Island, which became a Baptist stronghold. During the late 1650s, Rhode Island became a haven for Quakers, some two decades before establishment of the first

Quaker settlements in New Jersey and Pennsylvania. Further enriching this mixture were Dutch Reformed elements who founded New York, German Reformed and Lutherans who settled in Pennsylvania, and a host of German pietists who began arriving, particularly in the Middle Colonies, during the late seventeenth and early eighteenth centuries.

Although religion played a profound role in motivating settlement in North America, by the early eighteenth century many observers were beginning to detect a severe deterioration in the quality of spiritual life. This was particularly the case in New England, the bastion of Puritanism. The founders of Massachusetts Bay, under the leadership of John Winthrop, had hoped to fashion a Biblical Commonwealth—a "City upon a Hill"—whose example would help redeem the world from sin and create a model by which the Church of England could be reformed. Such a mission required strict discipline and adherence to a personal covenant between God and man. But vision and reality soon diverged.

Among a people so committed, differences of opinion over theological and political issues were inevitable. Such conflicts resulted not only in the exile of Roger Williams in 1636 and the expulsion of Anne Hutchinson in 1638, but also prompted Thomas Hooker's move in 1634 to the Connecticut River valley, where he established Hartford, one of a cluster of towns that eventually evolved into the colony of Connecticut. Several crises during the second half of the seventeenth century further undermined the Puritan mission. A particularly troublesome ecclesiastical issue was the question of church membership for the children and grandchildren of Puritan saints who were baptized but unregenerate. During the late 1650s and early 1660s, church councils in Connecticut and Massachusetts resolved the problem with the Halfway Covenant, which based church membership on baptism but confined communion and voting powers to the regenerate. A more tragic crisis was King Philip's War in 1675–1676, which interrupted a promising program of Indian evangelism and gave the Puritans a feeling that the conflict was a manifestation of divine punishment.

These crises occurred within a society that was experiencing the growing pains of immigration, mobility, town formation, and commercial expansion. As new opportunities appeared and more and more unregenerate persons arrived, the authority of ministers and the church declined. The collapse of the Puritan Revolution and the Stuart Restoration in England in 1660, revocation of the Massachusetts Bay Company charter by King Charles II in 1684, and the Salem witchcraft episode in the 1690s further contributed to the erosion of spiritual life in New England. As the eighteenth century dawned, a new generation of ministers, such as Cotton Mather, began calling for spiritual renewal.

In the Middle Colonies, already the most religiously diverse region in British North America, revival was rooted deeply in immigration. By the early eighteenth century, Pennsylvania, New York, and New Jersey were attracting large numbers of settlers from Scotland, northern Ireland, and various German states. The Scottish and Scotch-Irish newcomers were predominantly Presbyterian, but the Germans included a mix of Reformed and Lutheran people along with adherents of numerous pietist sects.

For the Presbyterians, Reformed, and Lutherans, like their Dutch Reformed cousins, development of a sound institutional structure was a major preoccupation. The Reformed and Lutheran churches accomplished this goal with a minimum of conflict. But among the Presbyterians, issues of church structure became a source of controversy. The first American presbytery was organized in Philadelphia in 1706. Its founders included ministers from Scotland, northern Ireland, and New England. Over the next decade, they established three new presbyteries and a synod. During the years that followed, however, a growing number of Scotch-Irish immigrants arrived in America, upsetting the denomination's ethnic balance and generating intense arguments over issues such as the amount of authority that should be exercised by presbyteries and synods, educational requirements and other standards for approving ministers and ministerial candidates, and the degree of adherence which should be given to the Westminster Confession, compared with the Bible, as a standard for faith and practice. By the mid-1720s distinct parties or factions had emerged around these issues, creating fertile ground for potential revivalists.

The challenges faced by the Lutherans and the German and Dutch Reformed leaders were not so much structural as doctrinal. The source of the threat was the radical pietists such as the Mennonites, Dunkers, Moravians, and Schwenkfelders. Although they disagreed among themselves on many points, these sects shared common beliefs that the simple form of first-century Christianity was the ideal model of church organization; that the major Protestant bodies, like the Roman Catholic church, had become too encumbered by the sacraments, ministers, and dogmas; that the true church consisted only of "visible saints," not the totality of society; that the use of force and state authority to advance religion was unchristian and illegitimate; and that Christians should not become too deeply involved in the civil and social affairs of the world. Above all, they believed strongly in the importance of personal conversion, observance of strict spiritual and moral discipline, and vigorous biblically based preaching.

The situation in the South differed substantially from both New England and the Middle Colonies. Although the South was dominated by the Anglican church, large numbers of newcomers from the coastal areas and Pennsylvania were moving into western parts of Virginia, the Carolinas, and Georgia. Some were Presbyterians, Baptists, or German pietists, but thousands more had no religious affiliation. These frontier settlers consisted largely of former indentured servants and small farmers, many of whom resented what they perceived as the haughty ways of predominantly Anglican provincial leaders. In addition, the South had a growing slave population that was largely unchurched. Both white frontier settlers and African slaves were prime candidates for a massive missionary effort.

The first stirrings of Awakening occurred in Northampton, Massachusetts, where Solomon Stoddard served as pastor of the Congregational church for nearly sixty years. Like other Congregational pastors, Stoddard had to reckon with the Halfway Covenant. But unlike Cotton Mather, who condemned it for undermining the spiritual integrity of both church and community, Stoddard took advantage of the compromise. Instead of limiting the Lord's Supper to visible saints, he invited all baptized Christians into full church membership. Then he employed powerful, emotionally charged sermons to stir his members to conversion. By the time of Stoddard's death in 1729, Northampton had experienced five periods of revival.

Meanwhile, the Middle Colonies began to experience the sparks of revival. The key figure in initiating the movement was Theodorus Jacob Frelinghuysen, pastor of the Dutch Reformed church at Raritan, New Jersey. A native of the Netherlands who had arrived in America in 1720, Frelinghuysen was strongly influenced by the German pietists. In addition to preaching the importance of personal conversion and of living a holy life, he also observed strict standards for participation in the Lord's Supper. By the late 1720s his preaching had not only influenced many lay persons in Dutch Reformed congregations around Raritan, but also inspired a handful of Presbyterian ministers who would carry his message to a much broader audience.

If Stoddard and Frelinghuysen ignited the sparks of Awakening, then their protégés were responsible for fanning it into full blaze. Taking the torch from Stoddard was his brilliant grandson, Jonathan Edwards. After graduating at age seventeen from Yale College, where he finished first in his class, Edwards remained there to study for the ministry. In 1724 he became head tutor. He moved to Northampton three years later and became his grandfather's assistant. When Stoddard died, his grandson assumed his pulpit. Despite Northampton's history of revival activity, it seemed to the young pastor that his community was "very insensible of the things of religion." Indeed, he observed, "licentiousness . . . greatly prevailed among the youth" and many were "much addicted to night-walking, and frequenting the taverns, and lewd practices, wherein some by their example exceedingly corrupted others."

Employing a powerful preaching style that moved his hearers' emotions as well as their minds, Edwards gradually began to detect a distinct change in the hearts of his parishioners. In late 1734, while he was preaching a series of sermons on justification by faith, the intensity of the response quickened, especially after the conversion of a young woman whose morals had left something to be desired. During 1735 news of the events in Northampton began to spread to nearby towns such as South Hadley, Suffield, and Sunderland. As word of revival in these and other towns in frontier Massachusetts got back to Northampton, it further stimulated and strengthened the Awakening at its source.

The revival was not limited to Massachusetts. Within a relatively short time, the fervor spread to Edwards' home town of East Windsor, Connecticut, where his father was the Congregational pastor, as well as to Lebanon and New Haven. From there the revival moved eastward, from town to town, through the Connecticut River valley, toward the Atlantic Ocean. Although it had considerable impact in western Massachusetts and the Connecticut River valley, the Awakening had not yet affected the whole of New England. Indeed, Edwards himself considered the religious excitement that he had helped create as little more than a frontier revival, and by 1738 the fervor had begun to wane. But events were already under way in the Middle and Southern Colonies that would spread to New England and create "a great and general Awakening."

The same year that Jonathan Edwards ascended to his grandfather's pulpit, the Presbyterian Synod passed the Adopting Act of 1729. This measure produced an uneasy peace between the orthodox faction, which favored literal adherence to the Westminster Confession as a standard for ordination and believed that sessions, presbyteries, and synods should exercise strong legislative as well as administrative authority, and the emerging revivalist faction, which embraced a much less rigid stance on both issues. To the extent that the compromise moved away from orthodox positions, it was a victory for the revivalists.

Into this uneasy situation stepped William Tennent, Sr., an Irish-born Scotsman who had been ordained in the Episcopal Church of Ireland. After emigrating to America in 1716 he married the daughter of a Presbyterian minister and was ordained by his father-in-law's denomination two years later. During the years that followed, he served pastorates in Bedford, New York, and Neshaminy, Pennsylvania. Deeply influenced by Theodorus Frelinghuysen, he embraced an "experimental" Puritanism which held that a true Christian was one who had gone through a definable experience of regeneration, followed by assurance of salvation. He further taught these views to his sons, Gilbert, John, and William, Jr., who followed him into the ministry. Between 1729 and the late 1730s the congregations pastored by Tennent and his sons experienced a wave of revival. Helping to spread the fervor were graduates of a "Log College," or unofficial seminary, established by the elder Tennent at Neshaminy in 1726.

As the Presbyterian revival spurred by the Tennents gained momentum, it generated opposition, especially from a new wave of Scotch-Irish immigrants. A heated controversy erupted in 1738 when the synod voted to require ministers who lacked a college degree, including Log College products, to undergo a review by a synodical committee. This and other measures calculated to weaken the revivalists' position created an ideal environment for the next phase of the Awakening—the coming of the Grand Itinerants.

Curiously, the events that helped transform a series of local revivals in New England and the Middle Colonies into a movement that engulfed the English colonies from Rhode Island to Georgia began in the South. In 1738 George Whitefield, an English associate of John and Charles Wesley, the founders of Methodism, arrived in Georgia to preach to the poor and homeless. He returned to the colonies the following year for a whirlwind speaking tour that took him from Savannah, Georgia, to Newport, Rhode Island, as well as to Charleston, Philadelphia, New York, and Boston. He also spoke in many smaller communities, including Northampton, where he preached from Jonathan Edwards' pulpit.

Whitefield's ostensible purpose was to raise money for an orphanage he had helped organize in Bethesda, Georgia. But his message was aimed more at his listeners' hearts than their pocketbooks. In contrast to most American ministers, who read unemotionally from tightly written manuscripts, Whitefield preached highly emotional, extemporaneous sermons that appealed across denominational loyalties, social stations, and other prejudices and connections. The power of his message could move his audiences to heights of joy and tears of despair.

There was more to Whitefield, however, than a highly impassioned speaking style. His message shook the authority of the clerical establishment to its very foundation. In one message, widely circulated in colonial newspapers, he charged that many preachers "do not experimentally know Jesus Christ," attacked the practice of preaching from notes, and challenged the spiritual integrity of university-trained ministers, especially Harvard and Yale graduates. Whitefield's attacks infuriated many prominent ministers, who not only answered back in public but also barred him from preaching or taking the Lord's Supper in their churches. But the converts Whitefield gained far outnumbered the enemies he made.

Whitefield attracted not only converts and opponents but imitators. Numerous clerical and lay evangelists embarked upon itinerant ministries, seeking converts of their own. The most influential of Whitefield's followers was Gilbert Tennent, son of William Tennent, Sr., and pastor of the Presbyterian church at New Brunswick, New Jersey. Whitefield and Tennent met at Staten Island, New York, in the fall of 1740, and Whitefield persuaded Tennent to continue the Englishman's evangelizing work with his own tour of New England. Tennent arrived in Boston in December and conducted a three-month tour that took him to towns in southeastern Massachusetts, Rhode Island, and southern Connecticut. Wherever he went, Tennent drew great multitudes, including large numbers of children and African Americans. During the months that followed his departure for New Brunswick, pastors of many of the congregations Tennent had visited reported substantial growth in membership and a significant increase in participation in other congregational activities.

In addition to gaining new converts, Tennent also copied Whitefield in attacking the spiritual commitment of many New England ministers. One particularly notorious sermon, "On the Danger of an Unconverted Ministry," was published in Boston in 1742 and brought severe denunciation from critics of the revivalist's enthusiasm. But the opposition Tennent attracted paled in comparison with that generated by his contemporary, James Davenport.

A native of Connecticut and a graduate of Yale College, Davenport became pastor of the Presbyterian church at Southold on Long Island in

1738. He met Whitefield at a Synod meeting in Philadelphia in early 1740 and heard Tennent preach later that year. In the summer of 1741, after a decision to follow their example, Davenport launched his own preaching campaign in Connecticut and Rhode Island. He imitated not only his mentors' powerful preaching style but much of their message as well. But where Whitefield and Tennent challenged orthodoxy and pushed convention to the limit, Davenport crossed the line to fanaticism. His sermons were frequently ill-prepared harangues, and he often attacked and embarrassed local ministers who were friends of the Awakening with the same invective that he showered on its enemies.

Finally, in May 1742 he was arrested at Stratford, Connecticut, for violating a recently passed law against itinerant preaching. After being found mentally disturbed by the General Assembly, he was deported to Long Island. Now a self-styled martyr, he went to Boston the following summer in hopes of resuming his itinerant ministry. When pastors of Boston and Charleston, many of whom were proponents of the Awakening, voted not to invite him to speak in their churches, he roundly condemned them as unconverted and unworthy of their calling. At this point, even Gilbert Tennent found it necessary to disavow his errant follower. In August a Suffolk County court charged Davenport with slander. After a brief trial, the court found him mentally incompetent and sent him back to Long Island, where he was tried for neglecting his own congregation.

By the time of Davenport's second exile, the Great Awakening had largely run its course. It ebbed primarily because the society in which it occurred was running short on new converts and could no longer sustain a high level of disorder. Nevertheless, the Awakening had profound impacts, both immediate and long-term, on American society. The most obvious immediate result of this extended eruption of religious enthusiasm was to create thousands of converts. Some were inspired by the powerful sermons of outstanding parish ministers such as Jonathan Edwards and the Grand Itinerants—Whitefield, Tennent, and Davenport. Many others were converted by a host of unsung lay and clerical itinerants who were little-known outside their own regions. But perhaps the most successful evangelizers were the many local pastors who used the power of personal evangelism to stir revivals in their own congregations and communities.

Another immediate consequence of the Awakening was an extended period of public controversy between revivalists and their opponents. Congregationalist Charles Chauncy, pastor of the First Church of Boston, and his Anglican colleague, Timothy Cutler, inveighed against such extravagances as lay exhorting, itinerant preaching, doctrinal errors, and the excesses of persons such as Davenport. In 1744 the faculties of Harvard and Yale, still smarting from George Whitefield's attacks against university-trained clergy after they had welcomed him warmly during his 1739 tour, closed their doors to him when he returned and condemned not only his message and methods but his character as well. Whatever the specific charge, opponents of the Awakening feared that it tended to undermine established clerical authority.

More significant than the immediate effects of the Great Awakening were its long-term consequences, both religious and secular. One of the most important consequences was the schisms that split the Congregationalists and Presbyterians into two distinct theological schools of thought. The former divided generally between "Old Lights" and "New Lights." The Old Lights, exemplified by Chauncy, favored a formal style of worship and moved increasingly toward rationalism in theology. The New Lights, while they deplored its excesses, embraced the revival and continued to employ an evangelistic style of ministry. This division in the Congregationalist ranks persisted, with periods of readjustment, until the onset of the "Second Great Awakening" and the withdrawal of the Unitarians during the early nineteenth century.

Meanwhile, the New Lights gradually experienced their own internal division. The conflict reflected differences of opinion regarding membership policies in light of the Halfway Covenant. While the revival impulse had begun with Solomon Stoddard, who embraced the membership compromise, the emphasis of the Awakening was on personal conversion. As a result, a growing number of ministers wished to make evidence of a personal conversion experience a prerequisite for church membership. However, many other ministers, and even more congregations, opposed tightening membership procedures and continued to receive and retain unconverted members. Perhaps the most dramatic manifestation of this split within the New Lights came in 1750 when the Northampton church dismissed Jonathan Edwards after he rejected the Halfway Covenant and began requiring applicants for church membership to sign a confession of faith and to acknowledge a personal experience of divine grace before they could be allowed to receive the Lord's Supper.

The Presbyterian schism occurred in 1741 when the Synod of Philadelphia, through highly questionable means, formally ejected the revivalistic Presbytery of New Brunswick in reaction to Gilbert Tennent's sermon "On the Danger of an Unconverted Ministry." Four years later the body joined with the Presbyteries of New York and New Castle to create the Synod of New York. Popularly known as the "New Side" party, the new synod affirmed revivals as God's work, made the presbytery responsible for ordination, and stressed the importance of strong educational, doctrinal, and experiential qualifications for ministry. It also declared a firm desire for church reunion.

The New Side grew quickly over the next dozen years, while the antirevival "Old Side" Presbyterians lost strength, particularly among the laity. The success of the New Side, combined with its moderate course, ultimately produced a favorable response by the Old Siders to conciliatory gestures made by Tennent and others during the late 1740s and early 1750s. In 1758, after extended negotiations, the two synods reunited to create the Synod of New York and Philadelphia.

Closely related to these schismatic tendencies was the flowering of denominationalism. Although both the Congregationalists and the Presbyterians eventually healed their major breaches, reunion was accompanied by secondary divisions that produced new institutional expressions of the body of Christ. In parts of New England, especially eastern Connecticut, New Lights unhappy with the refusal of some of their brethren to abandon the Halfway Covenant left the Congregationalist church and formed their own Separate Congregational churches, which practiced believers' baptism. Many of these congregations ultimately became Baptist churches. During the second half of the eighteenth century, Separate Baptist missionaries from New England moved south and began gathering adherents, with considerable success, in the Piedmont regions of North Carolina and Virginia.

The Awakening had little immediate impact upon the Anglicans, whose church was established in the South. However, during his tour of Georgia in 1738, George Whitefield attracted a substantial number of his fellow Anglicans with the rigorous devotional and evangelical methods advocated in England by John and Charles Wesley. Among those most impressed by Whitefield's message was Devereux Jarratt, who became rector at Bath parish in Dinwiddie County, Virginia, in 1763. Over the next several years, with the help of lay preachers sent by John Wesley, Jarratt began organizing converts into "methodist" societies. Between 1766 and 1775, with the leadership of Francis Asbury, the movement spread to New York and Maryland. In the short term, Jarratt, Asbury, and others brought many new adherents into the Anglican fold. But after the Revolution, much to Jarratt's dismay, many of the societies broke from Anglicanism in 1784 and created the Methodist Episcopal Church, with Asbury as the first bishop. The Anglicans responded nine years later by organizing the Protestant Episcopal Church.

Another long-term consequence of the Great Awakening was the emergence of the revival or evangelical style as an important component of American religious life. Characterized by an emphasis on converting sinners, stress on living a holy life, suspicion of ecclesiastical pretensions, and a preference for the emotional, extemporaneous preaching style, revivalism was a fundamental component of the second Great Awakening and related social reform movements of the early and mid-nineteenth century. More than 250 years after the Great Awakening, the evangelical style continues to find favor, especially among the various fundamentalist, Holiness, and Pentecostal Protestant bodies.

Although many exponents of the Awakening doubted the spirituality of many well-educated clerics, especially those who studied at Harvard and Yale, numerous revivalists were themselves highly educated and saw the need for their own institutions for educating ministers. Thus William Tennent founded his so-called Log College at Neshaminy. Tennent's college lasted less than two decades, but similar schools in other communities graduated a substantial number of ministers during the mid-eighteenth century.

In addition to its clearly religious consequences, the Great Awakening also had substantial secular implications. Despite its tendency to create schisms within existing denominations and to spur the creation of new ones, the Awakening had a profound unifying impact upon American society. As the Grand Itinerants and lay exhorters moved from place to place, people from Rhode Island to Georgia were caught up in the excitement, whether they approved or disapproved of the revivalists' message. As the movement swept across colonial boundaries, it generated a common interest and bound people together in a common cause. In the process it reinforced a growing conviction that God had a special destiny for America and fostered a sense of cohesion among the American people.

The Great Awakening also had a substantial democratizing effect. Although the fame of individual revivalists such as Edwards and Tennent added a degree of luster to the ministerial office, the Awakening also eroded ministerial authority by pitting clergy against each other while emphasizing the importance of personal religious experience. Revivalists also cooperated across denominational lines to establish charitable institutions for the poor and schools for Native Americans, African Americans, and the children of indentured servants. Such activities helped strengthen the average individual's sense of self-confidence and standing in the community.

In the political realm, the Great Awakening spurred the development of pre-Revolutionary parties in some colonies. In Connecticut, New Light Congregationalists and Separate Baptists dominated the political scene east of the Connecticut River and led the radical resistance against the Stamp Tax, the Townshend Duties, and other English impositions. On the other hand, Anglicans, Old Light Congregationalists, and some moderate New Lights in western Connecticut took a more conservative approach. While they opposed British taxes, they respected the Empire's power and feared that New Light radical tactics would bring retaliation and further erode colonial liberties. When the Revolution moved from a struggle for reconciliation to one for independence in 1776, the Old Light party collapsed as a political force.

Finally, the Great Awakening helped pave the way for religious freedom in America by undermining the position of the established churches. As long as Congregationalism remained the dominant religious force in New England and Anglicanism in New York and the South, legal ties between church and state remained strong. But the Great Awakening weakened those ties by causing major divisions within both denominations and generating new dissenting bodies whose members increasingly resisted the requirement that they pay taxes to support the established churches. This tendency was compounded in some colonies, particularly Connecticut, where certain dissenters, such as Baptists, Quakers, and Anglicans, were exempt from church taxes. When strict Separatists and Presbyterians withdrew from the Congregational fold, they asked for the same exemption, but the colony's General Assembly denied it. When they began changing their names to "Baptist" in order to take advantage of the exemption, the Assembly abolished it for all dissenters. Adding insult to injury were laws providing for the arrest and punishment of New Light itinerants and restricting ordination to graduates of certain schools.

In an increasingly diverse religious environment, state control over spiritual affairs became intolerable. When the Revolution came, several colonies swept away their establishment laws, and only Virginia, Massachusetts, Connecticut, and New Hampshire continued to collect church taxes. In all four states agitation for complete religious freedom continued through the Revolution. Virginia adopted Thomas Jefferson's "Bill for Establishing Religious Freedom" in 1786, but the three New England states did not grant complete religious freedom until the early nineteenth century, with Massachusetts holding out until 1833.

The Great Awakening transpired within a relatively short period, but it had a powerful impact on American society and culture. Encompassing the genius of Jonathan Edwards, the advent of revivalism, and the proliferation of denominational bodies, the movement added colorful new theological, rhetorical, and ecclesiastical threads to the American religious tapestry. Even if its effects had been limited to the religious realm, the Awakening would have been noteworthy. But its influence carried beyond the strict boundaries of religion into education, politics, and social reform. Simply put, the Great Awakening exemplifies the profound role that religion has played and continues to play in American life.

SELECTED BIBLIOGRAPHY

Ahlstrom, Sydney E. *A Religious History of the American People*. New Haven, CT: Yale University Press, 1972. This distinguished synthesis of American religious history devotes four informative chapters to the Great Awakening, including one each on events in the New England, Middle, and Southern colonies and one on Jonathan Edwards and New England Theology.

Bushman, Richard L. *From Puritan to Yankee: Character and the Social Order in Connecticut, 1690–1765*. New York: W. W. Norton, 1967. Analyzes the role of the Great Awakening in the political, economic, and social transformation of Puritan society in Connecticut.

Butler, Jon. "Enthusiasm Described and Decried: The Great Awakening as Interpretive Fiction." *Journal of American History* 69, 2 (September 1992): 305–325. Asserts that the link between the revivals of the Great Awakening and the American Revolution was virtually nonexistent and suggests that the concept of the "Great Awakening" itself is invalid because the revival failed to produce the dramatic religious and political changes commonly attributed to it.

Coalter, Milton J. *Gilbert Tennent, Son of Thunder: A Case Study of Continental Pietism's Impact on the First Great Awakening in the Middle Colonies*. Westport, CT: Greenwood, 1986. Explores the influence of Theodorus Frelinghuysen on Tennent's theological views and compares his role with those of George Whitefield and James Davenport.

Cowing, Cedric B. *The Great Awakening and the American Revolution: Colonial Thought in the 18th Century*. Chicago: Rand McNally, 1971. Examines the role of evangelical religion in the struggle for civil and religious liberty in eighteenth-century New England.

Elwood, Douglas J. *The Philosophical Theology of Jonathan Edwards*. New York: Columbia University Press, 1960. A comprehensive analysis of the philosophical depths of the single most influential exponent of the Great Awakening and one of the leading theologians in American history.

Gaustad, Edwin Scott. *The Great Awakening in New England.* New York: Harper and Brothers, 1957. A concise yet definitive account of the Great Awakening in New England.

Heimert, Alan. *Religion and the American Mind: From the Great Awakening to the Revolution.* Cambridge, MA: Harvard University Press, 1966. Argues that the Great Awakening filled the American people with the hope of a millennial era which would satisfy their desire for a new order characterized by fraternity and democracy.

Henretta, James A. and Gregory H. Nobles, eds. *Evolution and Revolution: American Society, 1600–1820.* Lexington, MA: D.C. Heath, 1987. A collection of essays dealing with various aspects of colonial and early national social history.

Hudson, Winthrop S. *Religion in America: An Historical Account of the Development of American Religious Life.* New York: Charles Scribner's Sons, 1981. Includes a concise account of the Great Awakening within the context of American religious history.

Lippy, Charles H. *Seasonably Revolutionary: The Mind of Charles Chauncy.* Chicago: Nelson-Hall, 1981. Views the Great Awakening through the eyes of one of its leading opponents.

Marty, Martin E. *Pilgrims in Their Own Land: 500 Years of Religion in America.* Boston: Little, Brown, 1984. Examines the Great Awakening as a struggle by colonial Americans to understand what it meant to be religious in an environment where decisions of faith were no longer determined simply by where one lived.

McLoughlin, William G. " 'Enthusiasm for Liberty': The Great Awakening as the Key to Revolution." In Jack P. Greene and William G. McLoughlin, *Preachers and Politicians: Two Essays on the Origins of the American Revolution* (Worcester, MA: American Antiquarian Society, 1977): 47–73. Argues that the Great Awakening prepared the way for the American Revolution by promoting intercolonial unity, religious rebirth, and democracy.

Miller, Perry. *Errand into the Wilderness.* New York: Harper and Row, 1956. A collection of essays on Puritanism and the Great Awakening by one of the twentieth century's premier interpreters of the Puritan mind.

Ver Steeg, Clarence L. *The Formative Years, 1607–1763.* New York: Hill and Wang, 1964. A concise overview of American colonial history that treats the Great Awakening as a clash between faith and reason.

Ziff, Larzer. *Puritanism in America: New Culture in a New World.* New York: Viking, 1973. Examines the Great Awakening in New England within the broader context of Puritanism's role in shaping American culture.

Jarvis Pinx.

Robert Walpole, prime minister of Great Britain for more than 20 years, presided over the policy known as "benign neglect." (Reproduced from the Collections of the Library of Congress)

2

The Era of Salutary Neglect, c. 1720s–1750

INTRODUCTION

In the early eighteenth century, the British government, under its first great prime minister, Robert Walpole (1721–1742), instituted a policy known as "salutary neglect," which had at its basis a relaxation of colonial regulations. This policy, it was hoped, would allow Britain to concentrate on European matters, and at the same time allow the colonists to buy more British goods and be of benefit to Britain and its merchants. The real effect of salutary neglect, as it turned out, was to allow the colonial assemblies to garner more and more independent authority, a circumstance that would come back to haunt the British a generation later.

In the sixteenth century, England, Spain, and the Netherlands developed an economic system known as mercantilism to further their national interests. In England's case, this involved the encouragement of investment in domestic manufacturing, so that fewer imported goods were needed and more goods were available for export. This worked to give England a favorable balance of trade, defined as having more gold and silver coming into the country than going out. This gold and silver could then be used to build up the military (and especially the navy) or bring about further economic expansion.

As the Spanish colonized Mexico and South America in the sixteenth century and supported a huge bureaucracy and military with the abundant gold and silver they extracted from their colonies, English adventurers made their first tentative forays into North America. Significant colonial expansion into North America, however, was not feasible for the English until financing was available to permit an entrepreneurial group to go overseas and establish a profitable outpost. The problem of financing was solved in the late sixteenth century by the development of the joint-stock company. Like a modern corporation, company managers would sell shares of stock in the company to a large number of investors. This would provide the capital necessary to undertake the colonial venture.

In this way, the colonies fell under the mercantilist system. This was the economic phase of nationalism, part of the broad movement of nation-making (and, indeed, empire-building), involving a communal rather than an individualistic view of society. The colonies were looked upon as supplements to the colonizing country, necessary to make it independent of foreign rivals. The main question was how the colonies could best serve the interests of Britain.

The best way was to have an abundance of gold and silver, like the Spanish colonies of Latin America two centuries earlier, but these precious metals were not readily available in the North American colonies. So the colonies served the mercantile system in other ways. They provided raw materials needed by Britain, which allowed the British to keep more gold and silver at home, and they served as a market for the finished products of British manufacturers, thus providing employment for British workers. In addition, the exchange of raw materials for manufactured goods stimulated the merchant marine and added to Britain's naval strength.

Two types of Parliamentary legislation were necessary to fit the colonies into the mercantilist scheme. A group of laws called Navigation Acts provided that all goods engaged in imperial trade had to be shipped on vessels built and operated by subjects of the crown. The first of these was passed in 1651 and aimed at the Dutch, Britain's chief commercial rival. It stipulated that any goods imported into England or its colonies had to be carried in ships of English, Irish, or colonial registry. In addition, another Navigation Act passed in 1660 provided that certain colonial products—sugar, indigo, and tobacco—could be shipped only to British possessions. No direct trade to other nations was allowed. This act was made even more restrictive in 1663 when the Staple Act required that "enumerated goods," as those colonial products were called, could be shipped only to Great Britain, from where they could be reexported to other countries. Similarly, goods from other countries destined for markets in the North American colonies also had to be shipped first to Britain and then reexported to the colonies. This gave Britain a monopoly on these goods and brought in more revenue through customs duties and the reexport trade. For the colonies, this meant higher transportation costs and pushed prices for these goods to a prohibitive level, thus forcing the colonists to buy British. To administer these acts, in 1696 Parliament created a new body called the Board of Trade, composed of individuals with political or commercial backgrounds, which oversaw colonial trade and proposed new laws aimed at American manufacturing enterprises that might compete with British companies engaged in the same trade. In the late seventeenth century, Great Britain enforced its mercantilist policies with zeal, fighting commercial wars with the Netherlands that eventually drove the Dutch from North America, and clamping down on violations of the trade regulations in North America. In the 1680s, for example, repeated violations of the Navigation Acts in Massachusetts resulted in the annulment of the colonial charter of that colony and its incorporation into a new administrative unit called the Dominion of New England, which was ruled by a despotic governor, Sir Edmund Andros. Happily for New England, the aftermath of the Glorious Revolution, in which James II was swept off the British throne and replaced by the dual monarchy of William and Mary, led to the dissolution of the Dominion and the creation of a new royal colony of Massachusetts, with a fairly democratic and autonomous assembly.

Another set of laws, the Manufacturing Acts, was designed to cut down colonial industry that might compete with British industry of a similar nature. These acts included the Woolens Act of 1699, the Hat Act of 1732, and the Iron Act of 1750. The first two of these acts banned the intercolonial or export sale of woolen goods or hats, while the Iron Act did allow the sale of pig iron to England but prohibited the building of new iron forges and mills in the colonies.

Why did the colonists tolerate a system seemingly so little in their interests? The answer is that it was not as disadvantageous as it might seem. First, the principal colonial agricultural commodities enjoyed a monopoly of British markets, which was certainly economically beneficial. British manufactured goods were at this time the best and cheapest in the world, and colonists would probably have bought them with or without foreign competition. The Royal Navy gave protection to colonial shipping, something the colonists could not have afforded themselves, and the Navigation Acts did not prevent American vessels from engaging in imperial trade, which they did with great zeal, eventually controlling more than 90 percent of the trade between mainland North America and the West Indies. Finally, most colonists were not affected by the mercantilist system anyway; they were engaged in subsistence agriculture, which had no bearing on foreign trade. It is also important to note that mercantilism was generally accepted as the way things were done, and in North America at this time, the colonies were thirteen separate entities with practically no intercolonial communication and no effective way to voice grievances.

Walpole's policies had a political side to them as well. A strong believer in the patronage system, he filled many colonial administrative posts with friends and political allies who were, perhaps, loyal, but who were at best mediocre bureaucrats. Many of them came to the colonies with the single goal of milking the system to their own financial advantage, and they were willing to act in corrupt ways or ignore obvious problems if it were profitable to do so. In many cases, they made friends with American merchants, involving themselves in their businesses and sharing in their profits, much of which came from the nonenforcement of mercantilist regulations.

Similarly, in London, Walpole's patronage system weakened the Board of Trade and other parliamentary bodies charged with overseeing colonial affairs. This had a negative effect on those British officials who went to the colonies determined to uphold British authority; when they found no support from the bureaucrats back in London, they became disillusioned and resigned themselves to accepting the system the way it was.

The policy of salutary neglect often meant that the mercantile acts were not enforced, allowing colonial traders to smuggle goods in or avoid customs payments by other means. New England traders were able to profit from the so-called triangular trade, in which they sent fish and lumber to the Caribbean colonies, which in turn sent sugar, molasses, and rum to the west coast of Africa, which in turn sent slaves to the sugar planters or tobacco planters in the warm weather colonies of North America. Profits from this trade allowed New Englanders to buy more goods from Britain.

One of the most profitable sectors of American trade might have been seriously compromised in 1733 had it not been for the policy of salutary neglect. By the 1720s, American merchants were enjoying a lucrative trade with the French West Indies, exchanging such items as flour, fish, and wooden barrels for West Indian sugar. The sugar was then used in the distilleries of New England, whose rum helped support the enthusiastic drinking habits of colonial Americans as well as serve as another profitable export product. British sugar interests, however, were upset that Americans were not buying sugar from the plantations of the British West Indies, as good mercantilist theory dictated, and they persuaded Parliament to pass the Molasses Act in 1733. This act placed a tax of six pence per gallon on molasses (the form in which sugar was usually purchased) imported from non-British possessions. American merchants protested the imposition of this tax, pointing out that it would, among other things, impair their ability to purchase British manufactured products, but Parliament was not impressed. As a consequence, most American merchants simply ignored the tax, either by smuggling molasses into New England or by bribing corrupt customs officials. Because sugar prices worldwide rose in the late 1730s and because there was no particular interest in London to enforce the Molasses Act, colonists could pretend that the Molasses Act did not exist.

Another problem exacerbated (as far as the British were concerned) by salutary neglect was the growing tendency in the colonies to establish land banks and issue paper currency. Much of the gold and silver that came to the colonies was sent to Britain to pay for manufactured goods. This left a currency shortage in the colonies, which the colonies attempted to solve by issuing paper currency. The land bank would print currency and then lend it to farmers who needed it and were willing to put up their land as collateral. Farmers thus had money to invest in land or supplies, and that money made its way into general circulation.

Some colonies printed too much money—more than was backed by the value of the land held as collateral. The money then depreciated in value. In Rhode Island, one of the worst offenders, local currency soon became worth only half its face value. Needless to say, creditors, some of whom were British businessmen, objected strenuously to being repaid with money that was worth significantly less than that which they had originally lent. Finally, in 1751, after Massachusetts, one of the larger colonies, had begun to abuse paper currency, Parliament passed the Currency Act, which prohibited the founding of new banks throughout New England and barred the use of local paper currency (called public bills of credit) to pay private debts. One consequence of this issue was that it awakened a number of high-ranking British government officials to the autonomy that colonial governments had assumed during the period of salutary neglect.

The French and Indian War (1754–1763) brought an end to the policy of salutary neglect. The war revealed to London how weak British administrative control had become and how independent many of the colonial assemblies now were. This was seen during the war when the Virginia assembly voted not to raise additional tax money to help pay the costs of the war but rather resorted to printing paper currency to meet its obligation. Too much currency was printed and it fell in value, yet creditors were bound by law to accept the bills in payment of debts. British merchants refused to accept the paper money and lobbied Parliament for assistance, but it was not until 1764 that that body passed the Currency Act, which prohibited the use of paper money in all of the colonies; henceforth, all debts would have to be paid in gold, silver, British currency, or bills of exchange (similar to an interbank transfer).

Toward the end of the war, British officials began to enforce more rigorously the Navigation Acts, the heart of mercantilism. Specifically, they went after the almost universal flouting of the 1733 Molasses Act. In 1762, Parliament passed the Revenue Act, which disallowed the practice of customs officials hiring corrupt deputies in their place. In addition, the Royal Navy was directed to stop all trade between North America and the French West Indies (in part, this was a wartime measure, as colonial food and supplies sold in the French West Indies were finding their way to the French armies fighting against the British).

The war left Britain deeply in debt, and this fact was the most important in inducing London to reassert its authority over its North American colonies. William Pitt had devised a marvelous strategy to bring victory to the British, but he had spent extravagantly to do so. Between 1754 and 1763, the national debt nearly doubled and the first postwar government had to find ways to make interest payments. Parliament raised import taxes for goods coming into Britain and imposed new excise taxes on popular items, such as tobacco, so that the tax burden fell on the common people. With respect to the North American colonies, there was a widespread feeling in Britain that imperial reform, by means of the more assiduous enforcement of existing rules and regulations, was needed, both to force the colonies to bear some of the cost of the war and to show them where the source of power lay. Thus, in 1764, Parliament passed the Sugar Act. This act, which represented a revised version of the old Molasses Act of 1733, actually lowered the tax on imported sugar from six pence to three pence per gallon but called for the vigorous collection of the tax. Colonial leaders protested, of course, but interestingly, they seemed to be more concerned about their right, as they saw it, to impose their own taxes. This, then, became one of the overarching disputes that propelled the colonies and Great Britain into war just twelve years later.

INTERPRETIVE ESSAY
Thomas A. Prasch

Edmund Burke, on the eve of the American Revolution, first framed the notion that "a wise and salutary neglect" had been central to the earlier success of British imperial aims in the American colonies. In his *Speech on Conciliation with America* (March 22, 1775), he declared:

> when I know that the Colonies in general owe little or nothing to any care of ours, and that they are not squeezed into this happy form by the constraints of watchful and suspicious government, but that through a wise and salutary neglect, a generous nature has been suffered to take her own way to perfection; when I reflect upon these effects, when I see how profitable they have been to us, I feel all the pride of power sink and all presumption in the wisdom of human contrivances melt and die away within me. . . . I pardon something to the spirit of liberty. (Burke, *Writings and Speeches*, 3:118)

Burke could well look back nostalgically to the relative peace and prosperity produced by British hands-off policies earlier in the eighteenth century from his vantage point in 1775. In Burke's day, an intensely interventionist British state sought to recoup the costs of colonial war with France through taxes and impositions that resulted not only in the disruption of profitable trade but also in massive resistance by American colonials and thus in greater military and monetary costs to Britain. To Burke, it was already clear by 1775 that the dominant policies of force applied to the American colonies would result in costly war and that war in the colonies would yet again mean war with France as well.

Burke's prescient analysis pinpoints a number of the central themes in the development of the American colonies from 1722 to 1742, including the importance of relatively unfettered free trade to the prosperity of both colonies and empire and the autonomous development of free political institutions within Britain's American colonies. The circumstances that produced two decades of "salutary neglect," however, are rather more complex than Burke's simple formulation suggests. A complex set of conditions in the British political sphere produced a period of relative neglect of colonial policy that was only partly an intentional effect of policy decisions; meanwhile, in North America, rapidly changing conditions were only partly the consequence of British imperial policies.

It is no accident that the decades historians identify with this "salutary neglect" correspond with the age of Robert Walpole's ascendancy in British politics. Walpole is often credited with inventing the prime ministership, although the term was not applied to him at the time; officially, he served as First Lord of the Treasury. On the surface, at least, Walpole's tenure presents a picture of remarkable stability between eras of destabilizing political infighting and intrigue. Walpole held his post at the Treasury for twenty-one years; over the seven years before he took office, five people held the post (including Walpole himself for two years), and in the two subsequent decades, eight men would hold the office. Similarly, in the post of Secretary of State (South Department), the cabinet officer largely responsible for policy in the American colonies, a single figure, Thomas Pelham-Holles, first Duke of Newcastle, held power through most of the Walpole years; five men held the post in the decade before Walpole selected Newcastle for the position, and nine would serve in the post over the next two decades.

The stability of Walpole's tenure in domestic politics and of Newcastle's dominance in American colonial policy was further reinforced by a new security in the royal succession, established with the ascension of the Hanoverians to the throne beginning with George I in 1714 and the rapidly diminishing threat of Jacobite challenges to the crown.

The Jacobite threat can be traced back to the Glorious Revolution of 1688, when Parliament invited William of Orange to replace James II, the last Stuart king, as British monarch. James fled to France, leaving the throne to his daughter Mary and her husband, William. However, with French support James established a rival monarchy in exile, ever ready to challenge William and Mary and their successors' claim to the English throne. After the French officially recognized the Hanoverian succession in 1713 and the Jacobite rebellion of 1715 failed, however, such claims had relatively little impact on English political life (at least until 1745, when a renewed Jacobite rebellion shook Scotland); no serious challenge was mounted, for instance, when George II took power in 1727. It is a further sign of Walpole's political skill that his ministry, too, survived this transition.

In a variety of ways, Walpole's explicit policy aims worked to reinforce this sense of security. One of the most important of these is Walpole's skill as a financial manager and his policies to promote expanded trade. It was, not coincidentally, a financial crisis that brought Walpole to power: the crisis of speculative investment known as the South Sea Bubble. The crisis had its origins in the chartering of the South Sea Company as a joint-stock venture in 1711. The company's stock prices soared after 1713, when Britain secured, through the Treaty of Utrecht, a monopoly on slave-trading with Spanish possessions in the Caribbean (part of the South Sea Company's territory). The directors of the company, however, were engaged as much in manipulation of public debt as in actual trade. With the assistance of Parliament and the direct involvement of key members of the cabinet, the company sought to exchange shares of stock for holdings of public debt, a workable scheme as long as stock prices continued to rise. When the crash came in September 1720, it provided the mechanism for Walpole to secure his supremacy through skillful crisis management. The Bubble Act that followed the crisis put joint-stock operations on more secure (and more state-regulated) ground, leading to two decades of slower but steady expansion of overseas trade.

Walpole firmly believed in the mercantilist system, by which colonial possessions served primarily to enrich the mother country. The system envisioned colonialism as a closed loop, in which colonies provided raw materials for home manufacturing and a market for the mother country's goods; trade with the merchants and colonies of other powers was discouraged through prohibitive legislation. In accepting mercantilist principles, Walpole was very much a man of his age. Until Adam Smith's denunciation of mercantilism and argument for unfettered free trade in *The Wealth of Nations* (1776), the mercantilist case dominated state policy. The doctrine was enshrined in a long series of legislative acts, from the Acts of Trade of 1660 and 1663 to the Navigation Acts of 1696. To these, Walpole would make his own additions, most notably the Molasses Act (1733).

But Walpole also sought to reconceive mercantilism, to reinvent a doctrine that presumed stable levels of production into one fitted for an era of expanding trade. He signaled his intentions in his speech from the throne (delivered by George I, but written by Walpole) in 1721, declaring the encouragement of trade and manufacturing as his goals. These aims were to be accomplished by measures reducing duties on both imports of raw materials from the colonies and exported manufactured goods, while meanwhile raising duties on foreign imports. Government preferments and subsidies further favored trading and manufacturing interests. The principal results were steady increases in the value of both imports and exports over the next two decades and widening prosperity, at least for interests involved in both trade and manufacture, on both sides of the Atlantic. An additional consequence of the policies was that Walpole gained the firm support of merchant and manufacturing interests and of London-based financiers (already beholden to him for his handling of the South Sea Bubble crisis).

Meanwhile, on the colonial side of economic development, the mercantilist system, had it been firmly enforced, would doubtless have both restricted the expansion of trade and exacerbated tensions between colonials and the British state. These eventualities were avoided during Walpole's tenure by a simple expedient: the restrictive legislation of mercantilist doctrine went largely unenforced. It is unclear to what extent this was a deliberate policy and how far it amounts to mere historical accident. Walpole's positions generally, above all else his belief in minimizing government action, were certainly closer to laissez-faire economics than those of his predecessors; he nevertheless regularly proved quite willing to implement legislation to secure the favor of important interests, especially the West Indies lobby, even at the expense of North American colonials, as in the case of the Molasses Act. But that act, even more than its predecessors, was more widely ignored than enforced.

Historians have pointed to a variety of institutional and personal factors to explain the relatively hands-off policies of the Walpole years. The Board of Trade, the body principally responsible for enforcement of mercantilist legislation, was in an institutionally weak position from the end of the seventeenth century, becoming weaker in policy decisions especially after 1714, and it would only become an effective enforcer of the law when reorganized in 1748. Newcastle, as Secretary of State (Southern Department), came to the post without preparation on the details of the system, resulting in a suspension of much administrative activity while he learned the duties of his office after 1724. Even after that, however, enforcement was very lax, and Newcastle's preferred approach to problems was to delay firm action. James Henretta, in his account of Newcastle's political career, attributes the "salutary neglect" of the era to a combination of accidental factors—"administrative inefficiency, financial stringency, and political incompetence"—as well as to some element of deliberate policy ('Salutary Neglect', 104). It is also the case, however, that Walpole's deliberate policies sought to avoid interference with the advancement of trade, and lax enforcement of the trade and navigation acts certainly fit this aim. In any case, for whatever reason, mercantilist legislation was easily evaded in the period, contributing to significant growth in American trade and giving the colonies a far more significant role in Great Britain's overall trading patterns.

Walpole's quest for stability is nowhere more clear than in his firm antiwar position. For Walpole, avoiding war was connected to a range of policy issues. Most central, doubtless, was Walpole's overall aim of reducing state expenditure; nothing balloons a national budget as surely as the cost of war. War also interfered with Walpole's aims of expanding trade, especially across the Atlantic, because it both diverted government expenditure in other directions and directly disrupted trading. Further, keeping out of European wars provided a means to alleviate the threat of Jacobitism to the security of the Hanoverian monarchy. War almost always put France and England at odds, and France could always employ the Jacobite court-in-exile to undermine its enemy across the Channel; staying out of conflicts made such direct challenges less likely.

In addition, and more directly linking antiwar and colonial policy, it was clear to Walpole that European conflicts could no longer be restricted to engagements on the Continent. Rather, European war always spilled over into the colonies, involving disruptions of the Atlantic trade, challenges to territorial boundaries at the margins of British North American colonies, and clashes in the West Indies. This was the lesson Walpole learned from the War of Spanish Succession (also called Queen Anne's War, 1702–1713), a conflict that began with the powers of Europe disputing who had proper title to the Spanish throne but that was fought not only in European battle theaters (the Danube Valley, the Low Countries, northern Italy, and Spain) and throughout the Mediterranean Sea, but also on the wilderness frontiers of North America and among the island colonies of the Caribbean. Indeed, Britain's gains from the war, concluded with the Treaty of Utrecht (1713), almost all benefited the colonies: they gained Hudson's Bay, Nova Scotia, and Newfoundland from France, and British merchants received a monopoly from Spain on slave imports to Spain's American possessions.

The Treaty of Utrecht ended nearly a quarter century of almost continuous warfare involving the European powers and Britain. Through Walpole's efforts, at least in part, Britain remained at peace almost until the end of his tenure in office. When, for example, the War of the Polish Succession (1733–1735) embroiled the major European powers, Walpole kept Britain out of the fray despite George II's prowar position. It was finally Walpole's staunch resistance to war, in fact, that ended his long tenure in office, when conflict between British merchants (and smugglers) and Spanish authorities led to the brink of war in 1738. Although both popular and parliamentary opinion favored war, Walpole resisted, negotiating the Convention of Pardo in 1739 to avert military conflict with Spain. But a revolt of key members of his own cabinet and continued prowar agitation in Parliament led Britain into war later the same year. The War of Jenkins' Ear (named for the ear Robert Jenkins lost to the Spaniards who had boarded his ship in 1731), a conflict that soon became subsumed within the broader War of the Austrian Succession (1740–1748), doomed Walpole's antiwar program, leading to precisely the sort of war he feared, one involving British military action on multiple fronts: in Europe, in Great Britain itself (with the Scottish revolt led by "Bonnie Prince Charlie"—Charles Edward Stuart, seeking to reclaim the throne for the Stuart line—in 1745), and in the colonies (this time not only in America and the Caribbean, but in India as well). Although Walpole remained in office for three years after the commencement of hostilities, the war eventually brought Walpole's resignation from office in 1742.

The ease with which that descent into war occurred despite the desperate resistance of Walpole himself as chief minister suggests how fragile, in fact, the security of his system was. On the domestic front, the solidity of Walpole's tenure required a cautious balancing act on Walpole's part between pleasing the king, still far more than a figurehead in the politics of the time, and keeping control of Parliament, especially the House of Commons, whose supremacy in the legislative field had been established through the course of the political upheavals of the seventeenth century. In Walpole's case, his political balancing act was also carried on in the face of vociferous opposition; no chief minister ever endured such an openly and personally hostile opposition and press.

Within the context of the unreformed parliamentary system of eighteenth-century Britain, it was never elections per se that determined power. The presumption that the upper classes constituted the nation's "natural" leadership was enshrined in the ideology of "virtual representation": the idea that members of Parliament represented not just specific constituencies, but the whole population. As a consequence of this idea, for instance, it was not necessary for a candidate to live in the place where he (for it was always he) stood for election. The greater part of the British population—roughly six out of seven people—had no role in elections whatever. The franchise was restricted to those with landed wealth, with the minimum being a forty-shilling freehold. Further, because the distribution of Parliamentary seats had been apportioned in the Middle Ages and left unchanged since, in some cases—the famous "rotten boroughs" that would finally be eliminated in the Reform Act of 1832—members stood for seats that had almost no population at all.

Influence and patronage were the keys for controlling this system at almost all levels. At the level of elections, the ability to buy votes and promise rewards determined to a large extent who served in Parliament. From Walpole's position, working to please interest groups and dispensing patronage were the means to maintain a parliamentary majority. That placement—those we would now call civil servants—served in Parliament, casting votes for the regime that provided their jobs, which was only the most obvious sign of patronage at work. We have seen already how Walpole used trade policy as an instrument to gain the support of powerful interests in Parliament, manufacturers and merchants as well as the increasingly influential West Indian lobby and the financial community that had benefited, too, by his intervention on the South Sea Bubble crisis. He also used his control of Treasury to secure patronage positions for allies and employed his links to the king to distribute honors and preferment to his supporters. And he paraded his own personal background, as a country gentleman, to keep the support of parliamentary independents who shared his class background (the landed gentry also, as major investors, benefited from Walpole's financial skills). Finally, Walpole knew when to beat a strategic retreat, as when he withdrew his proposed Excise Bill (1733) rather than see it face defeat in the House of Commons.

But Walpole's system, precisely because of its dependence on patronage and interest politics, was inherently unstable. There were limits on the total available patronage positions, much competition among cabinet members for the right to distribute favors, the need to constantly redeploy patronage to fit immediate needs, and the necessity to continue to please interest groups for whom long-past favors were apt to be forgotten. The rapidity with which Walpole's supporters and even fellow cabinet ministers deserted him when they believed others could provide for them better in the crisis that began in 1739 underlines how tenuous Walpole's power really was.

In the colonies, an oddly similar balance can be seen between a surface security and seething sources of instability. The general picture presented by the colonies during the Walpole years seems relatively placid. The major stages of the settlement process had been largely completed by the eighteenth century; only Georgia was added during Walpole's ten-

ure, in 1733. By the turn of the century, too, the basic dynamics of colonial politics was set: a see-sawing balance of power between bicameral
colonial assemblies, with far more popular elections than those of England determining the membership of at least the lower houses, and a
royal-appointed executive. Colonials chafed at the limitations imposed
by mercantile legislation, but their resistance was minimized both by
their knowledge of the limited standards of enforcement and by the security that Walpole's policies also promoted colonial trading interests.
The expansion of the colonial economy benefited similar interests in the
colonies to those that backed Walpole in England. More generally, expanded trade ensured the increasing prosperity of the colonies, if also
widening the gap between haves and have-nots. Walpole's antiwar policies further limited conflict on the colonial frontiers, the spillover effect
that resulted from European wars; the relative peace facilitated colonial
expansion westward, necessitated by the rapidly expanding colonial
population.

The security of the colonial system was, however, more fragile than it
appeared. A closer examination of colonial politics makes this clear: if
the broad form of colonial politics had become stable by the eighteenth
century, the practice of politics was far more fractious and contentious.
As opposed to Great Britain, where Parliament and the ministerial executive represented the same basic interests and shared a common place
in the social order, the interests of colonial assemblies and royal executives were far more sharply divided, with the assemblies promoting the
interests of colonials and the executive seeking to ensure the interests of
the British state. Further, the tenor of politics in America differed on the
level of political theory: the radical inheritance of the seventeenth century, reinforced by the wide circulation in the colonies of the opposi-
tional press in Walpole's era, gave colonial political discourse a more
radical, more democratic, and more antistatist edge.

Bernard Bailyn, in his classic study *The Origins of American Politics*
(1968), explores the specific differences between the practice of politics
in the colonies and Britain, emphasizing above all else the differences in
the informal structure of politics. Precisely those tools of influence and
patronage that were central to Walpole's hold on power in Britain were
not fully in the control of colonial executives. Their powers of patronage
were limited, largely because patronage was dispensed at the cabinet
level in Britain, and even at that level shared between several officers.
Even Newcastle's power of patronage was limited by the competing demands of Walpole himself and (through 1730) Charles Townshend, as

secretary of state for the Northern Department. Colonial governors also had limited flexibility in setting policy, which was determined back in Britain, or imposing it, especially with only limited access to military support. They thus could do little independently to cultivate influential interest groups, and the interest groups most vital to the security of officials back in England were not necessarily those who were most important in colonial politics.

Colonial legislatures, for the most part, lacked the ideology of "natural" leaders characteristic of British politics, and legislators were thus much more subject to popular opinion and electoral pressures. Such tendencies were reinforced by the more radical traditions of political theory, with their emphasis on the evils of any power that seemed absolute in character. In this, interestingly, Bailyn to a large extent reiterates the arguments Burke had made back in the 1770s concerning the development of autonomous traditions of representation in the colonies quite distinct from those of the mother country, reinforcing Burke's case with the evidence of modern historical scholarship.

The security of colonial boundaries and the dominant tenor of peace between major powers with colonial holdings was also less solid than it seemed through most of the Walpole years. As the colonial population rapidly expanded, westward settlement seemed an obvious solution to American colonials. This brought them increasingly into conflict with French claims to the American interior as well as with Native American groups threatened by displacement; the establishment of Georgia also produced boundary disputes with Spanish possessions to the south. The lack of full-scale war should not be taken to suggest the existence of full-scale peace. On the contrary, border skirmishes and minor conflicts with the representatives of other European powers and their allies among the Native American groups also being pressured by American expansion were almost continuous. Further, the complications of a Caribbean trading system that featured high levels of smuggling as well as legal trade produced similar minor conflicts at sea. Throughout the 1730s, indeed, a state of near war existed between British and colonial traders and Spanish authorities, as reflected in episodes such as that of Jenkins' ear. It is in part because trading interests had something to gain from conflict in both the western frontier and the Caribbean that Walpole's antiwar position failed to hold through the growing crisis of the late 1730s.

What ensued with the end of Walpole's primacy (and with it the end of the era of "salutary neglect") in many ways amply justified Walpole's wariness about war as well as Burke's later nostalgia for the bygone days of more minimal British colonial government. The war with Spain gradually extended until, by 1740, it had merged into the wide-ranging conflict of the War of the Austrian Succession (1740–1748). That war in turn was but a prelude to the almost continuous warfare on both the European continent and in America that ended with the Peace of Paris (1763). That treaty ensured British supremacy in North America, but at such cost that the colonies would soon after be lost. The expenses of the war itself and of the expanded need to police a wider colonial realm led the British state to abandon its policies of "salutary neglect" in favor of attempts to enforce strictly and even expand the mercantilist laws so neglected in the past and to impose taxes on the colonies to recoup the costs of the new empire. These new policies ignored the by-then-longstanding independent political traditions of the American colonies and, by doing so, broke down the fragile balance between assemblies and governors in colonial politics.

It is often to this later period of conflict that historians first look for the development of an independent American character, for the advent of colonists who thought of themselves first as Americans and only secondarily as citizens of the British state. But this basic shift can also be traced back to the era of "salutary neglect," when colonists, left largely to their own devices, began to forge an independent identity and an autonomous political tradition. It might be said that in the shadow of this neglect, then, in the opportunities offered by being ignored, the new shape of the New World first took form.

SELECTED BIBLIOGRAPHY

Bailyn, Bernard. *The Origins of American Politics*. New York: Knopf, 1968. Bailyn's classic treatment of the differences between British and American colonial political orders, although dated, remains a clear and useful discussion of the central issues.

Black, Jeremy. *British Foreign Policy in the Age of Walpole*. Edinburgh: John Donald, 1985. Black's discussion illuminates the role of European diplomacy and warfare in Walpole's regime and makes the impact of those policies on Walpole's tenure and colonial politics clear.

———. *Robert Walpole and the Nature of Politics in Early Eighteenth-Century Britain*. London: Macmillan, 1996. Black's brief survey presents a clear portrait of the structure of politics in Britain in the eighteenth century and the methods employed by Walpole to maintain his control.

Bowen, H. V. *Elites, Enterprise and the Making of the British Overseas Empire 1688–1775*. London: Macmillan, 1996. Useful discussion of how the key interest groups of the Walpole era—landed interests, the merchant elite, and financial figures—came into alliance on major policy issues after 1720.

Burke, Edmund. *The Writings and Speeches of Edmund Burke.* Paul Langford, gen. ed. Vol. 2, *Party, Politics, and the American Crisis, 1766–1774,* ed. Paul Langford. Oxford: Clarendon Press, 1981; vol. 3, *Party, Parliament, and the American War, 1774–1780,* ed. William Elofson and J. A. Woods. Oxford: Clarendon Press, 1996. Burke coined the term "salutary neglect" to refer to earlier British colonial policy, and his writings on the subject remain lucid arguments for the autonomous development of the colonies as a consequence of the minimal involvement of the British state.

Colley, Linda. *Britons: Forging the Nation 1707–1837.* New Haven, CT: Yale University Press, 1992. A valuable discussion of the emergence of British identity in the eighteenth century with interesting insights into the development of a distinctive American character as well.

Dickenson, H. T. *Politics of the People in Eighteenth-Century Britain.* New York: St. Martin's Press, 1994. A useful survey of the limitations and possibilities of popular politics in the period.

———. *Walpole and the Whig Supremacy.* London: English University Press, 1973. A solid political study of Walpole's place in and impact on the Whigs who dominated British politics from 1714 to 1760.

Engerman, Stanley L., and Robert E. Gallman, eds. *The Cambridge History of the United States.* Vol. 1, *The Colonial Era.* Cambridge: Cambridge University Press, 1996. This collection includes useful essays on economic developments in different regions of the colonies and on British mercantilism.

Henretta, James A. *'Salutary Neglect': Colonial Administration under the Duke of Newcastle.* Princeton, NJ: Princeton University Press, 1972. Henretta's detailed political biography is particularly useful for outlining the informal mechanics of British politics and colonial policy.

Plumb, J. H. *Sir Robert Walpole.* Vol. 2, *The King's Minister.* Rev. ed. New York: Augustus M. Kelley, 1973. The best available political biography of Walpole in the early years of his power.

Reitan, Earl A. *Politics, War, and Empire: The Rise of Britain to a World Power 1688–1792.* Arlington Heights, IL: Harlan Davidson, 1994. A brief survey that usefully emphasizes the imperial dimensions of British history in the eighteenth century.

Rothbard, Murray N. *Conceived in Liberty.* Vol. 2, *'Salutary Neglect': The American Colonies in the First Half of the Eighteenth Century.* New Rochelle, NY: Arlington House, 1975. Survey of early American history that offers particularly solid coverage of the Walpole years and the tensions beneath the surface of colonial government.

Speck, W. A. *Stability and Strife: England, 1714–1760.* Cambridge, MA: Harvard University Press, 1977. A solid treatment of sources of political conflict in eighteenth-century England, particularly useful on the topic of operation of patronage and influence in Parliament.

The French and Indian War secured Great Britain's dominance of North America. In this engraving, the British general at the Battle of Quebec, James Wolfe, lies mortally wounded. (Reproduced from the Collections of the Library of Congress)

3

The French and Indian War, 1754–1763

INTRODUCTION

France had been consolidating her hold on parts of North America since 1608, one year after the founding of Jamestown, when the explorer and geographer Samuel de Champlain founded Quebec. From that settlement, the French expanded their territory so that by Champlain's death in 1635 they controlled the St. Lawrence River and were poised to take possession of the Great Lakes. However, hard times fell on the French colonization efforts, and New France, as the area came to be known, remained chronically weak. The unfriendly climate and barren soil of eastern Canada were no drawing card, and Frenchmen seemed reluctant to leave France for the New World. Religious dissenters were forbidden to emigrate to Canada, and the whole colonial administration was hindered by a home government that interfered in all phases of colonial activity. Despite these difficulties, the French had great success as explorers and traders. They worked well with the Indians, willingly acquiring Indian ways and wives, factors that proved of significant military and economic value. Indians procured furs for them, fought battles against the British for them, and served as guides on expeditions all throughout the central part of North America. With Indian help, France could claim most of interior America and thus constitute a threat to British colonial security. But only 7,000 French lived in North America in 1700, and this meant for Canada an increased dependence on France for food and protection and more of that meddlesome French bureaucracy. The historian Francis Parkman, writing in the nineteenth century, summed it up: "It was the nature of French colonization to seize upon detached strategic points and hold them by the bayonet, forming no agricultural base, but attracting the Indians by trade and holding them by conversion. A musket, a rosary, and a pack of beaver skins may serve to represent it, and in fact, it consisted of little else."

Before 1660, there had been no serious conflict between the French and British in North America. Between 1689 and 1815, however, these two countries fought a series of seven wars. Why? The reasons for this long era of conflict lay partly in the general European rivalry over the balance of power (in all of these wars, other nations fought with Britain and France), partly in the basic conflict of interest produced by rival systems of mercantilism, and partly in direct colonial conflicts. Both Britain and France looked upon their colonies as integral and exceedingly valuable sectors of their whole national economies; colonial trade for each nation by the early eighteenth century amounted to nearly one-third of its entire foreign commerce, and the wealth of the influential merchant classes in both countries was due largely to profits made from that colonial trade.

The most important difference in the two colonial systems lay in the manner of settlement and administration. France, as we have seen, governed its colonies from Paris and, unlike Britain, made little effort to install a system of local government in North America. Commercial profit, and not immigration, was France's objective. Great Britain, on the other hand, permitted local self-government, and under the policy of salutary neglect (see Chapter 2), left the colonies very much on their own. In addition, Britain's desire to populate its North American colonies produced by 1750 a population imbalance of twenty to one in favor of the British.

In other ways the colonial systems were similar. Both used slave labor, both tried to regulate the economic life of the colonies for their own good by utilizing the mercantile system, and both found themselves competitors in several different economic areas. British and French fishermen competed off the coast of Newfoundland and Nova Scotia. In the back country, trappers vied for valuable furs and the friendship and support of the resident Indian tribes, the French allying with the Algonquins, and the British with their great rivals, the Iroquois.

By the 1750s, colonial possessions in North America were becoming

Peachtree Branch
404-885-7830
www.afpls.org

User name: LAGUNA,
MANUEL (MR.)

Title: Events that changed
America in the eighteenth
cen
Author: Findling, John E.
Item ID: R0080587676
Date due: 10/29/2018,23:
59
Current time: 10/01/2018,
11:16

increasingly important in the diplomatic maneuverings of Europe, and the colonies were often mentioned in discussions concerning the balance of power. A French minister said in 1758: "The King believes, Monsieur, that it is the possessions in America that will in the future form the balance of power in Europe and that if the English invade that part of the world, as it appears they have the intention of doing, it will result therefrom that England will usurp the commerce of the colonies, and that she alone will remain rich in Europe."

The ultimate contest between France and Great Britain was the Great War for Empire (called the Seven Years' War in Europe, where it was fought from 1756 to 1763, and the French and Indian War in North America, where it lasted from 1754 to 1763). This war was different in two major aspects from the earlier wars fought between England and France. First, in the earlier wars, the great British victories had been won in Europe; in this war, they were won in North America and India. This is explained by the growing naval power of Great Britain and the growing realization of the importance of colonial empires. Second, in the earlier wars, American colonists had fought without much British aid, reflecting Britain's lesser concern for colonies at the time. In this war, however, British regulars did most of the fighting, even in the early stages. Britain thus showed her recognition of the increased importance of its colonies and of the fact that the balance of power would be determined by events outside Europe.

It is worth noting that at this time wars were quite limited in scope; these were not wars of national survival such as the twentieth century has experienced. Each belligerent had limited aims, usually territorial, and fought with small professional armies, which were affordable in relation to the objectives of the war. And while no one cared much about the humanity of the soldiers involved, a good deal of money and time went into their training and the installation of discipline, and that was something not to be wasted. Consequently, battles were fought formally on fields carefully chosen to allow the disciplined movement of regular troops. To fight the Indians in North America (or later, the colonists) was altogether different in terms of tactics. And the nature of the war, fought in distant frontier sites, made logistics a potentially serious problem.

The French and Indian War also saw the first use of the Kentucky rifle, a better weapon for irregular or guerrilla war than the musket because of its much greater accuracy. One could hit a man's head at 200 yards if one was reasonably proficient. Although rifling (the practice of scoring the inside of the barrel to give a spin to the bullet, which produced greater accuracy) had been known for many years, the Kentucky rifle was the first to be developed that was light enough to carry comfortably and acceptably fast to load. But Kentucky rifles were never used widely because they were individually made, which meant that bullets had to be custom made for each rifle. Despite a greater ease of loading, the rate of fire was only one-third that of the musket, and the standard bayonet did not fit. Thus, the Kentucky rifle was no good for formal battle lines but fine for firing from behind trees or rocks.

The relative position of the two great powers on the North American continent was well-defined in 1756. English colonies still huddled along the Atlantic coast from present-day Maine to Georgia, heavily populated along the coast and extending only a short distance inland. French control stretched in an L-shaped pattern from Quebec down the St. Lawrence River, through the Great Lakes, and from there down the Mississippi River to its mouth near New Orleans. French expansion seemed to delimit strictly the English colonies and their potential growth.

Despite the disparity in population, the French in America were better prepared for war. French military power rested in its army, the greatest on the European continent, while Britain relied more on its navy. The French had a larger military establishment in America, and French soldiers were better trained and led than their English counterparts. Finally, France's Indian allies were more reliable.

Great Britain's best strategy was thus a war of attrition, using its navy to cut off as much as possible the flow of supplies from France to Canada, while building up its own troop strength and stock of supplies. No one, however, in London in the early 1750s seems to have figured this out, and instead, British troops made futile attempts to break out of the French encirclement in the early years of the war. Thus did General Edward Braddock's disaster at Fort Duquesne (near present-day Pittsburgh) happen, an event that gave young George Washington some good experience but contributed nothing but apathy and defeatism to British forces as they were pushed back along the whole perimeter.

Finally, under the astute leadership of the brilliant prime minister William Pitt, the British military machine began to function. Pitt diverted French attention (and troops) by aiding his European ally, Prussia. He built the colonial governments into important agencies in support of the war effort by reconciling many of the differences between the British army and the colonists. He strengthened both the fleet and the army and found good leaders within the officer ranks instead of looking within the circle of his political allies, as was the general custom. Finally, he worked out a unified plan of overall strategy for the conflict.

After their shaky beginning, British troops did relatively well in America, impressing Americans enough so that they created their own revolutionary army in the British image. British success also created overconfidence among the troops when they returned to fight Americans in the Revolution. But British discipline allowed them to withstand an Indian attack without breaking ranks and then outlast the Indians, forcing them into an open battle. Moreover, the British were flexible enough to adapt to the frontier setting of much of the war. Troops maneuvered in smaller units (companies rather than battalions), good use was made of reconnaissance, and care was taken to ensure march and camp security. Some troops were designated to learn ranger skills, and other regiments learned to fire from a prone position, an innovation for that day. Likewise, they learned to march single file through a forest and jump behind a tree in response to the command, "Tree all!" The British could, of course, still fight a traditional European battle and did in 1759, when Pitt's strategy culminated in a great thrust by land and sea at Quebec, the heart of New France, led by James Wolfe. At 32, Wolfe was already a leader of great reputation and considerable experience. At Quebec, he faced the equally able French general, the Marquis de Montcalm. The climax of the war came after a two-month siege when Wolfe and the British stormed the Plains of Abraham outside Quebec and captured the city. Both generals were killed, but the French were the real losers. Montreal fell a year later, and the Treaty of Paris officially ended the war in 1763.

In the treaty, Britain won all of New France (Canada) and all of interior America except for the port of New Orleans. France retained fishing rights off Newfoundland and the islands of St. Pierre and Miquelon as fishing bases. Britain returned to France the captured West Indian islands of Guadalupe and Martinique but acquired East and West Florida from France's ally, Spain, who, in turn, received from France all its territory west of the Mississippi River, as well as New Orleans (what later became, roughly, the Louisiana Purchase).

The consequences for the colonies were immense. The war removed the checks on the westward expansion of the colonists, except for the natural barriers of the forests and mountains. British institutions were bound to move westward across the Appalachian range. In addition, the war was something of a unifying force for the colonies. At the least, it made them more aware of each other and of the commonality of their problems. While response to the Albany Convention, called in 1754 to work out a common Indian policy, had ranged from indifferent to hostile, response to the Stamp Act in 1765, just two years after the war, was direct and united.

For the British, the war created the conditions that led to many of the disputes with the colonies between 1763 and 1776 that, in turn, led to the American Revolution. Britain had problems of how to administer, settle, and protect the land acquired from the French, how to run a much expanded global empire, and how to handle the great new burden of war debts, for Pitt had borrowed heavily to finance his successful war effort. These British problems would run headlong into colonial affairs and meet stout resistance from colonists, who found themselves much less dependent on Britain for protection from the French and therefore much bolder in fighting for their own rights and interests. Moreover, the limited enthusiasm of the colonists for the war had demonstrated serious flaws in the idea of salutary neglect.

Significantly, Great Britain had crowned a new king in 1760. He was George III, grandson of George II and the first of his dynasty to have any real English sympathies. George I and II had been far more attached to their native Hanover (a part of present-day Germany) than to England, spoke little English and cared little for England's problems. But George III was thoroughly British and proud of it and determined to be a king in deed as well as in name. He asserted his constitutional rights, maneuvered the normally antiroyalist Whig party out of Parliamentary control, where they had been since 1721, and by bribes and royal favors, installed his friends in positions of power in Parliament, thus gaining a personal control of government. In 1763, George III made George Grenville his prime minister. Grenville was William Pitt's brother-in-law, but he did not share Pitt's conciliatory attitude toward the colonies; rather, he felt that the colonies should be made to pay a part of the cost of defending and running the Empire and should also be made to obey the law, especially with respect to the various acts regulating commerce. His ministry, which lasted until 1765, thus initiated the chain of events that led to the Revolutionary War. Because of this, it can be said that the greatest consequence of the French and Indian War is that it set the stage for the American Revolution.

INTERPRETIVE ESSAY
Thomas Clarkin

Beginning in the late seventeenth century, the British and French colonies in North America became embroiled in a series of colonial wars that resulted from competition between Great Britain and France. King William's War (1689–1697), Queen Anne's War (1702–1713), and King George's War (1743–1748) were essentially European conflicts that spilled over into North America. Though these three wars caused hardship and suffering for many colonists, North American concerns played only a small role in the wider wars fought to determine which nation would gain political dominance in Europe. However, the final war, which began in 1754, grew out of the struggle to control the resources and the trading opportunities in the region between the Appalachian Mountains and the Mississippi River. The conflict in North America eventually spread to Europe and other parts of the globe, leading many historians to regard the event as the first true world war.

The final colonial war is known by several names. In Europe it was later called the Seven Years' War, although the violence lasted for nine years. Americans refer to it as the French and Indian War, which is somewhat misleading because Native Americans fought for both the French and the English. Regardless of its name, the conflict constituted a turning point in the history of North America. The Treaty of Paris, which ended the war, also ended any realistic French hope of remaining an imperial power in North America. Perhaps more important, the conduct of the war strained relations between the British colonies and the mother country. The tensions and resentments which developed helped to spark the American Revolution.

Though King George's War ended in a stalemate, French leaders realized that their power in North America was on the wane. The British population was growing at a rapid rate, and because British manufactured goods were of a higher quality than those of the French, English traders were successfully capturing a larger and larger share of the lucrative trade with Native Americans. British expansion posed a serious threat to the French empire—if the British gained control of the Ohio Valley, they could sever communications between the French possessions of Canada and Louisiana. In 1749, the French sent Céleron de Blainville through the upper Ohio Valley to impress the Native Americans of the region with French power and to instruct the tribes to expel British traders. Céleron buried lead plates bearing inscriptions that declared French sovereignty over various locations which he visited, but French leaders knew that a more concerted effort would be necessary. The following year French officials began arresting and jailing British traders who operated in the area, and in 1753 they authorized the construction of several small forts in the Ohio Valley.

Authorities in London and in the colonies reacted with alarm to the French activities, and the royal governor of Virginia received instructions to use force to meet the French threat. Because both the British and the French recognized the strategic importance of the Forks of the Ohio, where the Allegheny and Monongahela Rivers meet, both sides raced to occupy and defend the Forks. Though a small company of Virginians arrived first, a larger French force successfully routed them and began building an outpost which they called Fort Duquesne. Attempts to dislodge the French from the Forks failed, and in July 1754, Lieutenant-Colonel George Washington, leader of a Virginia militia force sent to attack Fort Duquesne, had to surrender to the French after a brief battle. To make matters worse for the British colonists, the French were gaining influence with Native American leaders who up to that time had remained neutral.

Despite these conflicts, Britain and France were not yet formally at war. The British government decided, however, that the French must be driven out of the Ohio Valley. Officials realized that the Virginians could not defeat the French without assistance; they also knew that a cooperative effort between the colonies was unlikely. The government decided to send British troops to resolve the conflict, and in late 1754 Major General Edward Braddock departed for Virginia with two regiments of British regulars. While making preparations for a 1755 offensive against the French, Braddock encountered several difficulties that indicated that working with the colonists would prove difficult and frustrating.

The British government had determined that civil authorities in the colonies would be subordinate to British military commanders in most matters concerning the conduct of war. However, Braddock soon discovered that the colonists and their representatives had no intention of complying with his demands. He met with resistance from the colonial governments and the people. Jealous of their powers over expenditures and over colonial armies, the colonial assemblies often refused to cooperate with Braddock and his officers. In April 1755, Braddock asked the royal governors to create a common defense fund to pay for supplies and other military costs. The governors informed him that the assemblies would never agree to such a plan, which was then dropped. Braddock also had difficulty procuring supplies for his army. He needed wagons and horses to prepare for the expedition to Fort Duquesne, but the colonists proved unwilling to rent their property to the army. Braddock threatened to take the wagons without payment, but Benjamin Franklin persuaded farmers in the region to rent their wagons to the army.

In addition to disputes over money and supplies, differences concerning the status of provincial troops also arose. In 1755 approximately 5,000 colonists enlisted in the British army, where they served as regulars. However, most colonists chose to serve in provincial armies, which remained under the authority of colonial leaders. In 1754 the British government had decreed that provincial officers would be subordinate to British army officers of the same rank. For example, colonial captains would have to obey the orders of British captains. The colonial officers regarded this as an insult, and the resulting resentment increased friction between colonial troops and British regulars and made cooperation difficult.

Despite the numerous problems he faced, Braddock managed to devise a strategy for defeating the French. Four different forces would strike at French garrisons in hopes of destroying supply and communication lines. William Shirley, the royal governor of Massachusetts whom Braddock appointed as his second-in-command, would lead an attack on the French outpost at Niagara, between Lake Ontario and Lake Erie. William Johnson, superintendent of Indian affairs, would take Crown Point on Lake Champlain. A third British force would move against Fort Beauséjour in Nova Scotia. Finally, Braddock would personally lead his troops in the attack on Fort Duquesne.

The British offensive failed. British and colonial troops captured Fort Beauséjour without great difficulty in the only successful campaign of the year, but Shirley never reached Niagara, and though Johnson engaged French troops in the Battle of Lake George, he never reached Crown Point. Braddock's expedition met with disaster. In June 1755, his army marched into the dense woodlands on their way to Fort Duquesne. On July 9, these troops encountered a force of French soldiers and their Indian allies. The Indian warriors fired from the forests on the British troops, who were confined to a narrow trail. The French and Indians sustained minimal casualties, while nearly 70 percent of the British troops were killed or wounded, with Braddock among the dead. The surviving British soldiers fled in a panic.

The failure of the 1755 campaigns in general and of Braddock's expedition in particular shocked and outraged officials both in London and in the colonies. Thomas Gage, a lieutenant colonel under Braddock, blamed the defeat on the colonists, who had refused to outfit and supply the troops. George Washington, a survivor of the expedition, claimed that the British regular soldiers had performed badly under fire. Regardless of the real reasons for the disaster, the squabbles between colonists and the British revealed an intense dislike and distrust that would only grow as the war continued. After Braddock's defeat the number of colonists who enlisted in the British army dropped dramatically, and colonial attitudes toward the redcoats became increasingly negative. At the end of 1755 the French held the upper hand in the Ohio Valley while the British and their colonial allies could not agree on a military strategy that would ensure victory. Thus, the first phase of the French and Indian War concluded without any significant shift in the balance of power in North America.

Great Britain formally declared war against France in May 1756. John Campbell, Lord Loudon, who was selected to lead the war effort in North America, arrived in New York in July. Loudon was determined to teach the colonial governments that they were subordinate to the Crown, but he quickly discovered that colonists were willing to defy British authorities at every turn. One particularly sore point was the recruitment of colonists into the British army. After Braddock's defeat, declining enlistments in the regular army led the British to use questionable means to acquire new soldiers. Some recruiters used threats or deception to induce colonists to enlist; others relied upon alcohol, signing up the recruit when he was drunk. Colonists grew so angry at such practices that that they sometimes attacked recruiters—in at least one instance an irate crowd killed a recruiting sergeant. Especially irritating to the colonial elites was the practice of recruiting indentured servants, who were often eager to leave their employers. Merchants complained that recruiting servants before their contracts expired was tantamount to theft. The British government asked the colonies to create a fund to reimburse masters for their losses, but, in typical fashion, the assemblies refused to comply. Loudon arrived in the colonies with a government decree that required recruiters to compensate masters, but, much to his frustration, colonial complaints about recruiting continued. Loudon did not improve his relations with the colonists when his troops assisted naval press gangs in New York in 1757. Press gangs seized citizens and forced them aboard ships for involuntary service, a practice which understandably infuriated the colonists and worsened relations with the military.

The housing of British troops, known as quartering, was another source of contention between Loudon and the colonists. In England the army had the right to quarter its troops in inns, but in the colonies they also had to make use of privately owned buildings such as barns and, in some cases, houses. Army officials maintained that in a time of war the citizenry had no cause for complaint about such practices, but the colonists thought otherwise. They argued that the forced housing of soldiers on private property was a violation of their rights, and colonial authorities agreed. Loudon and other army officers claimed that the colonists were merely stingy and unwilling to make the necessary sacrifices to fight a war. When the people of Albany, New York, protested the quartering of troops in their city, Loudon threatened force to end the complaints. He made similar threats to the citizens of Philadelphia and Boston, and the colonists grudgingly complied with Loudon's commands. Though Loudon usually won the arguments over quartering, the disagreements only led to more friction and animosity between the British and the colonists.

Trade restrictions also contributed to the growing tensions during Loudon's tenure as commander-in-chief. Fearing that colonial resources would end up in French hands and help the French war effort, several colonies imposed trade embargoes on provisions such as grain and war materials. These embargoes usually hurt local economies because farmers and merchants were unable to ship their merchandise to buyers. When Pennsylvania revised its embargo in 1756, Loudon responded with a total embargo on shipping in Virginia and all colonies to the north. Suffering from the resulting economic crisis, several colonial assemblies voted to lift the embargo. Loudon ignored their protests. The dispute between Loudon and the local governments over trade restrictions served as an example of the intractable problems that marred the British war effort. Concerned only with winning the war and convinced that he wielded total authority in that effort, Loudon ignored the economic impact of the embargo and the complaints of the colonial assemblies. The colonists perceived Loudon's actions as evidence that British officials did not respect their governments and were unconcerned with their needs and welfare.

Loudon's failure to control the colonies was matched by his inability to wage a successful war. Campaigns planned by William Shirley before

Loudon's appointment brought no victories in early 1756. In addition, Louis Joseph, Marquis de Montcalm, the new French commander, proved to be a capable adversary. In August 1756, he led an expedition against the British garrison at Oswego, located on the shores of Lake Ontario. After three days of battle the British force surrendered. The loss of Oswego denied the British a base of operations from which to attack French forces at Niagara, thus weakening the British ability to mount an offensive, and Montcalm rightfully claimed a great victory. In 1757, Loudon hoped to deliver a crippling blow to New France with an attack on Louisbourg, a French fort on Cape Breton Island off the coast of Nova Scotia. The capture of Louisbourg would allow the British to block French supply ships from reaching the St. Lawrence River, effectively strangling New France. In 1745 Louisbourg had fallen to a colonial force during King George's War but had been returned to France as part of the 1748 peace treaty. Though Loudon's plan was sound, preparations for the Louisbourg expedition took months. During that time the French received information about the planned attack and so deployed a naval squadron to defend the fort. Loudon had no choice but to abandon the expedition. To make matters worse, Montcalm scored another victory, forcing the British to surrender Fort William Henry, which was located north of Albany, New York.

Native American support for the French added to the bleak outlook for the British war effort in 1757. Many Native American communities regarded the British colonies, which were constantly expanding, as a greater threat to their interests, and so sided with the French. In addition, the French victories in the early years of the war convinced many Indians that the French would prevail. Indian support allowed the French to augment their armed forces. The Indians also waged an effective style of guerrilla warfare that wreaked havoc on outlying British settlements. Though some Native Americans allied with the British, the general trend of native support for the French was viewed with alarm in the British colonies. Thus, as the 1757 campaign season drew to a close, Lord Loudon could claim no major victories, no improvement in his relations with the colonies, and worsening relations with Native Americans. Given the status of the British effort in North America, Loudon had no hope of continuing as commander-in-chief. Management of the war became the responsibility of the brilliant William Pitt, whose strategies would turn the tide and ensure a British victory.

Pitt, who became prime minister in 1757, believed that British war resources were squandered in European battles. He maintained that victory in North America was far more important for protecting British interests as a shipping and trading nation. Though James Abercromby replaced Loudon, it was Pitt who planned strategy. Recognizing that squabbles with the colonial assemblies slowed the prosecution of the war, Pitt sought to improve relations with the colonists. He sent more British regulars to fight the war in order to end the disagreements concerning unpopular recruiting practices and British authority over provincial troops. He informed the colonial assemblies that the Crown would reimburse them for military expenses, a promise that resulted in an expansion of the provincial forces. To improve relations with these forces, Pitt ended the practice of subordinating provincial officers to their counterparts in the regular army. These initiatives reinvigorated the colonies and bolstered support for the war.

Pitt used the powerful British navy to prevent French supply shipments from reaching North America, preventing New France from receiving foodstuffs, war materials and new troops. With the French weakened, the 1758 offensive struck at several major French outposts, including attacks at Ticonderoga, Louisbourg, and Fort Duquesne. Ticonderoga proved to be a calamity as the British commander marched his troops in a frontal attack which resulted in enormous casualties, but all the other campaigns brought victory. Louisbourg fell in July after a siege of nearly two months; the British troops who arrived at Fort Duquesne in November discovered that the French had burned and abandoned the fort.

The British victories in 1758 marked a turning point in the war. Pitt's policies had not ended the disputes with the British colonies, but they had reduced their impact on the conduct of the war. The influx of British troops made it possible to attack successfully the French on several fronts, destroying their internal supply and communication lines. The naval blockade of French ports had pushed New France to the edge of starvation; and, unable to provide their Native American allies with trade goods and gifts, the French lost the support of several tribes. The stage was set for the expulsion of the French from North America. To achieve that end, Pitt focused his attention on the city of Quebec, situated on the St. Lawrence River. If Quebec fell, virtually all of Canada would belong to Britain.

The 1759 offensive involved attacks on all fronts, one against the western French outpost of Niagara, a second north through the Champlain Valley toward Montreal, and a third west along the St. Lawrence River to Quebec. British ships patrolling the St. Lawrence continued to prevent supplies from reaching the beleaguered French forces. Montcalm and his armies were forced on the defensive without the provisions or troop reinforcements necessary to battle the British. Niagara fell into British hands after a siege of three weeks. Realizing that they could not hope to defend Crown Point or Ticonderoga in the Champlain Valley, the French commanders used delaying tactics as they retreated toward Montreal. However, the most important victory came in September, when Major General James Wolfe and his troops captured the city of Quebec.

Recognizing the importance of defending Quebec, Montcalm had assembled most of his troops there. Wolfe and his men had no problems reaching the city, but once there they faced serious difficulties. Situated upon a high cliff overlooking the St. Lawrence, Quebec offered a strong defensive position for the French forces. Wolfe pondered the attack on the city for nearly three months, from June to September. A frontal assault in late July proved disastrous, and Wolfe was at a loss as to how to capture the city. However, in early September he discovered the existence of a tiny, steep trail that climbed the cliffs near the city. In a daring nighttime maneuver, British troops traveled in boats to the beach at the cliff's base, silenced the small French outpost they found there, and began to climb the plateau above. By daybreak Wolfe had assembled nearly 5,000 men on the Plains of Abraham, a flat area atop the cliffs adjacent to the city itself. When word of the British troop movement arrived, Montcalm rushed his force of French, Canadian, and Indian troops outside the city to face the enemy. What followed was the stuff of legend.

A classic European-style battle ensued, with the French slowly advancing on the British line. The redcoats held their fire until the French were almost upon them and then released a volley that destroyed the French line. Both Montcalm and Wolfe received mortal wounds, with the British commander dying on the field of battle. The French forces fell into a disorganized retreat, abandoning Quebec to regroup closer to Montreal. The garrison commander within Quebec had no choice but to surrender the city, and the British claimed a great victory. Historians have criticized the performance of both Wolfe and Montcalm, but the battle on the Plains of Abraham became the story of two brilliant, young generals dying in one of the most important battles in American history.

The French defeat at Quebec marked the end of any real French resistance in North America. Native Americans who had allied with the French now sought to repair their relations with the victorious British. In 1760 the British launched an attack from three directions on the remaining French forces assembled at Montreal. The French commander wisely surrendered before battle began. The Seven Years' War would continue for three more years, fought on the high seas, in Europe and in other spots on the globe, but with the capture of Montreal the North American phase of the war came to a close.

In 1763 Great Britain and France signed the Treaty of Paris, which ended the war between the two nations. In North America, France ceded Canada and its holdings east of the Mississippi save the city of New Orleans to England, retaining only two islands near Newfoundland and some sugar islands in the Caribbean. Pitt's strategy had proven effective, and the mood throughout the British Empire, in both England and the colonies, was jubilant. The colonists expressed great pride and pleasure at being members of the mightiest empire in the world. For the Native American communities in the Ohio Valley and in the southern United States, however, the future was not so bright. Most Native Americans did not benefit from the British victory. Because the British colonists were expansionist in their outlook, Indian sovereignty was not guaranteed and Indian land was at risk. For decades the tribes had retained their sovereignty and acquired valuable gifts by playing the British and the French against one another. When the French had posed a threat or refused to supply the Indians with desired goods, Native American communities cooperated with the British until the French changed their policies. Now that the French were gone, the Indians had no choice but to work with the British, who in many ways had less respect for Native Americans than the French did. British General Jeffrey Amherst held the Indians in contempt. In an attempt to reduce expenditures, Amherst curtailed the exchange of gifts with the Indians, a decision which caused much resentment among the tribes. Seeking to end conflicts between colonists and Indians, the British government announced the Proclamation of 1763, which established a boundary line that followed the Appalachian Mountains. Settlers were not to occupy lands west of the line. However, most colonists ignored the boundary, and the British found it impossible to enforce its decree. For Native Americans, the French defeat meant a loss of negotiating power and the continued loss of their lands.

The war also had negative consequences for relations between the colonies and Great Britain. The frictions between the Crown and the colonies pointed to divisions within the Empire that heralded trouble in the coming years, divisions which ultimately led to the American Revolution. Waging war against New France during the 1750s had required close contact and cooperation between the British and the colonists to a degree never before reached. The earlier colonial wars had necessitated some coordination of regular and provincial troops, which had resulted in disagreements. The scale and scope of the French and Indian War were far greater than those of the earlier wars, however, resulting in more tension between the allies. The disputes which arose revealed that the colonists perceived their role in the Empire in a completely different manner than British authorities did. In addition, the interpersonal contact between colonists and British regulars led each side to develop opinions that were often negative, offering little ground for cooperation in the postwar years.

Over the years the colonists' considerable distance from Great Britain had led them to rely on their assemblies for legislative and financial policies. Though the royal governors represented the interests of the Crown, they found it almost impossible to conduct government affairs without the agreement and support of the assemblies. British commanders such as Braddock and Loudon arrived in North America prepared to fight a war against an enemy of the Empire. Anticipating only cooperation from the colonial governments, they were shocked and angered to discover that the assemblies wanted an equal say in the conduct of military affairs. They had no respect for these colonial institutions, which they regarded as subordinate to the Crown. The assemblies took a far different view. Because colonial money was being spent, and the lives of colonists in the provincial forces were being risked, the assemblies maintained that they had the right and the responsibility to oversee the war effort. Thus, ongoing disputes about quartering, supplies, and recruiting were not merely the complaints of ungrateful colonists; they represented potentially irreconcilable differences concerning the power and authority of the colonial assemblies.

For many of the colonists in British North America, the war was the first time they had come into contact with a large number of people from Great Britain. Unfortunately, the British regulars were a rough lot, typically drawn from the lowest classes of society and sometimes having criminal backgrounds. The behavior of these redcoats, combined with the unpopular recruiting and quartering policies, created an attitude of contempt toward the soldiers and, to some degree, England in general. On occasion mobs attacked the British soldiers, even after Pitt's policies had brought popular victories. Relations between the regulars and the provincial troops were usually not much better. The British army relied upon strict discipline and unquestioning obedience to orders. Infractions were met with swift and extreme punishments which included execution. The provincial troops regarded themselves as volunteers and expected to be treated with respect, an attitude that the British could not understand. As a result, the regulars and their officers regarded the provincials as amateurs and bumpkins, while the colonists perceived the regulars as haughty and mean-spirited. In addition, the regulars were given to swearing and violating the Sabbath. Such behaviors shocked the colonists, who put far more stock in religion than did the British. While there were many occasions on which the regulars and provincials worked well together and even formed friendships, the general attitudes that each group held toward the other were ones of dislike and contempt.

These contacts between colonists and the British created negative perceptions that were to have tremendous consequences in the postwar years. Colonists saw the British authorities as despotic, willing to run rampant over their constitutional rights. Their experiences with the regulars led them to believe that the British were an irreligious and arrogant people. On the other hand, the British perceived the colonists as greedy and unprincipled. Throughout the war British officers claimed, in many cases correctly, that colonial merchants profited from the war by overcharging the army for supplies. They viewed the actions of the assemblies as unpatriotic obstructions to the conduct of the war. These perceptions lingered on both sides after the war ended, and shaped the reactions to the events that eventually culminated in the American Revolution.

The French and Indian War contributed to the coming of the Revolution in another fashion. Pitt's policies of using more regular troops and of spending money from the British treasury to fight the war did not resolve any of the deeper problems between the mother country and the colonies, but they did allow for a British victory. However, the price of success had to be paid at some point. After the war the British government found itself burdened with a tremendous debt of approximately £145 million. During the 1760s, the government turned to taxing the colonies to pay for the war. It was these tax increases that sparked the protests against taxation without representation.

The French and Indian War shaped the future of North America in ways that no earlier war had. The expulsion of the French from the continent liberated the colonists from the threat of invasion and the burden of economic competition and opened the way to the expansion in the west. It also reduced the colonial dependence on Great Britain for defense. The defeat of the French was thus a tremendous boon to the colonists and the British empire. However, the victory contained the seeds for future conflict between the citizens of the colonies and England, conflict which in a dozen years would lead to another war and the eventual creation of a new nation in North America.

SELECTED BIBLIOGRAPHY

Alberts, Robert C. *The Most Extraordinary Adventures of Major Robert Stobo.* Boston: Houghton Mifflin, 1965. A biography of one of the most unusual and interesting figures in the French and Indian War.

Anderson, Fred. *A People's Army: Massachusetts Soldiers and Society in the Seven Years' War.* New York: W. W. Norton, 1984. An excellent study of provincial attitudes toward the British and the war.

Bird, Harrison. *Battle for a Continent.* New York: Oxford University Press, 1965. Harrison offers a detailed military history of the war.

Donaldson, Gordon. *Battle for a Continent: Quebec, 1759.* Toronto: Doubleday Canada Ltd., 1973. A narrative history of the climactic battle of the French and Indian War.

Downey, Fairfax. *Louisbourg: Key to a Continent.* Englewood Cliffs, NJ: Prentice-Hall, 1966. A history of one of the most important forts in North America in the eighteenth century.

Fregault, Guy. *Canada: The War of the Conquest.* Toronto: Oxford University Press, 1969. Discusses the war from the perspective of Canadian history.

Furneaux, Rupert. *The Seven Years War.* London: Hart-Davis, MacGibbon, 1973. A brief and well-illustrated military history of the war.

Hamilton, Charles, ed. *Braddock's Defeat.* Norman: University of Oklahoma Press, 1959. A collection of firsthand accounts of Braddock's defeat in 1755.

Igneri, David S. *Sir William Johnson: The Man and His Influence.* New York: Rivercross, 1994. Examines Johnson's relationship with the Iroquois and its impact on the outcome of the war.

Jennings, Francis. *Empire of Fortune: Crowns, Colonies, and Tribes in the Seven Years' War.* New York: W. W. Norton, 1988. Jennings offers shrewd and sometimes caustic analyses of the interactions between colonists and Indians.

Keegan, John. *Warpaths: Travels of a Military Historian in North America.* London: Hodder & Stoughton, 1995. A leading military historian offers observations on the forts of New France.

Kopperman, Paul E. *Braddock at the Monongahela.* Pittsburgh: University of Pittsburgh Press, 1977. Includes several eyewitness accounts of the disastrous expedition to the Forks of the Ohio.

Leach, Douglas Edward. *Arms for Empire: A Military History of the British Colonies in North America, 1607–1763.* New York: Macmillan, 1973. A highly readable general history of the colonial wars with detailed descriptions of battles.

———. *Roots of Conflict: British Armed Forces and Colonial Americans, 1677–1763.* Chapel Hill: University of North Carolina Press, 1986. Focuses on the differences that arose between the British army and the colonists during the colonial wars.

Lewis, Meriwether Liston. *Montcalm: The Marvelous Marquis*. New York: Vantage Press, 1961. A brief biography of the leading French general.

Marshall, Peter, and Glyn Williams. *The British Atlantic Empire Before the American Revolution*. London: Frank Cass, 1980. A collection of essays that examines the relationship between the colonies and England through the Seven Years' War.

McConnell, Michael N. *A Country Between: The Upper Ohio Valley and Its Peoples, 1724–1774*. Lincoln: University of Nebraska Press, 1992. Contains useful information about Native Americans and their involvement in the war.

O'Meara, Walter. *Guns at the Forks*. Englewood Cliffs, NJ: Prentice-Hall, 1966. Discusses events at the Forks of the Ohio from 1753 to 1760.

Parkman, Francis. *Montcalm and Wolfe*. Toronto: Ryerson Press, 1964. Originally published in 1884, Parkman's account is considered a classic example of nineteenth-century historical writing.

Peckham, Howard H. *The Colonial Wars, 1689–1762*. Chicago: University of Chicago Press, 1964. Looks at each of the colonial wars and includes a timeline of important dates.

Rogers, Alan. *Empire and Liberty: American Resistance to British Authority, 1755–1763*. Berkeley: University of California Press, 1974. Discusses disputes over issues such as recruiting, quartering, and Indian affairs.

Sherrard, O. A. *Lord Chatham: Pitt and the Seven Years' War*. London: Bodley Head, 1955. The second volume in a multivolume biography examines Pitt's role in managing the French and Indian War.

Stacey, C. P. *Quebec, 1759*. Toronto: Macmillan, 1966. A detailed account of the battle for Quebec.

Steele, Ian K. *Warpaths: Invasions of North America*. New York: Oxford University Press, 1994. Steele's final chapters are devoted to the French and Indian War.

Warner, Oliver. *With Wolfe to Quebec: The Path to Glory*. Toronto: Collins, 1972. Examines the 1759 campaign from the perspective of the British general.

White, Richard. *The Middle Ground: Indians, Empires and Republics in the Great Lakes Region, 1650–1815*. Cambridge: Cambridge University Press, 1991. A difficult but rewarding book which considers the cultural interactions between Native Americans and Europeans, with material on the "playing-off" of the French and English.

Few British acts aroused as much colonial resentment as the Stamp Act of 1765, as revealed in this print showing colonists making a tax collector's life miserable. (Reproduced from the Collections of the Library of Congress)

4

The Stamp Act, 1765

INTRODUCTION

The French and Indian War had left the British an undisputed world power, but one with great and complex new problems. There were the tremendous war debts, compounded by the loud objections of British merchants to the imposition of more taxes. The limited enthusiasm of the colonists for the recent war had demonstrated serious flaws in the idea of salutary neglect (see Chapter 2). The great acquisitions west of the Appalachians created new problems of administration and defense; many feared that France might arise again in an attempt to recover some of its lost territory and pride.

The British approach to handling the postwar problems was not helped by the turbulent state of politics in London during the 1760s. George III, who became king in 1760 at the age of twenty-two, was the first of his line to put his own stamp on British government. As a youth, he had observed some of the machinations of Whig and Tory politicians, and he felt that George II and his followers had not treated his mother very well after his father's death in 1751. He came to the throne, therefore, determined to cleanse British politics of those who had been loyal to his grandfather. His youth and inexperience at conciliation soon taught him that the only way he could deal at all successfully in the

political world was by being stubborn in defense of his views. Surrounding himself with politicians who had been in the opposition under
George II, he found himself nesting with those who, in general, advocated a tough stand toward the colonies, particularly with respect to
measures designed to reduce the horrendous debt problem left over from
the war. Among these politicians was George Grenville, never a personal
favorite of George, but an individual determined to fight Britain's debt
problem by all means possible. Grenville believed that the colonies
should bear at least part of the cost of their own administration and that
it would be fiscally responsible to make the colonies obey existing mercantilist regulations. The chain of events that led ultimately to the American Revolution began in 1763, during Grenville's ministry.

Among the various British-American disputes in the immediate postwar period, three are of particular significance: the Proclamation of 1763,
the Sugar Act of 1764, and, most importantly, the Stamp Act of 1765.

The most urgent problem following the Treaty of Paris concerned the
western lands acquired from France, because a federation of Indian tribes
under Chief Pontiac had attempted to defend their hunting grounds by
striking violently at the earliest English settlers to cross the Appalachians.
Although Pontiac's Indians were put down, largely by British troops, the
government in London issued the Proclamation of 1763, which temporarily banned settlement beyond a line drawn roughly along the ridge of the
Appalachians. The Proclamation was the first effort to control arbitrarily
the westward movement of colonists, and it was soon extended and elab-
orated. A fixed Indian boundary was to be drawn in agreement with the
tribes, and western lands were to be opened for settlement only in a gradual and closely supervised manner. This offended colonists for several
reasons. First, certain colonies, notably Virginia, had had western lands
granted to them in their original charters and now were liable to lose control over these lands. Second, the new Proclamation threatened the economic interests of a number of prominent colonists who had speculated in
western lands. Third, those who wanted to go west, and those who already had, were greatly inconvenienced.

The Sugar Act of 1764 imposed a tax on imports of various products
made from West Indian sugar. It replaced the Molasses Act of 1733,
which had provided a tax on imported foreign molasses but had never
been strictly enforced. The new Sugar Act reduced the tax rate but extended it to all sugar products, and more importantly, called for rigorous
enforcement. As a response to the Sugar Act, colonists boycotted the
products that fell under its tax. Among these were many imported liq-

uors, including the colonists' favorite, Madeira wine, which was now to be taxed at £7 the double hogshead as opposed to a mere 10 shillings for a like amount of port wine imported through England. In November 1764, the *New York Gazette* announced: "The young gentlemen of Yale College have unanimously agreed not to make use of any foreign spirituous liquors. . . . The gentlemen of the College cannot be so much commended for setting so laudable an Example. This will not only greatly diminish the Expenses of Education, but prove, as may be presumed, very favourable to the Health and Improvement of the Students. . . ."

Designed to raise revenue, the Stamp Act of 1765 placed a tax (in the form of a stamp) on virtually all paper products, including newspapers, legal documents, pamphlets, and even decks of cards and dice. American reaction to this act was surprisingly hostile, largely because the most powerful and articulate groups—merchants and businessmen, lawyers, journalists, and clergymen—were most directly affected by it. Business came to a temporary standstill with widespread nonimportation; trade with England fell off by £300,000 in the summer of 1765 alone. Violence was carried out by groups called Sons of Liberty, who coerced collectors into resigning, burned the stamped paper, and incited the people to turn against locally unpopular figures. In New York, they did it to the tune of "An Excellent New Song for the Sons of Liberty in America":

> In Story we're told, How our Fathers of Old,
> Brav'd the Rage of the Winds and the Waves
> And crossed the Deep o'er, To this desolate Shore
> All because they were loth to be Slaves; brave Boys,
> All because they were loth to be Slaves.
>
> The Birthright we hold, Shall never be sold,
> But sacred maintained to our Graves
> Nay, and ere we'll comply, We will gallantly die,
> For we must not and will not be Slaves; Brave Boys
> We must not and will not be Slaves.

Though violence was so widespread that law and order seemed to be completely nullified for a while, individual incidents stand out. One of the worst occurred in Boston the night of August 26–27 at the home of Thomas Hutchinson, then lieutenant governor and chief justice of Massachusetts. His three-story house was one of the finest examples of domestic architecture in America; it was massive, fronted and supported by Ionic pillars and surmounted with a large cupola. Two separate mobs, having been active earlier in the evening, joined forces and converged on Hutchinson's house. He had been warned of the impending danger and had fled, claiming that he did not deserve to be made a party to the Stamp Act. His pleas notwithstanding, the mob axed down the heavy front doors and destroyed everything that could not be carried away, including a great collection of manuscripts relating to the early history of Massachusetts. Next, the rioters climbed to the roof, determined to raze the house, but it was so well built that it took them three hours to tear down the cupola and the rest of the night to break a hole into the roof. Finally, sunrise came and everyone went home. A town meeting the next day brought forth expressions of sympathy for Hutchinson and resentment toward the rioters, but not one of them was ever punished, despite the posting of rewards, nor were the victims ever compensated for their losses.

The riots occurred sporadically from midsummer until November, and were a serious concern, but the real pressure for repeal of the Stamp Act came from the merchants of England, who saw significant economic losses in the situation. Many colonial importers owed large sums of money to the English merchants, and payments would not resume until normal trade was reestablished. The merchants petitioned Parliament to modify or repeal the Stamp Act, and after a long debate, Parliament decided that the act was inexpedient, because it necessitated the use of the military against British subjects for enforcement, and if civil war did come, the commercial situation would, of course, be even worse. At the same time, Parliament unanimously passed the Declaratory Act, confirming its right to levy revenue taxes on the colonies, regardless of the resumed authority of colonial assemblies.

In May 1766, news of the repeal reached the colonies, and a time for cheering was at hand. In New York, the King's birthday and repeal were celebrated on the same day; candles lit every window, two oxen were barbecued, and free beer and grog were distributed. The assembly voted to commission an equestrian statue of George III, as well as a statue of William Pitt, who had engineered the repeal act through Parliament. The Sons of Liberty also celebrated repeal. At a large dinner in Massachusetts, John Adams noted that these affairs "tinge the minds of the people; they impregnate them with the sentiments of liberty; they render the people fond of their leaders in the cause, and averse and bitter against all opponents." Forty-five toasts were drunk at the dinner, but Adams said he "did not see one person intoxicated, or near it." While how much Adams could see at all may be open to question, it is clear from the celebrations over repeal of the Stamp Act that the colonists in 1766 retained a fundamental sense of loyalty toward Great Britain and George III.

INTERPRETIVE ESSAY
Thomas C. Mackey

In the long, hot summer of 1765, mobs controlled the streets of Boston, Massachusetts. To intimidate the Crown's officers, the "People," acting out-of-doors, built bonfires, paraded in the streets, tore down fences, broke down windows and doors, and hung effigies of key royal officials from trees. On August 14, 1765, merchant Andrew Oliver became the target of the mob's wrath because of the rumor (later confirmed) that he had accepted the post of "Distributor of Stamps for Massachusetts." As the mobs knew, this minor governmental position was not as harmless as its title might sound to today's observer. Oliver was not a postman, nor were the stamps he was to distribute postage stamps. Oliver had agreed to administer the distribution of official royal paper and to collect the royal taxes on that paper. Such paper was "stamped" with the royal impression, much like the impression made today by notary publics on official documents. Such "stamps" could not be scraped off, discarded, or ignored, since they were quite literally impressed into the paper. Further and more important for the people of Boston, not only could the "stamps" not be ignored, neither could the principle behind the stamps be ignored. Bostonians (like all the colonists living in British North America) had to pay for this official stamped paper because Parliament had decided to raise revenue for the British empire by levying a stamp tax on the colonies. By resisting the stamp tax, one was really resisting the power and right of the British Parliament to make laws for its empire. And the easiest way to resist the stamps and to deny Parliament the precedent of paying this Stamp Act tax was to bully and to intimidate any local person who agreed to administer the tax in the colonies—and Andrew Oliver had committed that sin.

In colonial and revolutionary America, mobs were not groups of men (and women) who formed for the mere excitement of destroying property and frightening people. In the eighteenth century, mobs did not act arbitrarily, but rather with directed purpose and to political ends. Middle- and upper-middle-class persons directed and led mobs composed of dock workers, day laborers, and the generally idle of the city, many of whom had been fortified with strong drink. The Boston mob of August 14 was just such a mob. It was led by a secret group of merchants and "respectable" men, the Loyal Nine, who sought to stop the payment of the Stamp Act tax and to put the royal government on notice not to impose revenue acts on the local population. The mob first moved on a small house owned by Oliver near the docks; by the time the mob left the docks, nothing remained of the house. They then moved on to the street in front of Oliver's home, where they displayed an effigy of the new stamp distributor and ceremoniously beheaded the symbol, all the while throwing rocks through the house's windows. From there the mob advanced to a nearby hill, where the crowd symbolically "stamped" on what was left of the effigy before tossing it onto a bonfire.

The mob's work, however, was not yet done. Having disposed of the effigy of Oliver, they moved back to his house. Oliver and his family fled from the building, taking refuge with a neighbor. A few of Oliver's friends stayed in the house and barricaded the doors, but to no avail. The mob tore down the garden fencing, uprooted the garden, and, using the wood from the fencing, broke down the doors and the windows of the house. Frustrated at not finding Oliver (whom they claimed they would kill if found), the mob took revenge on him by further destroying his house. All of Oliver's furniture was either pilfered or broken, a particularly large mirror was destroyed, all the surviving doors and windows were removed, and even the fine wood paneling, known as wainscot, was torn out and carried off or burned.

At about 11 P.M. that night, the lieutenant-governor of Massachusetts, Thomas Hutchinson (who was also the chief justice of the colony), joined the local sheriff, Stephen Greenleaf, in urging the mob to go home. Unfortunately, when the crowd recognized them, Hutchinson and the sheriff had to beat a hasty retreat as a shower of rocks rained down upon them.

Hutchinson's behavior had irritated the leaders of the mob; his actions made him appear, as historians Edmund S. and Helen M. Morgan state, "a friend of the Stamp Act and the enemy of colonial rights." It was thus probably only a matter of time before the mob struck at Lieutenant-Governor Hutchinson. A few days later on August 26, 1765, after attacking customs and admiralty offices that evening, the mob moved on to his home. He and his family barely had time to escape out of the back of their house, leaving their unfinished evening meal on the table, before the mob entered the house and started destroying it. Once again, the mob removed or broke apart the furniture; they removed the windows and doors, £900 worth of sterling silver disappeared, and all of Hutchinson's public and private papers were either destroyed or scattered. The mob's fury continued throughout the night as it removed the house's wainscot; dawn found the mob trying to remove the cupola from the roof. Their message of intimidation to all persons who might support either the stamps or their purpose was heard loud and clear by all but the most loyal to Parliament's authority.

To understand these dramatic outbursts of politically directed violence requires understanding the context of the historical times. To understand those times, it is necessary to go back a few years. In 1763, Great Britain ended a period of warfare with France, the Seven Years' War (as it was called in Europe) or the French and Indian War (as it was called in British North America). Like all wars, the conflict proved costly, and Britain ended the war in debt. In order to pay off its debt, the British wanted to cut governmental costs and to tap new sources of revenue. To limit the cost of defending settlers against native attacks in North America (Pontiac's rebellion of early 1763 convinced everyone of the need for British troops), the British implemented the Proclamation of 1763 along the crest of the Appalachian Mountains. The British hope was to prevent, or at least slow down, the movement of people into the western areas and thereby reduce the costs of defending those settlers against the natives. To provide that protection, the British estimated that 10,000 troops were needed at a cost of £220,000 per year, and the money had to be found somewhere. In the colonies, the perception of British motives and actions was different: colonials saw the Proclamation Line and the troops to enforce it as a device to limit their economic expansion and to impose a standing army on them. While probably a good idea on paper, Britain's Proclamation of 1763 was bad policy, because it appeared to hem in the colonists while establishing a standing army on their western border. Instead of viewing the Line and the troops as a beneficial measure, the colonials viewed the policy as an affront to their own interests.

A new First Lord of the Treasury, George Grenville, became prime minister in Great Britain in 1763. He understood well the magnitude of the British war debt and the need to find new taxes and methods to pay it off. It is important to remember that at no time did Grenville or Parliament ever ask the North American colonists to pay all of Britain's war debt. Nor did Britain ask the colonists to pay even the interest on the debt used to support the troops on the western border. Grenville and his government sought to raise revenues from other sources, not just from their North American colonies, such as a tax on hard cider in Great Britain (which Britons strongly and successfully opposed). All that Grenville wanted was for the colonists to pay their fair share of the costs of the empire; that goal meant new taxes and better enforcement and collection of the taxes then in place. But this desire and the decisions that flowed from it changed British policy toward the colonies from a policy of "salutary neglect" to a policy of purposefully directing colonial affairs from London. In order to meet the reasonable needs of running the empire, Grenville fundamentally changed British policy toward its North American colonies, which, in turn, resulted in one of the key events that changed eighteenth-century America, the Stamp Act crisis of 1765–1766.

Since the colonists carried less of a tax burden than did their fellow subjects in Great Britain, raising new revenues from the colonists and tightening the collection of their taxes made sense to Grenville. Also, colonial shippers and businessmen had thrived under lax British rule and benefited from the protection that the British navy provided colonial shipping. Through successful smuggling, bribery, and fraud, many colonial traders regularly paid little or no customs duties on their economic activities. To enforce the customs regulations already in place (and start collecting more revenue due the Crown), Grenville acted to tighten compliance with the customs laws. He ordered all customs officers to take up their posts and not hire substitutes. He ordered more customs and naval patrols to cut down on smuggling activities. He urged, and Parliament passed, a bill in 1763 entitled "An Act for the Encouragement of Officers Making Seizures" to aid customs officers in collecting the taxes. In particular, this legislation created a new vice-admiralty court in Halifax, Nova Scotia, with jurisdiction over customs issues arising from all of the British North American colonies. This court proved especially threatening to the colonists because first, the trials of accused smugglers would occur not in their traditional local courts (with local judges and juries sympathetic to the smugglers), but far away in Halifax, and second, vice-admiralty courts did not employ the common-law jury system used throughout the colonies. Instead, in vice-admiralty courts, crown-appointed judges heard the case and reached a decision on its merits. Further, if the accusation by the customs officers failed to be proven in the vice-admiralty courts, the Act specifically forbade merchants from bringing damage suits against the customs agents to recover the costs of defending themselves. This act went a long way toward Grenville's goal of limiting colonial interference with the collection of imperial taxes.

If tightening the customs regulations, better enforcement of the tax laws, and new courts to hear customs violations were not enough, Grenville also wanted new taxes. This desire meant that an old tax came under new scrutiny. Back in 1733, to prevent trade in molasses with the French West Indies, Parliament had established a six-pence-per-gallon duty on molasses. Molasses, liquefied sugar shipped in bulk in barrels, was needed to make rum in the distilleries of New England. Once the sugar was distilled into rum, the rum was then sold throughout the greater Atlantic world of Europe, Africa, South America, and the Caribbean. The high tax rate in 1733 was aimed not to raise revenue but to stop trade in sugar with the French West Indies and thereby encourage North American colonial sugar production. Unfortunately, the high tax rate only produced more smuggling of West Indies sugar into colonial ports and more opportunities for the bribery of and fraudulent dealing with the royal customs agents. Grenville understood that the six-pence rate was too high and unenforceable, so he proposed and Parliament passed new legislation, the Sugar Act of 1764. This legislation *lowered* the tax on sugar by half, from six pence to three pence. By lowering the tax, Grenville actually hoped to collect *more* revenue, since colonial merchants would be more willing to pay a reasonable tax rate. Further, Grenville reasoned, this lower tax rate would remove the incentives to bribe and corrupt the customs officials. In addition to lowering the molasses duties, the Sugar Act of 1764 placed new taxes on a variety of other items such as wines (especially Madeira from Portugal), foreign (meaning French) textiles, coffee, and indigo (a blue dye). Add to this legislation the increased customs patrols and new courts to litigate tax disputes, and Grenville believed that he was on the correct path toward meeting the financial needs of the British empire. He estimated that the lower tax on molasses combined with the other taxes and better enforcement of the customs laws would bring the British Treasury £45,000 per year. That figure, Grenville calculated, would provide a good income to the Crown but would not be so high as to seriously hurt the flourishing colonial trade.

While the Stamp Act of 1765, the resulting riots, and consequent developments have received the most attention (from the participants and ever since from scholars), the Sugar Act of 1764 must be recognized as the point when British colonial policy regarding the North American colonies altered. On its face, the Sugar Act looked like just another routine trade act which Parliament had every right to impose on the colonies, but in substance, the Sugar Act (as well as the Stamp Act) was different. With the Sugar Act, Parliament deliberately taxed the colonies to raise revenue for the empire—an action not previously undertaken by Parliament. In addition, colonials had to pay the tax, a tax dictated by Parliament and not approved by their own local colonial governments. This parliamentary action was new. It marked a turning point in imperial relations both for what it actually achieved (the Sugar Act actually raised far less revenue than Grenville had hoped it would) and for the many questions it raised about the relationship of colonies (potentially any colonies throughout Britain's worldwide empire) to Parliament and the Crown. Britain's Sugar Act did not seek merely to regulate commerce between the home country and its overseas colonies; it sought to raise revenue for the empire.

Parliament passed another measure in 1764 which further raised suspicions among the colonists and threatened to hurt their thriving economy. Because the colonies exported raw products and imported more expensive finished products, the colonies regularly ran a debt to British merchants. To cover their debts, many of the colonies printed their own money, but British creditors refused to accept it. In 1751, Parliament prohibited the New England colonies from printing their own currency, and in 1764, at Grenville's direction, Parliament passed the Currency Act, which prohibited all the colonies from printing their own money. This legislative action meant that hard money continued to flow out of the colonies, further weakening their economy. To the colonists, the Currency Act appeared to be just another device to hinder their economy and favor that of Great Britain.

But Grenville's scheme for solving the debt problem confronting the British empire was not yet complete. Had the American colonists been paying close attention during the debate concerning the Sugar Act, they might have noticed the fifteenth resolution offered by Grenville which read that "towards further defraying the said Expenses, it may be proper to charge certain Stamp Duties in the said Colonies and Plantations." Such stamp duties, defined by historians Edmund S. and Helen M. Morgan as "an excise tax on various documents and articles made of paper," had occasionally been used in Great Britain but had never been applied to the colonies. Further, while it could be argued that a molasses tax was a type of trade regulation and not really a tax to raise revenue, a stamp tax lacked that argument. Stamp taxes had one purpose, raising revenue, and the tax could not be hidden behind the argument that it was a regulation of trade. Grenville and Parliament decided against implementing a stamp tax in 1764, hoping that the Sugar Act might be sufficient, but that hope proved short-lived. While evidence exists that Grenville made some overtures to the colonies to provide the needed monies on their own, other evidence suggests that by 1764 Grenville had already made up his mind to implement a stamp act in the colonies. At no time in 1764 and into 1765 did Grenville formally ask the colonies to meet the revenue needs he expected and at no time did he discuss a specific sum of revenue with the informal agents of the colonies in London. It is easy to understand why Grenville acted in this slippery fashion; he sought more than just revenue. Grenville sought both the tax and the precedent that Parliament could tax the colonies not merely as part of trade regulations but as part of the normal maintenance of the empire. Grenville knew that if he could establish the principle of Parliamentary taxation, then future taxes could be levied more easily.

By early 1765 the colonies had become aware of the changed British policies. Colonial merchants and social elites expressed their fears of more taxes from London and challenged Parliament's "right" to tax for revenue-raising purposes. And the more the colonists challenged Parliament's right to tax them (expressed to Grenville and the members of Parliament through letters, pamphlets, and the colonial agents residing in London), the more the feeling grew among the members of Parliament that the colonists needed to be reminded of their place within the British empire. As British subjects they too had to carry their fair share of the debt burden; their days of light taxation were nearing an end.

On February 6, 1765, Grenville appeared before the House of Commons and reminded the House about his 1764 resolution about the need for a stamp tax for the colonies. A short debate ensued with only three speeches given: two in favor and one opposed. Only Colonel Isaac Barré, who had served in the military in the North American colonies, spoke against the Stamp Act. Barré expressed the hope that the monies could be raised by the colonists themselves. When Charles Townshend, who would come to prominence a few years later with his own program of colonial duties, asked Barré a snide question about why it was that the "Americans, Children planted by Care" would not contribute to relieving the debt burden of the state, Barré snapped back that the Americans were hardly children and that Britain had hardly cared for them in the wilderness of America. At one point, Barré referred to the Americans as "those Sons of Liberty," a phrase which gained him the friendship of the colonists. Grenville brought the formal bill to the House of Commons on February 13, 1765, when, according to procedure, it received its first reading.

The stamp bill received its second reading on February 15. Numerous colonies and colonial agents had presented petitions to the House of Commons asking the House to reconsider or postpone the bill before the second reading, but Grenville and the House refused even to read those petitions, which caused the colonists to feel unrepresented and humiliated; they did not forget the insult and the lack of responsive representation. With little fanfare, the House of Commons passed the bill on February 17, 1765, voting 205 to 49. On March 8, the House of Lords unanimously approved the bill without debate. King George III was ill when the bill reached him, so the Stamp Act received royal approval by special commission on March 22, 1765. It would take effect on November 1, 1765.

The Stamp Act covered a wide variety of paper items that would have to be purchased from special stamp agents and paid for in sterling rather than colonial paper money. Taxed under the Act would be various documents used in court proceedings, including attorney's licenses, which at £10 each, were the highest taxed item. In addition, the stamp tax applied to documents involved in clearing ships from harbors, appointing people to public office, and certifying land ownership. Even mundane items such as playing cards, dice, pamphlets, newspapers, and almanacs fell under the umbrella of the Stamp Act's taxes, so that nearly everyone in the colonies was affected by the measure.

Although the amounts of the individual taxes were not large (the colonists could have easily paid the fees and taxes), the tax stamps provided a vivid visual reminder of the power of Parliament to tax and to control the colonies. The Act taxed not just formal court papers, but also paper products used by all social segments, from the documents of lawyers and merchants to the newspapers, playing cards, and dice of working people. This tax would reach all and threaten all. Further, a provision of the final Stamp Act provided a tax on documents used in courts "exercising ecclesiastical jurisdiction." While this provision was not clearly specified, many colonists worried that the British Crown might in the future establish Anglican Church bishops in the colonies. Was this Stamp Act the wedge to establish one church for all the colonies? No one knew for certain, but the Act suggested it might be so. Further and more troubling still, violations of the Act were left to the local royal prosecutor to prosecute either in the local common law courts or the vice-admiralty courts, away from local influences and juries. On close inspection by the colonists, the Stamp Act of 1765 established a principle they could not tolerate—parliamentary taxation for revenue purposes—and the Act threatened to establish bishops among them while potentially denying them trials by juries of peers. It is not surprising, then, that the Stamp Act set off alarm bells among colonists of all social strata.

One final act of Grenville's administration guaranteed such was the case. All the money raised by the Stamp Act was to be spent within the colonies to support the troops on the frontier. But those troops needed more than money, so Parliament passed the Quartering Act of 1765. This Act required each colony to support British troops with provisions and barracks. Further, the troops could make use of inns and unused buildings for their quarters, at colonial expense. This Act fell most heavily on New York, where the troops had their headquarters, but it applied to all the British North American colonies.

The Quartering Act of 1765 threatened all the colonies in another way, more than just in their pocketbooks; it threatened their right to be free from, and not to support, a standing army. Although the British claimed that the troops would be stationed on the frontier, the colonists feared that the British might use troops against them in order to force compliance with the new British taxes. In this way, then, the Quartering Act threatened the colonists' property and their rights, and coming on the heels of the Stamp Act, the Quartering Act appeared part of a plan to use troops to impose parliamentary taxes on them.

What Parliament and George Grenville failed to anticipate adequately was the firestorm the Stamp Act caused in the colonies. While the colonists grumbled at the Proclamation Line and the Sugar Act and while they worried about the vice-admiralty courts and the tighter customs restrictions, the Stamp Act united the colonists as never before. Stamps raised legal and constitutional issues about taxation and about which level of government in the empire (their own governments or Parliament) truly possessed the "right" to tax them. Stamps raised issues about representation and whether the "virtual representation" of Parliament (where members of Parliament acted and thought in terms of the whole empire and not just the voters who cast ballots for them) or the "actual representation" of the colonies (where representatives to legislative bodies directly represented those who elected them) formed the true basis for taxation.

Unintentionally the opposition to stamps led to the "people acting indoors" and the "people acting out-of-doors." Through the spring and early summer of 1765, colonists acted out-of-doors by attending parades, demonstrations, bonfires, and mass meetings, and participating in mob actions to protest the Stamp Act. Led by the "better sort" of society such as the lawyer/merchant John Hancock of Boston, these mobs adopted the name given them by Colonel Barré, "Sons of Liberty." Up and down the coast, mobs designated a tree in each city's center as the "Liberty Tree," from which they hung effigies of the Stamp Tax or its agents. It was in Boston that the mobs went to their greatest and most dramatic lengths of intimidating stamp agents, customs agents, and other royal officials.

As impressive as the mobs were in their intimidations and enforcing a boycott on British goods, the people acting indoors took impressive steps as well. In the Virginia House of Burgesses, Patrick Henry took the floor and spoke against the Stamp Act and in favor of the colonial right to self-taxation. On May 30 and 31, 1765, Henry proposed four or five resolutions (official records and newspaper reports of the exact number disagree) in which he stated the colonial argument against the Stamp Act. Henry did not oppose taxes; in fact, he supported them and the roads and bridges and military protection that they provided. What he opposed was the fact that Parliament had imposed the Stamp Tax. As British subjects, Henry argued, they had the right to tax themselves through their own representatives. Virginians, like Englishmen, could not consent to an unrepresentative scheme of taxation. If Parliament could impose a tax upon them, then Virginians (and by implication all other colonists) did not govern themselves. Their property (taxes) could be taken from them without their consent and without their representation, and that Henry opposed. Not surprisingly, the debates in the Virginia House of Burgesses on Henry's resolutions proved contentious, so much so that at one point the Speaker of the House stopped Henry's speech and suggested that he had committed treason with his line of argument. Henry apologized and maintained his loyalty, but he did not step back from opposing the principles underlying the Stamp Act and what it represented.

Newspapers picked up Henry's resolutions, and they, in turn, pressured the colonial governments to oppose the Stamp Act. Action came on June 8, 1765, when Massachusetts' legislature sent a circular letter to the other colonial governments urging them to meet in congress in New York "to consider of a general and united, dutiful, loyal and humble Representation of their Condition to His Majesty and the Parliament; and to implore relief."

In all, only nine colonies (several colonial governors refused to allow the colonial legislatures to meet to choose delegates) responded to the call for a Stamp Act Congress to meet in New York City. Twenty-seven delegates met from October 7 to 25, 1765, and conferred on the crisis of the stamps. While the mobs, the people acting out-of-doors, informally controlled the royal officials, the Stamp Act Congress, the people acting indoors, formally challenged the stamp tax and Parliament's right to legislate for the colonies. Its members prepared a petition to the king for relief and another to Parliament urging the members to repeal the Stamp Act, but most importantly the congress approved a "Declaration of the Rights and Grievances of the Colonies." Consisting of a preamble, thirteen grievances, and a conclusion urging repeal of the Stamp Act, this declaration clarified the colonial position. While the Congress recognized that the colonies owed "due Subordination" to Parliament and that Parliament could indeed regulate colonial trade, it denied that Parliament could levy taxes on them for raising revenue. As the third resolution succinctly put the issue, "That it is inseparately essential to the Freedom of a People, and the undoubted Right of *Englishmen*, that no Taxes be imposed on them, but with their own Consent, given personally, or by their Representatives." Taxes must be free gifts to the sovereign, not taken from the colonies by Parliamentary edicts.

Ironically, by the time the mobs ruled Boston and before the Stamp Act Congress even met, the political situation in Britain had changed significantly. Because of a petty dispute with King George, Grenville fell from the king's favor in July 1765 and a new prime minister, the Marquis of Rockingham, came into power. Rockingham sympathized with the colonists and their concerns about the Stamp Act and sought to find a solution to the colonial problems, but by that time, a solution meant finding a way to repeal the Stamp Act. More and more merchants in colonial cities were cooperating with the Sons of Liberty boycotts of British goods. Those boycotts hurt the British merchants who, in turn, began to pressure their representatives in the House of Commons to repeal the Stamp Act.

Rockingham needed to find a way to assert parliamentary authority *and* to abandon the stamp tax. When William Pitt, one of the most powerful members of the House of Commons, made it clear that he supported a plan to abandon internal taxes on the colonies while maintaining the right to levy external taxes that were designed to regulate trade, Rockingham saw the opportunity to put forward a plan. This distinction made no logical sense, because trade regulations were no less taxes than a Stamp Act and, therefore, if the colonists opposed stamps then they would also have to oppose further parliamentary trade regulations since they had not directly consented to them. While lacking true substance, the internal/external division made it easier for members of

Parliament to vote to repeal the Stamp Act because they could claim to be repealing not Parliament's power to legislate for the colonies, but only a flawed policy, the internal taxation feature of the stamps. Under pressure from British merchants, colonial merchants, mob actions, and the British military's assessment that enforcement of the stamp tax was impossible, Parliament backed away from the stamp tax. Rockingham proposed two pieces of legislation: a repeal bill and a declaratory bill. Fundamentally, Rockingham sought to distinguish between the power to tax (which Parliament could revise to meet the changing needs of the Crown and the empire) and the constitutional duty to legislate (which Parliament could not abandon). To this end, his ministry drafted a bill to repeal the Stamp Act and a Declaratory Act, asserting Parliament's authority to legislate for the entire empire. In part, the Declaratory Act stated that Parliament had "full power and authority to make laws and statutes" for the realm "in all cases whatsoever." It was that last phrase, a blanket assertion of parliamentary authority and power, which the members of Parliament wanted and which the colonists came to regret in time.

In the early hours of February 22, 1766, after lengthy debate, the House of Commons passed the repeal bill and Declaratory bill by a vote of 275 to 167. It would not be until the middle of March 1766 that the bills received the King's signature and became law. Church bells rang out on both sides of the Atlantic when news of the repeal arrived. At the time, most colonists ignored the Declaratory Act, considering it simply a gesture by Parliament to maintain its dignity, but the British understood the Declaratory Act to mean that they could tax the colonies any time they wished and "in all cases whatsoever."

British colonists up and down the eastern seaboard celebrated the repeal of the hated Stamp Act. Their in-door and out-door actions paid off—or had they? In reality, while Parliament repealed the Stamp Act, it did not yield to colonial ideas about taxation and parliamentary authority. The Declaratory Act of 1766 reaffirmed Parliament's commitment to govern and to tax for the entire empire. British and colonial merchants supported the repeal as it reopened trade, but the harder question of who could tax whom and when was not settled by the Stamp Act crisis of 1765–1766. Colonists continued to deny Parliament's power to tax them to raise revenue regardless of whether the tax was an internal or an external tax.

Besides raising to consciousness important questions such as the problem of virtual versus actual representation and the nature and reach of the taxing power, the Stamp Act crisis succeeded in one other important area: it unified the previously disparate colonies in ways they had never experienced before. Instead of believing that each colony's primary tie was to Great Britain, the Stamp Act crisis and the Stamp Act Congress suggested that intercolonial issues were of primary importance. In 1767 in the face of the Townshend Duties and later still when opposing the Coercive Acts of 1774, the colonies drew on the precedent of unity forged in the summer of 1765. They looked back on the mobs intimidating the stamp agents and on the intercolonial petitions and learned from the experience.

America's revolution was not inevitable, and colonial separation from Great Britain did not have to occur. Britain's need for the stamp tax and the colonies' resistance to that taxation demonstrated that the imperial relationship was tense by 1765. Both sides reached an appropriate solution in 1766 wherein a repeal of the Stamp Act satisfied the colonists about the limits of Parliament's taxation while the Declaratory Act satisfied the members of Parliament about the legitimacy and reach of their power. To prevent even more dangerous problems in the future, to prevent the violence of the mobs, and to prevent the potential separation of the colonies from Great Britain, policymakers in Britain and the colonies would need more solutions and answers as they faced these key challenges ahead of them in the stormy future after 1766. The Stamp Act crisis was behind them, but the storm warning flags it raised continued to fly.

SELECTED BIBLIOGRAPHY

Bailyn, Bernard. *The Ordeal of Thomas Hutchinson.* Cambridge, MA: Harvard University Press, 1974. Discusses one of the key policymakers and royal officials in Boston, and how he and the British responded to the changing political sentiments in that flash-point city.

Bullion, John L. *A Great and Necessary Measure: George Grenville and the Genesis of the Stamp Act, 1763–1765.* Columbia: University of Missouri Press, 1982. Reassesses George Grenville's rise to power and his "vision" for the Stamp Act as a way to deal with the British debt problem.

Matthews, John C. "Two Men on a Tax: Richard Henry Lee, Archibald Ritchie, and the Stamp Act," in Darrett B. Rutman, ed., *The Old Dominion: Essays for Thomas Perkins Abernathy.* Charlottesville: The University Press of Virginia, 1964. Details how key Virginians, other than Patrick Henry, responded to the Stamp Act crisis of 1765.

Morgan, Edmund S., and Helen M. Morgan. *The Stamp Act Crisis: Prologue to Revolution.* Chapel Hill: University of North Carolina Press, 1953. Still the best analysis of the origins, progress, and results of the Stamp Act crisis of 1765–66.

Reid, John Phillip. *Constitutional History of the American Revolution.* Abr. ed. Madison: University of Wisconsin Press, 1995. This abridgment of Reid's four-volume *Constitutional History of the American Revolution* reemphasizes the constitutional and legal issues involved with the Stamp Act.

Seymour, William. *The Price of Folly: British Blunders in the War of American Independence.* London: Brassey's, 1995. Includes the Stamp Act in a list of British political and military mistakes during the era of the American Revolution.

Thomas, P.D.G. *British Politics and the Stamp Act Crisis.* London: Oxford University Press, 1975. Surveys the British political maneuverings that swirled around the Stamp Act and its repeal.

Tyler, John W. *Smugglers and Patriots: Boston Merchants and the Advent of the American Revolution.* Boston: Northeastern University Press, 1986. Examines the influence of the Stamp Act and other British measures on the merchants of Boston.

Weslager, C. A. *The Stamp Act Congress.* Newark: University of Delaware Press, 1976. Collects the key documents of the Stamp Act Congress, such as the journal of the Congress, and provides a historical introduction to the crisis.

Wood, Gordon S. *The Creation of the American Republic, 1776–1787.* Chapel Hill: University of North Carolina Press, 1969. One of the best assessments of how the issues raised during the Stamp Act crisis of 1765–66, such as representation and taxation, came to be resolved during the American Revolution.

———. *The Radicalism of the American Revolution.* New York: Alfred A. Knopf, 1992. Builds on the arguments of Wood's earlier book stressing the changed world of the American Revolution which had its origins in the crises of the 1760s.

5

The Boston Tea Party, 1773

INTRODUCTION

The Boston Tea Party, held on December 16, 1773, was an outlandish act of vandalism that had at its base the colonial objection to taxation for purposes of revenue without the assent of the colonial assemblies. Its roots go back to the Stamp Act of 1765, which provoked enough protest in the colonies to bring about its repeal the following year. In 1767, Parliament passed the Townshend Duties, which were revenue taxes on imports of certain commonly used commodities, such as glass, lead, paint, and tea. These duties were designed to take advantage of an apparent American willingness to pay external taxes (on imports from outside the colonies) as opposed to internal taxes (such as the taxes provided for in the Stamp Act). Moreover, Charles Townshend, the Chancellor of the Exchequer and the person for whom the duties were named, was aware of the prevalence of colonial smuggling. As a firm believer in Parliamentary authority over the colonies, he oversaw the establishment of a board of customs commissioners in America, whose task it was to put an end to smuggling. This board was headquartered in Boston and was most effective there, to the dismay of the local merchants.

Americans in general and Boston merchants in particular did not like the Townshend Duties, but resorted to less violence than they had with

The Boston Tea Party was an overt act of civil disobedience that brought a strong response from Great Britain, which in turn pushed the colonies closer to outright rebellion. (Reproduced from the Collections of the Library of Congress)

the Stamp Act, employing instead a policy of nonimportation of the affected products. Boston merchants took the lead in organizing the boycott. They were later joined by New York and Philadelphia traders, and still later, those from more southern cities and ports. Fashion and furniture fads suddenly became American, and English luxuries were definitely out of style. Townshend himself died in September 1767 and was replaced by Lord North. Meanwhile, British merchants complained, and in early 1770, all the duties, except that on tea, were repealed. By this time, Lord North had become prime minister, a post he would hold throughout the 1770s.

Americans were upset about taxation for revenue because:

a. If Parliament were given the right to tax the colonies for revenue, unrepresented American taxpayers would be discriminated against in favor of British taxpayers who were represented.

b. Americans realized that one objective of revenue taxation was to raise money to pay colonial officials and thereby take these officials out of the control of the colonial assemblies, which had become accustomed to paying them. To the assemblies, this represented the surrendering of a considerable amount of authority—the exclusive right to tax Americans and allocate the receipts.

All of this boiled down to the fundamental belief in the ancient British constitutional principle of "no taxation without representation." The British argument that the colonists were indeed represented in Parliament through the notion of "virtual representation," widely discussed at the time of the Stamp Act, found little acceptance among Americans.

In 1770, the year of the repeal of most of the Townshend Acts, British-colonial relations took another tumble with the Boston Massacre, as the colonial propagandists termed it. In this incident, British authorities in Boston sent armed troops to the customshouse to disperse a group of colonists who were harassing customs officials. Shots were fired, and five Bostonians were killed in the melee. John Adams, already a prominent colonial leader, defended the responsible troops, arguing that they had fired only under extreme duress. His defense was effective and the troops were given light penalties. Meanwhile, John Adams's cousin, Sam Adams, soon to become the leading propagandist for the colonies, was distributing his pamphlet on the incident under the title of "Innocent Blood Crying to God from the Streets of Boston."

Born in 1722, Sam Adams attended Harvard and failed in several private business ventures, but he was widely read in the political theory of the day. He intensely supported the democratic cause, hated any form of aristocratic privilege, and was the first to organize the political machinery needed to establish democracy in practice. He felt strongly that the liberties of the colonies could be preserved only through the force of an aroused public opinion and set about doing that through the encouragement of open discussion of political issues and British policy, the organization of Committees of Correspondence to allow for intracolonial communication, and the writing of countless letters, pamphlets, and newspaper articles. He was a signer of the Declaration of Independence, and after the war he served as lieutenant governor and then governor of Massachusetts. Personally, he was unkempt and unattractive and suffered from a form of palsy that made his hands tremble all the time.

Despite the unpleasantness caused by the Boston Massacre, the years between 1770 and 1772 saw a lull in active colonial opposition to British policies. Trade had revived after a postwar slump in the mid-1760s, and in the colonies distant from Massachusetts, the massacre had lessened impact. Smuggling was still possible for the discreet, New England fishing and shipbuilding prospered, and there was dissension between merchants and radicals, as merchants lost their zeal for reform as their profit margins increased.

Still, the radical agitators did enough to remind Britain that not all was forgiven and forgotten. The boycott of English tea continued with considerable effectiveness as a protest against Parliamentary authority. In 1771, a group of unidentified colonists set fire to a grounded British ship, the *Gaspee*, off the Rhode Island coast, and throughout, the irrepressible Sam Adams continued to organize Committees of Correspondence, while in Virginia, Patrick Henry and Thomas Jefferson urged their legislators to organize intercolonial Committees of Correspondence.

The relative calm was suddenly broken in 1773 by Parliament's passage of the Tea Act and the response in Boston to that act—the Boston Tea Party. The Tea Act was expressly designed to aid the debt-ridden East India Company, a leading importer of tea, which at that time had lots of unsold tea but no money. The Tea Act promised to reverse that situation by removing the normal English duties on all tea imported by the East India Company. With these duties removed, the company could sell its tea in America at a lower price than other tea companies could and, logically, have a monopoly on the American tea market. While this did indeed mean cheaper tea for the colonists, they objected for three reasons:

1. Since the East India Company worked with only a select group of merchants in America, those merchants who had contracts with other companies felt they were victims of discrimination;

2. Without payment of duties, the East India Company could even undersell tea, and there was a lot of it, that had been smuggled into America;

3. Most importantly, colonists feared that if Parliament could grant the East India Company a monopoly in tea, what could prevent it from granting other monopolies for other commodities at its will?

In many ports, mobs led by agitators merely prevented East India Tea from being unloaded or sold, but in Boston, on the night of December 16, 1773, a group of about 150 men, organized and probably led by Sam Adams, and loosely disguised as Mohawk Indians, boarded three British ships in Boston Harbor and threw overboard some £20,000 worth of tea. Though this was clearly destruction of private property, the local government condoned the act and no one tried to apprehend the "Indians." But to British public opinion (and Parliament), this was an outrageous incident that showed the colonists in their true colors, and it brought a loud outcry from the House of Commons to punish Massachusetts and to show the colonists once and for all where real authority lay.

Within a short time, Parliament passed four punitive measures:

1. The Boston Port Act, which closed Boston's harbor to all commerce until the East India Company was reimbursed for its lost tea;

2. The Massachusetts Government Act, which nullified the liberal 1691 Massachusetts charter that had established the form of local government in that colony. Under the new act, town meetings were forbidden without the consent of the governor, and members of the upper house of the Massachusetts assembly were to be appointed by the governor and no longer elected.

3. The Administration of Justice Act, which provided that British officials accused of capital crimes committed while performing

their duties could not be tried in Massachusetts but had to be sent back to Britain or to another colony to stand trial.

4. The Quartering Act, which applied to all colonies and required them to provide adequate housing in private residences, if necessary, for resident British troops within 24 hours after their arrival, without compensation to the property owner.

To these was added an act that was not intended to be punitive in nature, but was so interpreted by the colonists:

5. The Quebec Act, which administratively attached the whole Great Lakes region to the province of Quebec, thus making the Proclamation of 1763 permanent and nullifying many colonial land claims. The act also recognized certain features of French law for Quebec and granted complete toleration to all Catholics.

This series of acts was all the agitators needed. They quickly made the Quebec Act seem like a plot to Romanize the colonists, something that aroused the deep-seated prejudices of American Protestants. Furthermore, the agitators readily created the believable impression that the Quebec Act was meant to hem in the colonies and cut off their growth. With good reason, colonists quickly labeled the acts the Intolerable Acts.

To make sure Massachusetts buckled under, the British sent General Thomas Gage and four regiments of redcoats to the colony, with Gage as governor and the troops as a kind of palace guard. Gage had long been a strong believer in Britain's authority over colonial affairs. He had been in the colonies off and on for nearly twenty years, and from 1764 he had served as commander-in-chief for North America, with large responsibilities and frequent contact with London authorities. In 1767, he wrote, "The Colonists are taking great steps toward Independence; it concerns Great Britain by a speedy and spirited conduct to show them that these colonies are British colonies dependent on her and that they are not independent states." In 1770, somewhat more bluntly, Gage wrote, "My private opinion is that America is a mere bully, from one end to the other, and the Bostonians by far the greatest bullies, and I think you will find them so upon trial." And by 1774, the year of the Intolerable Acts, Gage had become a real hawk: "If you will resist and not yield, that resistance should be effective at the beginning. If you think ten thousand men sufficient, send twenty, if one million pounds is thought enough, give two, [and] you will save both blood and treasure in the end." Other British officials had similarly low opinions of the colonists. A Boston customs official, Henry Hulton, wrote in 1775: "They [the colonists] are a most rude, depraved, degenerate race, and it is a mortification to us that they speak English and can trace themselves from that stock."

The American response to the Intolerable Acts was to convene the First Continental Congress at Carpenter's Hall in Philadelphia on September 5, 1774. A total of fifty-five delegates from twelve colonies attended, with only Georgia unrepresented. The most important practical achievement of the Congress was to form a group called the Continental Association to impose a complete ban on the importation of British products unless Parliament repealed the Intolerable Acts by December 1. If the impasse continued after the imposition of nonimportation, then nonexportation to Britain would be put in place September 10, 1775, although everyone hoped that the British would come to terms before that time. The Congress spent a great deal of time discussing the issue of authority over the colonies but passed only two acts of a revolutionary nature. One was to advise the people of Massachusetts, hard hit by the Intolerable Acts, to form their own government and pay no attention to Governor Gage, and the other advised all colonists to arm themselves and take steps to organize militias free of royal authority.

INTERPRETIVE ESSAY
Henry E. Mattox

In Boston, Massachusetts, on the nearly moonless night of December 16, 1773, some one hundred men crudely disguised as Indians mounted a demonstration against British authority that had far-reaching consequences. The incident, lasting less than three hours, marked the beginning of the end of the American colonies' dispute with the Crown. Watched by numerous interested onlookers, the group raided three merchant ships docked in Boston Harbor. Seizing 342 chests of a commodity on which duties levied by the Parliament in London were coming due, they split open the containers and heaved their contents overboard. When the anonymous members of the raiding party had completed their work and had returned to their homes, virtually nothing remained of the forty-five tons of bulk tea contained in the ships' holds. The despised product now clogged the shallow tidal waters of the harbor, ruined and useless for both consumption and taxation.

It was Boston's famed salt-water Tea Party. Although the raiders avoided harming anyone or damaging the ships, their depredations cost the owners of the tea the substantial sum of nearly £10,000. Even more importantly, the action signaled that the collection of the duty on the imported product required by the government in London would not be possible.

The exact number of individuals involved and their identities remain uncertain to this day. Estimates range from 60 to as high as 200, with Paul Revere the only well-known name cited in lists of participants. Coming after close to three years of relative calm in relations between Great Britain and her thirteen North American colonies, the Boston Tea Party initiated a series of actions and counteractions that led soon to an irrevocable breach. Armed clashes between American militiamen and British regulars lay only sixteen months in the future.

As complicated as a close study reveals the parliamentary maneuverings and financial details leading to the Boston Tea Party to be, the origins of the episode can be stated simply: The British government wished to rescue from impending bankruptcy the private-sector East India Company, while at the same time confirming Parliament's taxation authority over the colonies. Given that the American colonists in recent years had developed an avid taste for tea, and that the Company had 17 million pounds of unsold tea in its London warehouses, the required course of action seemed evident.

Enacted by Parliament on May 10, 1773, the Tea Act in effect gave the East India Company a monopoly on the sale to the colonies of the commodity. By authorizing the Company to name consignees in the colonies, the measure shunted aside the dozens of importers currently involved in the trade. Those favored few chosen to receive consignments stood to receive a six percent commission on sales; the arrangement required each to deposit immediately one-eighth of the value of his shipment and to make a final settlement with the Company within two months of taking delivery of the tea. In addition, the Act lifted duties on tea landed in Britain destined for North America, retaining only the three-pence-per-pound tax on tea left over from the Townshend Duties of 1767. These duties, designed as a revenue measure by Chancellor of the Exchequer Charles Townshend, were imposed on colonial imports of glass, lead, paints, paper, and tea. The measure encountered immediate, widespread opposition in the colonies, leading in 1770 to their repeal—with the exception of the levy on tea, which was retained as a token of Parliamentary authority over the colonies.

The proposed cost formula would lower the price of tea in the colonies, thereby undercutting the smugglers who had captured much of the American market with tea brought in illegally from Dutch sources. The popular Bohea variety was to sell for two shillings a pound, compared with a current smuggled price seven pence higher. This would constitute an inducement, London expected, for the colonies to pay the duty, despite continuing objections to taxation imposed by the distant London government.

Lower prices on tea availed the authorities nothing, however; the colonists reacted negatively and emphatically, if not always for the same reasons. Committees of Correspondence, the first of which had been organized in Boston the previous year at the behest of patriot leader Samuel Adams, spread the word to oppose tea imports. The Sons of Liberty, a radical, sometimes violent organization dating back to Stamp Act protests in 1765, vehemently opposed the Act. Not only did large numbers of politically aware colonists object to what they interpreted as another instance of taxation without representation, artfully introduced as cheaper tea, but numerous commercial tea importers, including those who were not above a bit of smuggling, saw their livelihoods threatened. Still further, the monopoly aspect of the Tea Act resulted in the Company consigning the product to unpopular diehard loyalist Tory merchants, notably in Boston the relatives and friends of Governor Thomas Hutchinson. The Boston-born Massachusetts governor, able in many respects but more British than the British, opposed the colony's patriot element. He, like the government in London, underestimated the extent of the increasing opposition to the terms of the Act.

Widespread protest developed swiftly, and not just in Massachusetts. The East India Company named consignees in New York and Philadelphia, noted as centers of the illicit trade in tea, and in Charles Town (now Charleston), South Carolina, in addition to Boston. The Company dispatched substantial shipments to all four ports. In the first three cities named, patriot factions held public protest meetings, warning in sometimes violent terms the designated Tory importers and shippers involved that they would be enemies of their country if they brought in the taxable tea. By the beginning of December, these admonitions had brought the resignation of the consignees in New York and Philadelphia; the ships that transported the tea to those ports eventually returned to London. In Charles Town, after protracted negotiations, the shippers landed the tea, but in the absence of consignees, who had resigned, they had to store the chests in a warehouse unsold.

The scene developed differently in Boston. There one found in direct conflict the stubborn Governor Hutchinson and the equally inflexible Adams, the latter a Harvard-educated lawyer who, after a record of failure in virtually every endeavor, now devoted himself effectively to agitating against continued British rule. In early November, opponents of the Tea Act demanded of the Boston consignees (who included two of Hutchinson's sons and one of his sons' father-in-law) that they abandon their roles as agents for the Company, but to no avail. Rioters thereupon attacked and damaged the warehouse of one of the consignees, Richard Clarke. Two days later, more than 1,000 persons attended a town meeting in Faneuil Hall at which they repeated the call for resignation; the consignees again refused. On November 5, two committees, one chaired by John Hancock, called once more upon the consignees and asked them to resign. Again, they refused.

Protests continued. On November 17, a street mob smashed windows at the home of the luckless Clarke. At the end of the month, a town meeting overflowed Faneuil Hall and had to move to the more capacious Old South Church (or Meeting House); this mass meeting adopted a resolution that the tea not be landed nor duty paid, calling for it to be returned to England in the same vessels that had brought it. John Singleton Copley, the artist, then attempted to mediate between patriot leaders and his father-in-law, Clarke; he too failed to get anywhere.

Three ships loaded with East India Company tea heightened the crisis when they arrived at Boston, the *Dartmouth* at the end of November, followed by the *Eleanor* and the *Beaver* in early December. (A fourth tea vessel, the brig *William*, ran aground at Cape Cod; one of the Boston consignees had its cargo of fifty-eight chests transported overland to safety at the Castle William army post, where it played no role in the Tea Party.) By this time the consignees had found it expedient to flee the city, but they still refused to quit, unlike the designated importers in the other three tea ports. Governor Hutchinson prudently repaired to his country home on Milton Hill outside Boston.

Also unlike the situation elsewhere, the ships in Boston Harbor loaded with tea did not have the option of turning around and going back to England in the face of local opposition; the governor insisted on the letter of the law that required payment of the duty before the ships could receive port clearance and set sail. On December 14, leaders of the largest meeting ever held in Boston, including Adams, called for one of the owners of the *Dartmouth*, Francis Rotch, to apply for port authority clearance to take his ship and tea cargo back to England. The following day, a reluctant Rotch, accompanied by Adams and other protest leaders, approached port officials, only to receive an official refusal. Two days later, a reconvened mass meeting, again held at Old South Church, in a charged atmosphere dispatched Rotch to seek from the governor himself permission for his vessel to leave Boston harbor for England (according to regulations, the duty on the *Dartmouth*'s tea had to be paid the following day, the seventeenth). Late that afternoon, he returned to report to the assembly that Hutchinson had flatly refused the necessary approval.

At that point Adams exclaimed, "This meeting can do nothing more to save the country!" The huge throng broke up, to the unexpected sound of Indian war whoops in the galleries and outside the doors of the meeting house. The "Mohawks" headed in three prearranged and well-organized groups for Griffin's Wharf and the three tea ships, accompanied by a body of spectators eventually numbering several thousand. By seven o'clock that evening, the fateful Boston Tea Party, an action in direct defiance of British rule in the colonies, was underway. Somewhat inexplicably, none of the British troops stationed just outside Boston attempted to intervene, nor did the determined, but sensibly cautious, Governor Hutchinson.

There can be little question as to the importance of the Boston Tea Party in the countdown to the Revolution; virtually all historians of the era have remarked on its paramount significance as the spark that set off the powder train of events that turned the colonies from dissatisfaction and resistance to outright opposition and revolution. The action of the "Mohawks" in Boston Harbor presented the most direct and tumultuous challenge yet to British imperial authority in the increasingly troubled relationship between the mother country and her thirteen colonies, far more than the Stamp Act or Townshend Duties disputes of the 1760s or the violent incident in 1770 known as the Boston Massacre. Colonists of all persuasions, the British government, and the English people alike perceived the Tea Party as the crisis that would precipitate a decision on whether the North American provinces would remain British colonies or would break away to become independent, separate states.

Viewed from the colonists' perspective, Boston's strong stand had the immediate effect of dramatizing radicals' claims that the duty on tea represented a conspiracy to compel recognition of Parliament's powers of taxation. The Boston patriots' action stiffened the spines of other Tea

Tax resisters, and as the news of their action spread, by early 1774 opposition to the tax had spread to all corners of the colonies. The example
in Massachusetts overcame the lethargy that had beset radicals to this
point elsewhere in the colonies, especially on the question of paying
Parliament's impost on imported tea. Before the year ended, virtually
every colony had been the site of violent protest against dutiable tea.

From London's standpoint, of course, the crisis presented quite another aspect. Given an extraordinary degree of patience, good will, and
foresight, the ministry of Lord Frederick North might have turned the
raid, an unusually destructive action among the responses of the several
colonies directly affected by the Tea Act, against the patriots in Boston.
Many colonial merchants—and not only Tory loyalists—condemned the
destruction of private property; Benjamin Franklin, then a colonial agent
in London, suggested that Boston might prudently pay for the tea.

Such a turn of events did not come about, however; the Crown, while
adopting the minimum response it thought appropriate (with no concessions on the tax on tea), took somewhat unexpectedly severe action.
When word of the Boston Tea Party reached London a month after the
event, the news affronted much of the public and most members of Parliament, as well as King George III. In March 1774, the prime minister
announced that Boston and Massachusetts alone would be penalized.
Despite the expression of unacceptable doctrines elsewhere in the colonies, North said, only at Boston had violence taken place, and even
though the policy would affect those innocent of transgressions, a principle of British law made communities answer for public crimes committed with such impunity.

Parliament's sanctions began with the Boston Port Bill, which passed
both Houses at the end of March after considerable debate on details
and nuances but little basic opposition; it received the king's formal assent on March 31. This measure closed Boston Harbor, effective June 1,
until the East India Company received compensation for its losses. A
ministerial spokesman termed the Bill a "coercive" measure adopted to
deal with an act of rebellion, hence the appellation "Coercive Acts" for
this and the other acts that followed in short order.

In mid-April, the North government made known other portions of
its policy toward the recalcitrant New England colony. It introduced the
Massachusetts Government Bill, designed to negate the long-standing
elective nature of Massachusetts' 128-member Council by empowering
the governor to appoint council members, judges, and sheriffs. That act
also required the governor's permission for town meetings to be held.

Another measure, the Massachusetts Justice Act, provided for the trial in England, not locally, of Crown officials accused of a crime committed in the line of duty. Finally, the Secretary at War, Lord Barrington, on April 29 introduced a bill transferring billeting authority from local magistrates to the royal governor. After extended and sometimes heated debate, all three measures passed in Parliament with substantial majorities and received royal assent at the beginning of June.

Also in April, Thomas Gage, the commanding general in North America, departed for Massachusetts with four regiments of reinforcements. In mid-May he took over the additional duties of acting governor of the colony. Hutchinson departed for England on June 1 never to return to America.

Clearly London designed the "Intolerable Acts," as the colonists termed the new laws, to punish and isolate one colony. In June, Parliament adopted yet another measure, the Quebec Act, that served further to aggravate relations with the colonies. Although intended to focus on the situation of the French in that far northern area and a reform long under consideration, it placed within the boundaries of Quebec lands on which Pennsylvania, Virginia, and Connecticut had claims, and the Act's implementation soon placed restrictions on the sale of lands not yet formally granted to colonists. The measure also confirmed French law and the position of Roman Catholics in the province. Americans viewed these provisions as further proof of British designs on their freedom.

Massachusetts and the other colonies reacted quickly, even before the totality of Parliament's actions became evident. As soon as the terms of the Port Bill were known, Adams, Hancock, and other leaders convened Committees of Correspondence in Boston and surrounding towns to condemn the measure. They sent a circular letter to the other colonies calling for support and united opposition to British violations of liberty, including a proposed mutual nonimportation agreement. A Boston town meeting formally refused to pay for the tea tossed into the harbor. While few colonial leaders elsewhere agreed to the usefulness of a boycott against Britain at this early stage, contributions of funds and food arrived from various regions. Patriot leaders throughout the colonies expressed support for Boston, despite the city's reputation for contentious ways.

The movement needed, however, a means for a unified approach to Boston's sought-after Solemn League and Covenant in opposition to Britain. This unity became more feasible when the Virginia House of Burgesses, dissolved by the governor, moved to Williamsburg's Raleigh Tavern and joined with other colonies (notably New York and Pennsylvania) in a call for concerted action in the form of a congress similar to the one that had met ten years previously, at the time of the Stamp Act crisis.

Sentiment moved in this direction during the summer, and in September 1774 the First Continental Congress met at Philadelphia, with delegates from twelve of the thirteen colonies (all except distant Georgia). This extralegal body considered, and rejected, a compromise Plan of Union which would have established a governing council in the colonies under ultimate parliamentary authority. The Congress then resolved, after spirited debate, to ban trade with Britain, Ireland, and the West Indies—unless England provided redress for American grievances. In October, the delegates adopted two measures which made explicit the differences between the two parties: The Continental Association established procedures for enforcing the commercial boycott; and what came to be known as the Declaration of Colonial Rights and Grievances conceded to Parliament limited authority to regulate the colonies' commerce, but (in a clause written by John Adams) asserted the right of the colonies to govern themselves in matters of taxation and internal law; further, a measure demanded the repeal of the Coercive and the Quebec Acts. Finally, the Congress petitioned the king, demanding a return to the previous freedoms that they had enjoyed as loyal English subjects.

Upon adjournment, the First Continental Congress called for another meeting in May 1775. By resolution, the Congress urged all colonies to choose their delegates immediately.

Events had moved beyond recall in the colonies' deteriorating relations with George III's government, despite efforts at conciliation by members of Parliament such as Edmund Burke and William Pitt. Before year's end, the king had come to the conclusion that armed conflict would have to decide the issue. In February 1775, Lord North nonetheless offered a concession: his government, he announced, would restrict its taxation measures to the regulation of colonial trade, and would provide each colony the revenues collected within its borders—provided the colonies agreed to contribute to a common defense fund. It was too little, too late. Colonists viewed the offer as nothing more than another attempt to divide and rule. The British government thereupon increased its military forces and took measures to restrain the commerce of all of the colonies, not just those in New England.

Colonial patriot leaders took further initiatives, establishing provincial congresses; organizing their militias as fighting forces, including the formation of special units called Minutemen; and stockpiling military stores. Royal officials and loyalists everywhere steadily lost control. At the principal trouble spot, Boston, Governor Gage controlled only the city itself. In April, when ordered by London to take action against the "open rebellion" in Massachusetts, he sent a force of 700 soldiers to confiscate military supplies stored at Concord, twenty miles away. On the nineteenth, British army troops and the Minutemen clashed at Lexington and Concord, with the result that a day's hard fighting cost the Redcoats more than 270 casualties and the Minutemen nearly one hundred. Colonial forces laid siege to Boston, held by Governor Gage and his troops. As unthinkable as the idea had seemed even a short time before, Americans, after more than a century and a half as British colonial subjects, had entered into warfare against their mother country, England.

A few additional acts in the drama remained to be played out. News of the sanguine clash near Boston thoroughly shocked British politicians, although Parliament, being in recess, took no immediate action. The king espoused a hard line, the cabinet decided on reinforcements, and further war preparations followed, including the hiring of foreign troops. In America, colonial forces in June inflicted serious losses on the British regulars at Bunker Hill, just outside Boston, the first set-piece battle of the war. The Second Continental Congress met soon afterward, again in Philadelphia. In an "Olive Branch Petition," it proclaimed loyalty to the king and asked that he repudiate his ministers' actions. At the same time, however, Congress formed a Continental Army with George Washington at its head and issued a Declaration of Causes and Necessity of Taking Up Arms (drafted in part by Thomas Jefferson), which served all too well to show that the time for conciliation had passed.

Later in the summer of 1775, George III ignored the Olive Branch Petition and again declared the colonies in open revolt. Movement and countermovement of troops and warships followed. At year's end, Parliament passed the American Prohibitory Act, a drastic measure possibly intended as a means to force reconciliation, but one which provocatively banned all colonial trade and authorized the seizure of American ships. The news of the Act's passage, combined with London's dispatch of thousands of foreign troops to North America, tended to unite the colonies in opposition. For Americans, the only possible result seemed more and more to be complete independence, but it took Thomas Paine, in his January 1776 pamphlet, *Common Sense*, to articulate the colonies' grievances against Parliament and, importantly, the king as well. That spring, the Continental Congress prepared a Declaration of Independence (drafted mainly by Jefferson) and formally adopted the 1,300-word document on the Fourth of July. With its adoption, a period of limited armed conflict ended and open warfare began.

The first of the modern world's great revolutions was underway. As historian Peter D. G. Thomas puts it, "the crisis of 1774 became the war of 1775 and the revolution of 1776" (p. 297). These developments had been set off at the very end of 1773 by an incident destructive of property but bloodless. A relatively small band of colonial insurgents, acting at the behest of a radicalized Boston Town Meeting and directed by Sam Adams, one of America's early patriot leaders, made a signal protest against British rule from afar, one that could not be overlooked in London, by tossing case after case of dutiable imported tea into Boston's harbor. That December night marked a great divide in the thirteen colonies' relations with England, relations that had become increasingly strained after the French and Indian War by the government's efforts to raise tax revenues in the colonies. The Crown's handling of the tea tax and the timing of its imposition, following by a few years the Stamp Act and Townshend Act crises, aroused American resentment once again. Patriots effectively pointed out to their compatriots their belief that the plan of taxation indicated a conspiracy between the North ministry and the East India Company to force American acceptance of parliamentary taxation. In time it could have been some other measure originating in London that colonists viewed as onerous, or some other violent expression of noncompliance by American radicals, but it was the Boston Tea Party that triggered the American Revolution.

SELECTED BIBLIOGRAPHY

Ammerman, David. *In the Common Cause: American Response to the Coercive Acts of 1774.* Charlottesville: University Press of Virginia, 1974. Best treatment of the aftermath of the Boston Tea Party.

Bailyn, Bernard. *The Ordeal of Thomas Hutchinson.* Cambridge, MA: Harvard University Press, 1974. A sympathetic biography of the Massachusetts governor.

Griswold, Wesley S. *The Night the Revolution Began: The Boston Tea Party, 1773.* Brattleboro, VT: The Stephen Greene Press, 1972. A short account but one that provides useful detail and a good bibliography.

Hoerder, Dirk. *Crowd Action in Revolutionary Massachusetts, 1765–1780.* New York: Academic Press, 1977. A social history overview, with a chapter on the Boston Tea Party.

Labaree, Benjamin Woods. *The Boston Tea Party.* New York: Oxford University Press, 1964. A work of careful scholarship that is still the standard study.

Maier, Pauline. *From Resistance to Revolution: Colonial Radicals and the Development of American Opposition to Britain, 1765–1776*. New York: Alfred A. Knopf, 1972. Stresses the limits and control of American resistance to British policies.

Marston, Jerrilyn Greene. *King and Congress: The Transfer of Political Legitimacy, 1774–1776*. Princeton, NJ: Princeton University Press, 1987. Covers the aftermath of the Boston Tea Party from the American viewpoint, beginning with the Boston Harbor Act.

Miller, John C. *Sam Adams: Pioneer in Propaganda*. Boston: Little, Brown, 1936. Classic biography of the important Massachusetts leader.

Thomas, Peter D. G. *Tea Party to Independence: The Third Phase of the American Revolution, 1773–1776*. Oxford: Clarendon Press, 1991. Final volume of a trilogy on British policy toward America prior to the Revolution, with extensive use of British sources.

Warden, G. B. *Boston 1689–1776*. Boston: Little, Brown, 1970. Emphasis on the prerevolutionary years and on the importance of town meetings during that time.

Winston, Alexander. "Firebrand of the Revolution." *American Heritage* 18, 3 (1967): 60–64, 105–110. A popular and accessible account of Sam Adams's role in the Revolution.

The segmented snake banner represented the necessity for colonial unity at the time of the Declaration of Independence. (Reproduced from the Collections of the Library of Congress)

6

The Declaration of Independence, 1776

INTRODUCTION

The Declaration of Independence was written and published more than a year after serious fighting between colonial militias and British forces had begun. The First Continental Congress, convened in response to the Intolerable Acts (see Chapter 5), adjourned in late 1774, and in the spring of 1775, county militias in New England began to collect arms and ammunition and hold training sessions. Governor Thomas Gage of Massachusetts learned of an arsenal of colonial arms at Concord and sent several hundred troops there to seize it. As the soldiers marched through the town of Lexington on April 19, several dozen militiamen, warned the night before by Paul Revere and William Dawes, waited silently on the Lexington commons, an open grassy area in the center of town. No one knows who fired the first shot, but after a short encounter, in which eight colonial "minutemen" (so called because they were reputedly able to be ready for action in a minute) were killed and ten wounded, the British moved on to Concord and burned what was left of the supplies, although the forewarned colonists had moved most of the weapons to a safe place. On the march back, colonists fired upon Gage's men from behind trees and fences, and in the end, the raid on Concord cost the British 233 dead, wounded, or missing; the colonists lost 93. The real significance of the affair was the propaganda value Sam Adams and others made out of it; by exaggerating reports of British atrocities, they convinced many people in other colonies that the British were nothing more than cruel barbarians. Meanwhile, back in Massachusetts, colonial militias from counties in various New England colonies came together and laid siege to Gage and his forces in Boston by occupying two pivotal hills overlooking the harbor. In the misnamed Battle of Bunker Hill (the fighting actually took place on the other hill, called Breed's Hill), the British dislodged the Americans but only at a terrific cost. They lost over 1,000 men to the Americans' 400, and the battle showed that the raw, largely untrained Americans could hold their own against the professional British army.

The skirmishes at Lexington and Concord in April had brought about the convening of the Second Continental Congress in Philadelphia on May 10, 1775. Its chief purpose was to organize resistance capable of meeting the new military situation in New England. George Washington, accordingly, was chosen as commander-in-chief of a yet unformed continental army; indeed, his first duty was to organize that army. Washington was chosen because he had had just about as much military experience as any colonist and because he came from the largest and most important of the colonies, Virginia, whose support was needed in the fighting in New England. Washington took command almost immediately, traveling to Massachusetts to lead the assembled militias in a new siege of Boston, which lasted until the spring of 1776, when Gage went to Halifax, Nova Scotia, after the colonists mounted artillery on the hills overlooking the city.

The Second Continental Congress remained America's national government until nearly the end of the Revolutionary War, although its personnel changed constantly. It was an extralegal body, never really authorized by anyone, but it assumed the attributes of a national government. It raised an army, printed money, opened relations with foreign governments, and concluded treaties. It had initially been called as an ad hoc body, and it had to depend on the good will and cooperation of the colonial (soon to be state) governments to accomplish its aims. After the appointment of Washington as commander-in-chief, the Congress sent a petition to King George III—the Olive Branch Petition—which, despite its name, was less peaceloving and humble than earlier petitions from the colonies, blaming all the recent troubles on the king's ministers and their policies. But it went unheeded, since Parliament would not negotiate with what it considered to be an illegal government. Thus the drift toward complete separation continued. In August 1775, Parliament concluded that the colonies were "in open and armed rebellion." George III, for his part, issued a proclamation declaring the colonies in rebellion and denouncing their leaders as traitors.

The Congress now announced that the colonies would engage in free and open commerce with the rest of the world, thus abolishing mercantilist ties with Great Britain and the empire and abandoning the last economic reason for staying within the empire. Many colonists remained proud of their British heritage, but after combat started, this position was not very practical. Yet, as late as mid-1775, most colonial leaders were still not thinking in terms of complete independence. Although hopes for reconciliation were all but abandoned, the colonies were in a kind of transitional state, where all agreed that Britain was the enemy but few could agree where the momentum of events would take them. For many, it was not a question of home rule, but rather one of who should rule at home, and many merchants and upper-class colonists were afraid of the radicals and activists who had the support of the mobs. What would happen to them and their property if these mobs took control?

On the other hand, the very fact of independence was becoming increasingly evident. Sentiment for it grew under the careful pushing of the radicals, and the newspapers were almost unanimous in their support of it. Unless Congress acted swiftly, said one colonial leader, a great mob would march on Philadelphia, purge the Continental Congress, and set up a dictator.

The most eloquent of the spokesmen for independence was Thomas Paine, whose pamphlet, *Common Sense*, appeared in January 1776. Paine wrote clearly and persuasively as he argued for the advantages of a separate national existence. With independence, a new nation could enjoy free trade with all the other nations of the world. With independence, a new nation would be free from Europe's wars, since there would be no need to fight with the British, and with independence, Americans were freed from the absurdity of having a continent ruled by a small island 3,000 miles away. Paine summed his argument up with an analogy: "To know whether it be the interest of this continent to be Independent, we need only ask this simple question: Is it the interest of a man to be a boy all his life?" For the first time in anti-British literature, moreover, Paine's pamphlet ridiculed the monarchy, calling George III a "royal brute," and showing that the policies of Lord North, the prime minister, were really the policies of the king. This countered traditional colonial thinking that drew a distinction between a good king and evil ministers. *Common Sense* was an important piece of propaganda; Americans bought an astonishing 150,000 copies, and it helped prepare the public for the final break.

In the spring of 1776, several colonies instructed their delegates at the Continental Congress to vote for separation from Great Britain if the issue came up. In June, Virginian Richard Henry Lee moved the resolution of separation, and the Congress appointed a five-member committee to work out the details of the resolution and stipulate the causes for separation. This committee included Benjamin Franklin, John Adams, and Thomas Jefferson, whose leadership abilities were widely recognized. Jefferson, the best stylist, was given the task of writing up the committee's report on the reasons for separation. On July 2, 1776, Congress formally declared independence, and on July 4, the members adopted the report prepared by Jefferson's committee, which was then signed by the members of the Congress over the next several weeks. It is this committee report that we know as the Declaration of Independence.

The Declaration of Independence is deservedly famous in American history. One would hardly expect to find in it an unbiased resume of grievances; it was meant as propaganda aimed at the undecided both in America and abroad, especially the French. In France, England's long-standing rival, intellectuals were already talking about independence and freedom from an oppressive monarchy and aristocracy.

In the Declaration Jefferson tried to convince people that there were certain times when revolution might be justified. He derived much of his argument from seventeenth- and eighteenth-century philosophers, especially John Locke, who had written to justify the Glorious Revolution in England in 1688. Jefferson, like his predecessors, looked at the very nature of government and decided that initially government was a social contract made to protect certain rights and liberties, including the natural rights of life, liberty, and property (although Jefferson changed property and its elitist implications to pursuit of happiness). In a state of nature, before government, certain men had tended to deprive others of their liberties, so a body of people came together and agreed to give up some rights in order to organize a government and protect the remaining rights and liberties. A few were chosen to lead the government and maintain law and order, and were rewarded with wealth and power, but their essential purpose was to protect the natural rights of the people; this too was a contract, set up by the people and their rulers.

By the end of the eighteenth century, the natural rights philosophy, as it became known, had become part of the accepted ideological patterns of the age. There was so little quarrel about it that Jefferson could refer to natural rights as being "self-evident." It was, he said, the right of the people to alter or abolish the government when it (or its rulers) failed to fulfill their end of the contract. In the Declaration of Independence, Jefferson asserted that George III had indeed violated his contract, and much of the Declaration is a list of grievances against the king, indicating all the ways in which he had done so. Jefferson pointed out, moreover, that it was not the catalogue of abuses that made revolution necessary, but rather what they stood for—an intention to place the colonies under the autocratic will of a despot.

Independence thus came slowly, more than one year after the outbreak of fighting, and it came reluctantly in many places, as there were many Loyalists in the colonies, including groups around the colonial governors, backlands people in the South, and Philadelphia and New York merchants with important financial ties to London. These groups looked askance at independence, but several important groups or factions worked to propel the colonies toward separation from Britain and independence. These groups included the Continental Congress itself, and especially a vocal and dominant minority within it, including Sam and John Adams, Jefferson, Franklin, John Hancock, Patrick Henry, and Richard Henry Lee. In addition, by 1776 the army was an important catalyst for independence. By mid-1776, it was truly a continental army—not just a collection of local militiamen—that camped outside Boston, and its very existence was a powerful symbol of a new nation. Before he took command, Washington had been among the least revolutionary-minded of colonial leaders, but in quite a short time the army instilled in him a spirit of popular sovereignty more liberal than most. With the presence of an army that included men from all over colonial America, continental unity, so important for nationhood, was an inspiring reality. Finally, the press contributed much to the march toward independence. Nearly unanimous in their desire for separation, the thirty-odd colonial newspapers in 1776 were more journals of opinion than fact, and they became more opinionated as the war drew nearer. Newspapers were widely read and discussed in the taverns of every town and village, and their role as opinion-makers cannot be overlooked.

INTERPRETIVE ESSAY
Rick Kennedy

"Yesterday," John Adams wrote excitedly to his wife in July 1776, "the greatest question was decided, which ever was decided in America, and a greater question perhaps, never was or will be decided among men." That was the day the Second Continental Congress passed the resolution that created a new nation. It is awkward to note, however, that the date of that letter was July 3, 1776. The "yesterday" was July 2. The United States was legally created on July 2. On July 4 the Congress approved a propaganda pamphlet to explain the July 2 vote. No better evidence exists of the power of the Declaration of Independence than that our Independence Day is July 4 and not July 2. But that power is the power of cultural influence, not legislative statute. The power of the Declaration of Independence is actually not even in the main argument of the document; rather, the amazing influence of the Declaration of Independence is found in just two sentences in the second paragraph. Much of the rest is wrong, or at least misleading. This essay focuses on the power and importance of the Declaration, first as a document *inventing* America and second as a logical structure with great influence in the world but losing power in the twentieth century.

British and American soldiers began shooting each other on April 19, 1775. Killing people, however, does not found a new nation. On June 7, 1776, Richard Henry Lee of Virginia proposed the resolution that would be put to vote and passed on July 2 by the duly appointed representatives of the colonies. Such legislative action, though, does not necessarily found a new nation. At the time some delegates did not think that the congressional debate was very important. Richard Henry Lee, for example, the man who proposed the resolution on June 7, actually left town on June 13! Lee, like many congressional delegates, considered state resolutions of independence and state constitutions more important than national ones. So a diminished Congress representing twelve future states voted on July 2. The New York delegates got permission from their legislature to give assent on July 15.

Back on June 10, the Congress appointed an ad hoc committee to draft an announcement of independence if the June 7 resolution was eventually approved. Five representatives of various regions were put on the committee: Benjamin Franklin, John Adams, Roger Sherman, Robert Livingston, and Thomas Jefferson. After voting on the resolution on July

2, the Congress set to work editing and discussing what the ad hoc committee called a Declaration of Independence. Jefferson wrote in his autobiography that on July 4 the Declaration was "agreed to by the house and signed by every member present except Mr. Dickinson," who still held hope of reconciliation with Britain. This is a justification for the picture in many people's minds of the signers all gathered in one room lining up to sign the Declaration—but the picture is false. As already noted, a number of delegates were not in the building on July 4 and did not take part in the editing. The Declaration that was sent to the printers that evening bore only the signatures of John Hancock, president of Congress, and Charles Thomson, secretary. On July 19, Congress decided that a copy of the Declaration should be "engrossed and signed." This parchment copy of the Declaration that was received on August 2 is the one displayed in the National Archives. For the next few months, it collected the signatures of the delegates who participated at different times in the process of voting on the June 7 resolution. One signer, Matthew Thornton, was not a member of Congress until after independence was declared.

The printed versions of the Declaration were distributed around the country and to ships heading to England and Europe. Newspapers published it. General George Washington had it read to his troops. Most people heard it read aloud, and it is still better heard than read.

In Garry Wills' terms, the Declaration of Independence *invented* America. The date on top of the Declaration of Independence is the proper beginning of the United States because the United States is not just a political unit with a Gross National Product (GNP) rating. America is an idea; more than just an idea, it is an abstraction of what we want to mean to the rest of the world. The Declaration of Independence *invented* America in the minds of its citizens and the citizens of other nations. Nobody cared then or should care now about the exact wording of the June 7 resolution passed on July 2. That resolution is boring and does not tell Americans what they are about. The troops under Washington rallied to the July 4 Declaration, not the July 2 resolution.

Thomas Jefferson was the principal author of the Declaration. John Adams explained in his autobiography that the young Jefferson was asked to draft the Declaration because he had "a masterly pen." Benjamin Franklin certainly wielded the most famous pen in colonial America; however, Franklin was seventy years old, a bit tired, and had a reputation for wit, not gravity. Adams himself had a reputation for writing weighty prose—too weighty. On May 15, 1776, Adams had proposed a type of independence declaration to Congress. It was filled with lawyerly "whereases" and so many dependent clauses that finding a verb was as hard as discerning the point. Jefferson, however, was a "felicitous" writer. Jefferson had shown in his *Summary View of the Rights of British America* an ability to fashion a memorable argument that did not get bogged down in the facts.

"When in the course of human events," Jefferson grandly began the Declaration. He knew his audience was not only eighteenth-century Europeans but also all future generations, everywhere. Although grandly garbed, Jefferson clearly stated the purpose of the document: to explain to readers and listeners what the Congressmen had done on July 2, because "a decent respect to the opinions of mankind requires that they should declare the causes which impel them to the separation."

The "causes" are actually rather embarrassing. The most inaccurate statements by Jefferson—that the king was responsible for American slavery and colonial legislatures wished to mitigate the evils of slavery—were edited out by the Congress. The fundamental error, however, remained. This error is the statement that "The history of the present King of Great Britain is a history of repeated injuries and usurpations all having in direct object the establishment of an absolute tyranny over these states." The Declaration states that because of this objective of King George III, the colonists had the right and duty to create their own government—to make a preemptive strike before the king actually accomplished his goal.

This theory of a plot in Great Britain is completely false. More cynical readers have been willing to say that this is evidence that the Declaration is merely propaganda and constructed around a conscious lie. Robert Middlekauff in *The Glorious Cause* writes more sympathetically that the notion of a conspiracy in Britain "was too widely disseminated and accepted to be dismissed as propaganda; and virtually every sort of colonial leader—ministers, merchants, lawyers, and planters—sounded them through all the available means." Middlekauff goes on to offer some historical and psychological reasons for the "almost paranoid delusions of covert designs and evil conspiracies" that are the foundation of the Declaration of Independence. Certainly something deep inside Americans made them unable to see the truth about British intentions.

Responding to a supposed plot in Britain, the initial role of the Declaration of Independence was to offer a well-written, compelling, logical demonstration of why Americans should continue shooting at British soldiers. The basic structure of the Declaration follows this standard Aristotelian form:

> *Major Premise*: Individuals have self-evident rights and equality that governments are organized to protect. When governments don't protect these rights, people have the right to change their government.
>
> *Minor Premise*: The King of England is engaged in a conspiracy to slowly reduce the American colonists to a position similar to that of slaves under a tyrant.
>
> *Therefore*: People in Colonial America have a right to change their government.

In the above structure, the minor premise is false and the whole of the demonstration falls apart. The Declaration succeeded in rallying troops to a cause, but it was by a faulty logical demonstration. In one sense, the *invention* of America was done through faulty argument. However, when people talk of the Declaration *inventing* America they do not mean the whole Declaration, especially the erroneous factual material about the King's plot. What *invented* America was the major premise found in three sentences in the second paragraph:

> We hold these truths to be self-evident, that all men are created equal, that they are endowed by their Creator with certain unalienable rights, that among these are life, liberty, and the pursuit of happiness. That to secure these rights, governments are instituted among men, deriving their just powers from the consent of the governed. That whenever any form of government becomes destructive of these ends, it is the right of the people to alter or to abolish it, and to institute new government, laying its foundation on such principles and organizing its powers in such form, as to them shall seem most likely to effect their safety and happiness.

Jefferson did not make these ideas up. They were commonly believed by colonial leaders. They could not be claimed to be self-evident unless people assumed them almost without thinking. Richard Henry Lee accused Jefferson of plagiarizing the English political theorist John Locke for the "life, liberty, . . ." line; Jefferson insisted he consulted no books. Adams more correctly noted that the ideas and phrases in the Declara-

tion were well known and accepted in Congress before Jefferson wrote
them.

The Declaration's major premise stated more succinctly and forcefully
than ever before an assumption that people increasingly *felt* was true:
Individuals *are* equal and *do* have unalienable rights, and governments
should protect those rights. French revolutionaries and the progressive
revolutionaries in Latin America and Europe that later followed America's example were inspired by the Declaration of Independence, not because the ideas were new, but because, as one Frenchman wrote:
"America has given us this example. The act which declares its independence is a simple and sublime exposition of those rights so sacred
and so long forgotten." The revolutionaries did not think the Declaration told them anything new; rather, the Declaration reminded them of
what God had already written on their hearts. After the war, George
Washington declared that in the American Revolution "the rights of
mankind were better understood" and "are [now] laid open for our
use." Even later Thomas Jefferson wrote: "The Revolution of America,
by recognizing those rights which every man is entitled to by the laws
of God and Nature, seems to have broken off all those devious tram-
mels of ignorance, prejudice, and superstition which have long de-
pressed the human mind. . . . Every door is now open to the sons of
genius and science."

If, as Adams knew, the Declaration was born out of colonial American
commonplace ideas, Jefferson should be credited with the feat of distill-
ing those commonplaces into words and phrases that not only affirmed
what was already assumed but also inspired further development. The
Declaration transcended its own context. The two key sentences ceased
to be part of a flawed document and became a cornerstone, a motto, a
maxim for modern society.

In the history of the United States no two sentences are more radical.
Gordon Wood in *The Radicalism of the American Revolution* shows that
many citizens of the newly created United States took seriously the individualistic and egalitarian implications of the Declaration. The Declaration seemed invariably to point in the direction of pure democracy.
The authors of the Constitution successfully hedged these implications.
However, Jefferson's election to the presidency in 1800 and especially
Andrew Jackson's election in 1828 showed that democracy, individual-
ism, and egalitarianism remained powerful forces pushing further than
the authors of the Constitution wanted.

In most people's minds July 4, 1776, was the founding day of American government, not some day in 1787 or 1789 when the Constitution formed our present government. Soon after the Revolution, July 4 celebrations began to be an American ritual, and in them democracy, equality, and liberty were praised. Gordon Wood writes that a social revolution resembling "the breaking of a dam, releasing thousands of pent-up pressures" quickly swept the country, overwhelming the more hierarchical and controlled systems of the Founding Fathers. Wood is amazed: "Perhaps no country in the Western world has ever undergone such massive changes in such a short period of time." The speed of this revolution is largely due to the power of the Declaration of Independence.

Robert Owen, creator of one of the first and most famous early American utopian communities, gave a speech on the Declaration's fiftieth anniversary, July 4, 1826, called a "Declaration of Mental Independence." He declared that the signers of the Declaration had wanted to lead further but that the people at that time were not ready. His new society would show the way to the final stages of implementing the Declaration of Independence. Ralph Waldo Emerson in 1837 called for American students to finally throw off their Old World chains and start thinking for themselves. His speech was called a "Declaration of Intellectual Independence." In Seneca Falls, New York, on July 19, 1848, Elizabeth Cady Stanton and some other women wrote a "Declaration of Sentiments and Resolutions" that exactly paralleled Jefferson's Declaration, beginning with "When in the course of human events it becomes necessary for one portion of the family of man to assume among the people of earth a position different from what they have hitherto occupied." The second paragraph begins: "We hold these truths to be self-evident: that all men and women are created equal." The list that follows parallels the original complaints except that the plot to reduce women to slavery was perpetrated by men in general, not just the king.

On July 4, 1845, Henry David Thoreau moved into a cabin on Walden Pond to live deliberately as a free individual. He, like Owen, Emerson, Stanton, and thousands of others, wanted to push America further, to jump-start progress beyond Constitutional compromises. In the conclusion to "Civil Disobedience," Thoreau wrote, "Is it not possible to take a step further towards recognizing and organizing the rights of man? There will never be a really free and enlightened state, until the state comes to recognize the individual as a higher and independent power."

In 1846 Abraham Lincoln wrote to a friend that the writers of the Declaration of Independence

meant to set up a standard maxim for a free society, which
should be familiar to all, and revered by all; constantly looked
to, constantly labored for, and even though never perfectly
attained, constantly approximated and, thereby, constantly
spreading and deepening its influence and augmenting the
happiness and value of life to all people of all colors everywhere.

As president, Lincoln took part in spreading, deepening, and augmenting the influence of the Declaration of Independence in the Gettys-
burg Address where he called for the Civil War to end with a "new birth
of freedom."

What Lincoln called a "maxim" for America, William Henry Seward
called a "higher law." In 1850 on the Senate floor, Seward, one of the
great leaders of mid-century America, delineated the fundamental tension in American history between the Declaration of Independence and
the Constitution:

The Constitution regulates our stewardship; the Constitution
devotes the domain to union, to justice, to defense, to welfare,
and to liberty. But there is a higher law than the Constitution,
which regulates our authority over the domain, and devotes
it to the same noble purposes.

Seward astutely separated the working, day-to-day law of the land
from the guiding ideals of that law. The former is founded in the Constitution and the latter in the Declaration of Independence. For the most
part, Seward would say, the Constitution and the Declaration of Independence work well together; however, when in conflict, such as in the
case of legal slavery, Americans must follow the Declaration of Independence instead of the Constitution. In his essay on civil disobedience, Thoreau offered a stark example of the principle: Every good American
should be sent to jail every once in a while.

This tension between the Declaration of Independence and the Constitution, between higher law and working law, still exists in America.
The tension reflects the difference between the July 2 resolution and the
July 4 declaration. In law, the United States was created on July 2. In the
minds of most Americans, the United States was invented on July 4. On
the latter date, a higher law than courtroom law was recognized as the
purpose for the new nation.

Higher law is known in one's conscience, one's intuition, one's soul.

Higher law is sometimes called natural law, and its force comes from being "self-evident." In Jefferson's language, higher law was the law of "God and Nature." For early Americans from Jefferson to Lincoln, that higher law was a communication from God, self-evident because God the creator put it in every conscience. In modern terms, God hard-wired it into people. The Declaration simply helped people recognize what they already knew: the individual has unalienable natural rights and government must protect those individual rights.

For Jefferson, Thoreau, Lincoln, Seward, and probably almost all Americans before more recent times, self-evident higher law was known by intuition and communicated by a creator God. In this sense, the power of the Declaration of Independence for its first hundred years can be considered to be dependent on belief in a creator and sovereign God.

For Jefferson, most other early Americans, and most people in the history of Western civilization, powerful and compelling demonstrations had to begin with knowledge that God put in one's mind. Aristotle constructed his logic on the foundation of self-evident intuitions. At the end of his *Posterior Analytics*, one of the seminal books of Western logic, Aristotle declared that intuition was higher and more important than science, since intuition is the "originative source" of knowledge. Euclid followed Aristotle in this by constructing geometry on self-evident axioms known by intuition. For Jefferson, Lincoln, and most other early Americans the certainty of geometry and logic depended on intuitions, and those intuitions were created in humans by a God who does not deceive people. The certainty and power of the Declaration of Independence were similar to the certainty of geometry and stark Aristotelian demonstration.

For early Americans, the construction of an argument that compels assent began with a major premise of self-evident truths, then linked those truths to consequences through facts. As already noted, we now know that the Declaration's logic failed because it linked its major premise to a wrong fact: the king was not plotting to place Americans under tyranny. This did not matter in the long run. What mattered is that the Declaration of Independence clearly stated some self-evident truths that were accepted as intuitional, higher law.

Americans quickly began to use the Declaration as a model to prove other things: Given the major premise, *then* American slavery must end, *then* democracy must be enhanced, *then* women must be given their rights, *then* immigrants must be accepted as full citizens, then . . . then

...then.... The radical social changes demanding more equality and democracy that Gordon Wood shows quickly spreading after the Revolution and the governmental reforms of the Jacksonian era were empowered by the compelling logic of the major premise of the Declaration of Independence.

In more recent times, however, the Declaration's power to compel has diminished. If the power of the major premise is founded on self-evident truths communicated by "nature's God," then a declining belief in a God that communicates truths diminishes the power of the Declaration to compel society to reform. In the twentieth century, fewer and fewer American leaders have been willing to make a logical case based on the higher law of self-evident truths. The major premise of the Declaration of Independence has increasingly become more a rhetorical ploy or ineffective faith than a self-evident truth. Laura Kalman, in *Legal Realism at Yale, 1927–1960*, quotes a law professor matter-of-factly noting that "legal concepts" such as Jefferson's self-evident truths "are supernatural entities which do not have a verifiable existence except to the eyes of faith." For people who believe this, the Declaration of Independence is only a weak statement of faith and not compelling logic.

Since the middle of the nineteenth century, demonstrations founded on self-evident truths have no longer commanded assent among many leading intellectuals. Modern philosophers such as John Rawls in his *A Theory of Justice* try to argue that civil rights such as equality and liberty can still be affirmed as a foundation for a just society; however, the fact that he must argue so strenuously and against so many critics shows how far our public intellectuals have moved away from simple assent to the Declaration's logic.

The Declaration, we should remember, is not a statute passed by Congress. It has no force of law. The Declaration was not Congress's instrument of creating a new nation. The Declaration was only a statement of what had already been done on July 2. The Declaration is not a working part of the laws of the United States. The power of the Declaration has always been its role as a statement of higher law which could influence by compelling logic the course of normal law. Certainly people still quote the Declaration on equality and rights. It is most often quoted, however, as a vague faith or hope, not as a truth. As such, it has less power.

The best example of the diminishing political power of the Declaration of Independence is the history of civil rights for African Americans. Before the Civil War, the most powerful abolitionist argument was that a higher law stated in the Declaration of Independence demanded that

Constitutional slavery must end. There was no legal basis to force the end of slavery.

There was only the compelling logic of a higher law. With the end of slavery, the Declaration of Independence helped change the law of the land. In the twentieth century, the demand for African American civil rights moved on two parallel tracks. Martin Luther King, Jr., exemplifies a cultural track that used the Declaration of Independence as a rhetorical tool to stir American sensibilities. In local, state, and federal courts, however, where reality was at work and fundamental changes were brought about, lawyers from the National Association for the Advancement of Colored People (NAACP) such as Thurgood Marshall kept higher law arguments about equality in the background. In the courts, Marshall used such concepts as "stigmatic injury" to show that black children suffered in segregated schools. Marshall himself believed in the self-evident truths of equality and rights, but to get things done he focused on normal manipulation of legal arguments. Certainly the cultural exhortations of Martin Luther King, Jr., and Marshall's intermittent quotations from the Declaration were influential, but a significant change in the power of the Declaration of Independence occurred between the early nineteenth century and the late twentieth.

Internationally, the core statements of the Declaration of Independence are still revered, but there, too, the power of the logic is diminished. The United Nations (UN) in many ways is the greatest monument to the influence of the American Revolution in the modern world. The UN charter echoes the Constitution; both begin, "We, the people(s) of the United . . ." In 1948 the UN echoed the Declaration of Independence with the Universal Declaration of Human Rights. In the preamble the terms, phrases, and ideas parallel Jefferson's declaration—even to the point of using Jefferson's term "inalienable rights." (Somewhere between Jefferson's draft of the Declaration and the final version his "inalienable" became "unalienable.")

But the UN Declaration is constructed on lawyerly "whereases" and does not have the full force of demonstration in the manner of Jefferson's logic. The "inalienable rights" of humans are simply associated with a vague "recognition of the inherent dignity" of people. The UN Declaration's logic is not founded on claims of transcendent truth. At best, the UN Declaration's logic accepts being founded on a vague faith and hope.

The newer way of viewing individual rights and equality as a weak faith and hope is most often considered "being realistic." Maybe it is. We must take stock, however, of what that means for the Declaration of

Independence. The major premise of the Declaration had great power in early America—in the words of Gordon Wood, power to break the dams, to explode and quickly revolutionize society with a new radical order. Without a strong foundation in self-evident truths and a society that believes in self-evident truths, the United Nations Declaration cannot have the power to change the way people think the same way the Declaration changed America between the Revolution and the Civil War. The Declaration of Independence used to be able to compel assent in a society that honored demonstrations constructed on self-evident intuition. The Declaration of Independence no longer has that power in America, and neither does the UN Declaration have that power in the world.

On July 4, 1826, the fiftieth anniversary of the Declaration of Independence, Thomas Jefferson and John Adams both died. Most Americans then believed that God, with the act of taking these two men, had stamped the Declaration with a seal of approval. Most people raised in American schools today simply smile at the foolishness of their ancestors' thinking a mere coincidence to be a sign from God. In this change of perception lies the fate of the Declaration of Independence. If the self-evident truths stated by Jefferson no longer anchor logical arguments that compel assent, then the Declaration will increasingly be only a historical artifact and no longer a force in American history.

SELECTED BIBLIOGRAPHY

Becker, Carl L. *The Declaration of Independence: A Study in the History of Political Ideas.* New York: Random House, 1922. The classic work on the intellectual background of the Declaration of Independence by one of the greatest American historians.

Donovan, Frank. *Mr. Jefferson's Declaration: The Story Behind the Declaration of Independence.* New York: Dodd, Mead, 1968. One of the clearest point-by-point narratives of events surrounding the Declaration.

Fliegelman, Jay. *Declaring Independence: Jefferson, Natural Language, and the Culture of Performance.* Stanford, CA: Stanford University Press, 1993. Examines how Thomas Jefferson wrote the Declaration of Independence as an oratorical performance as well as an eloquent published document.

Gerber, Scott Douglas. *To Secure These Rights: The Declaration of Independence and Constitutional Interpretation.* New York: New York University Press, 1995. An analytical work that suggests the Founding Fathers wrote the Constitution in order to implement the natural-rights principles expressed in the Declaration.

Hawke, David Freeman. *Honorable Treason: The Declaration of Independence and the Men Who Signed It.* New York: Viking, 1976. Excellent bicentennial account of the most important events along with biographical information about each signer.

Howell, Wilbur Samuel. "The Declaration of Independence and Eighteenth-Century Logic." *William and Mary Quarterly* 38 (1961): 460–484. One of the rare studies of the way in which logic was structured in the Declaration by one of the best historians of modern British logic.

Maier, Pauline. *American Scripture: Making the Declaration of Independence.* New York: Alfred A. Knopf, 1997. A detailed study of the social context in which the Declaration of Independence was conceived and written that de-emphasizes Jefferson's role.

Middlekauff, Robert. *The Glorious Cause: The American Revolution, 1763–1789.* New York: Oxford University Press, 1982. A comprehensive narrative of the causes, military aspects, and consequences of the American Revolution.

Peterson, Merrill D. *Adams and Jefferson: A Revolutionary Dialogue.* New York: Oxford University Press, 1976. The best biographer of Jefferson presents a clear study of the divergent minds and personalities of the two most politically influential authors of the Declaration.

Wills, Garry. *Inventing America: Jefferson's Declaration of Independence.* New York: Vintage, 1979. A deeper and broader study than Becker and Howell of the intellectual context of the Declaration.

Wood, Gordon S. *The Radicalism of the American Revolution.* New York: Alfred A. Knopf, 1992. Emphasizing radicalness, Wood shows that the implications of the Declaration of Independence helped bring rapid change to the social and political structure of the new nation.

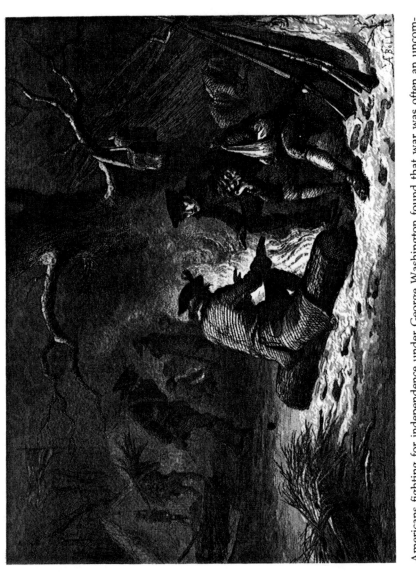

Americans fighting for independence under George Washington found that war was often an uncomfortable experience. (Reproduced from the Collections of the Library of Congress)

7

The American Revolution, 1775–1783

INTRODUCTION

One of the myths of the American Revolution is that all American soldiers were sharpshooting riflemen who won the war by shooting British soldiers from behind trees and rocks and using the tactics of irregular warfare, a real innovation for the age. Military historians agree that this account is nothing more than a myth, that the tactics employed by the militiamen were already known in Europe and had been used by Austrians against Frederick the Great of Prussia and by the Turks against all of their enemies. In reality, Americans used less accurate muskets and were no more skilled in marksmanship than the British. Many who were sharpshooters with their own rifles were uncooperative soldiers overly impressed with their own talent.

When George Washington assumed command of the yet unformed continental army in the summer of 1775, he faced major challenges just in the organization of his forces. There was very little money available to pay soldiers and buy provisions, and the term of enlistments had to be quite short; it would not work to ask soldiers to sign up for the duration. As a result, many soldiers did not reenlist, but left the continental army and joined their colonial militias, where pay and benefits were often better. Lack of money left most troops ill-fed, ill-clothed, and ill-shod during much of the war, and there was no guarantee of veterans' benefits, although national leaders spoke of a bonus and possible land grants.

Tactically, Washington realized that he could not succeed by meeting the British head-on in the classic manner. Instead, he adopted a strategic defense policy, hoping to hold out long enough to break the morale of the British government and army. Washington and his troops moved around a great deal and usually tried to avoid pitched battles, although there were exceptions, such as the Battle of Trenton, late in 1776, undertaken as a surprise attack with a good chance of success in order to raise morale and enhance recruiting.

Once war was formalized after the Declaration of Independence, British military leaders considered three strategic options in formulating their war plans. The first was a plan to divide the colonies in half through coordinated invasions from the north and south along the Hudson River. The second was a similar plan to divide the colonies by invading up Chesapeake Bay, and the third was a plan to invade the southern states, where loyalist sentiment was highest, and move north from there. The British chose the first option, and in the early months of the war, they nearly succeeded, capturing New York City and stalling only on account of American victories at Trenton and Princeton just before each army retired for the winter, a situation necessitated by the lack of food and other supplies during the winter months.

In 1777, the British continued with their attempt to split the states through New York, this time placing emphasis on the drive southward from Canada and some diversionary moves on New York state. But the attempt failed with the disastrous British defeat at Saratoga in October. That battle, which many consider to be the turning point of the war, pitted British forces, led by General John Burgoyne, against an American army, commanded by General Horatio Gates. Burgoyne's army, moving south along the Hudson River, had stalled near Saratoga while waiting for reinforcements from the west and south. Meanwhile, Gates's army had been gathering strength, and Gates was aware of Burgoyne's plight. When Burgoyne learned, to his dismay, that the reinforcements he had been expecting were not going to arrive, he was in desperate straits. His food was running out and he had only 6,000 men opposing Gates's 10,000. A tentative battle resulted in heavy losses for the British, who retreated toward Saratoga. American forces managed to get around to the rear of Burgoyne's position and cut his supply lines, making his position untenable. On October 17, Burgoyne surrendered, handing over nearly 6,000 prisoners and a large amount of military supplies to the

Americans, and effectively ending the British offensive plan. The British loss at Saratoga undercut support for the war in Britain and probably ensured that France would sign an alliance with the revolutionaries.

In 1776, the Continental Congress had sent a diplomatic mission to France to try to negotiate a treaty of alliance. Consisting of Benjamin Franklin, already a European celebrity, Silas Deane, a friend of Franklin's from the Congress, and Arthur Lee, a troublesome figure representing Virginia and the powerful Lee family, this mission sought to convince the French foreign minister, Count Charles Vergennes, that France (along with Spain) needed an alliance with the United States in order to improve their position in North America, which had been badly weakened by the 1763 Treaty of Paris. Initially, Franklin's arguments did not succeed in gaining an alliance, but they did generate new and badly needed loans from France.

During 1777, Franklin and Deane worked to deepen Franco-British hostility, mostly by encouraging naval harassment of British shipping. Every time an American privateer captured a British merchant ship and hauled it into a French port, Franklin knew it annoyed the British, and especially the king, who often acted rashly in a crisis. By the end of the summer, George III was very annoyed, and France and Britain were on the verge of war, which might have happened had not Spain, an ally of France, balked. Meanwhile, Lee had gone to Spain, where he received some material aid but failed to secure an alliance, and then went to Prussia, where an agent of the British minister stole his official papers. Lee returned to France, having convinced himself that Franklin and Deane had to be sent home, so he could conclude the work and take all the credit. In this he failed, although he did cause Deane to be called back to Philadelphia for questioning, which Lee's friends managed to extend for two years, ruining Deane financially and turning him into a British loyalist.

Finally, in December 1777, news of the American victory at Saratoga reached Paris, and the people cheered in the streets as if it had been their own victory. Vergennes invited Franklin to present his treaty proposals again, which he did, and on December 12, the French government accepted the idea of an alliance with the United States, with the proviso that the United States make no peace with Britain that compromised its independence. This, the first major American diplomatic achievement after the Declaration of Independence, committed France to join in the war until American independence was secured. France was of considerable help during the rest of the war. While only several thousand

French troops came to fight in America, French money flowed across the Atlantic, and French naval support was an important factor in that aspect of the war.

Following the Franco-American alliance, the British adopted a southern strategy for the balance of the war. Loyalist sacrifices in the south were used as an argument to send British troops there, and initially, the effort was successful. American forces were beaten in several battles, the important ports of Savannah, Georgia, and Charleston, South Carolina, were captured, and there was a surge of optimism among the British that the war might nearly be over since the winter of 1779–1780 was a bad one for American forces. By this time, however, there was a significant body of opposition in Parliament to the war, with its leaders arguing that it was time to cut losses, both human and financial, and befriend America in order to destroy the Franco-American alliance. Also, in 1780, some 5,000 French troops came to fight in America, helping to maintain morale in the American army.

The Battle of Yorktown changed all that, however, and brought a military end to the war. In this decisive battle, a combined French and American land force numbering about 15,000 trapped a British force of 8,000 under Lord Charles Cornwallis on a narrow peninsula between the York and James Rivers near the Virginia coast, while a sizeable contingent of French naval forces blocked Cornwallis from effecting an escape by sea. On October 19, 1781, Cornwallis surrendered his army to Washington, ending the active military campaigning in the war.

After the British defeat at Yorktown, Lord North resigned as prime minister and was replaced by Lord Rockingham, who was more responsive to the increasing public demand for a negotiated end to the war. In April 1782, Lord Shelburne, the secretary of state for colonial affairs, sent out peace feelers to Benjamin Franklin, still in France. The American was interested and listed some fairly excessive demands as part of the proposed peace, such as the British cession of Canada to the United States.

In June, John Jay joined Franklin in Paris, where the negotiations were to be held, but he was very suspicious about everyone, especially the French, who he thought wanted to keep the United States weak and dependent. To forestall this, Jay opened secret negotiations with the British, leaving Franklin in the dark, and the British rushed to exploit this schism between the two American diplomats. Franklin was annoyed, but he was ill and opted instead to preserve diplomatic harmony with Jay and John Adams, who had recently arrived from Holland. Although Jay's tactic technically violated the Treaty of Alliance with France, it may have been justifiable, since Vergennes was doing the same by carrying on his own negotiations with the British.

In November 1782, the United States and Great Britain signed a preliminary peace treaty, which would not take effect until the French and British had arrived at their own peace terms. The final treaty, therefore, was delayed until September 3, 1783. In the treaty, Great Britain recognized the independence of the United States and granted the new nation all the territory west to the Mississippi River, south to the Spanish frontier at 31 north latitude, and north to the Great Lakes and Canada. The treaty recognized certain American fishing rights off the Canadian coast, but the language was ambiguous and caused diplomatic problems for the next hundred years. The American negotiators agreed that the United States would not stand in the way of British creditors seeking to collect debts from Americans, which amounted to £5 million, a provision that helped win British commercial support for the treaty. Finally, the treaty only "recommended" that the property of the 80,000 Loyalists who had fled America during the war be returned, a recommendation that was generally ignored in practice.

In Britain, the treaty was viewed naturally as a national disgrace and dishonorable surrender; in the United States, there was some grumbling about the Loyalists being treated too generously and the failure to win any West Indian trade concessions, although the general feeling was very positive. The British military emerged from the war still very strong and would soon enter into a protracted series of European wars. Most military historians think that the British could have won the war but they underestimated America's numerical strength, its will to resist, and the amount of Loyalist support they could count on. The British also misunderstood the problems of trying to conquer a decentralized society; without a strategic center in America, Britain had to control a vast territory, which was simply too much for the resources Britain was willing to commit to the war. The British also had to depend on an overly long line of communication; when supplies from Britain lagged, they had to forage or plunder at the local level, practices that alienated Americans and increased support for independence. Finally, the British lacked unity at home concerning the war, which led to difficulties in raising troops and in putting together a coherent strategy to deal with the American problem.

INTERPRETIVE ESSAY
Steven E. Siry

Late in his life, John Adams asserted that the American Revolution was more than a military conflict. The Revolution, according to Adams, had taken place "in the minds and hearts of the people. . . . This radical change in the principles, opinions, sentiments, and affections of the people, was the real American Revolution." He meant that changes in American social values and political ideas had been as important as battlefield victories in creating the American nation.

Adams and most of the other leaders of the Revolutionary generation perceived history as a continual struggle to preserve republican liberty against the encroachments of power. They based their republican ideology on ideas from the Roman republic, the Florentine Renaissance, and certain eighteenth-century English writers, such as John Locke. American leaders primarily worried that self-interest would subvert civic virtue and consequently cause the republic to degenerate until tyranny, probably after a period of anarchy or oligarchy, would gain control.

To achieve their goal of protecting civic virtue and limiting governmental power, the Revolutionary generation decided to create constitutions for the states. After deleting all references to Great Britain, Rhode Island and Connecticut continued to use their colonial charters which were republican in their structure. But the other states created new documents.

As a result of this process, the Revolutionary generation established many of the basic ideas of American constitutionalism. These included sovereignty residing in the people, written constitutions produced by conventions and ratified by the people, constitutional limits on governmental functions, and the protection of religious liberty. Consequently, most of the new state governments were significantly more democratic than the colonial regimes. Indeed, the Revolutionary generation did not believe that elected officials should conduct themselves in an independent fashion. Instead, they were seen as the people's direct representatives. Moreover, the assemblies had additional power which was gained at the expense of the governors. Most importantly, every state prevented any executive officer from also having a position in the legislature. This ensured that the legislative and executive branches would be completely separate.

However, by the late 1770s, many Americans were increasingly concerned by the ineffectiveness and instability of the state governments. Believing the problem was one of too much democracy, most of the states in the 1780s significantly strengthened the executive branch. The people would now directly select the governor, who was to have a fixed salary and thus not be dependent on the legislature for his wages. Furthermore, the governor's powers included the right to veto legislative acts.

As a significant part of their effort to protect civic virtue and thus preserve the republic, Americans also made the national government relatively weak in relation to the states. For six years, the Second Continental Congress, which had been created in 1775, was the only institution of national political authority. This was then replaced in 1781 by the Articles of Confederation government which lacked sufficient power to deal with many important issues. It had the authority to conduct foreign relations, to declare war, and to borrow and to issue money. But only the state legislatures could raise troops or levy taxes. The Articles of Confederation government did not have a separate executive or judicial branch. The government consisted of a single legislative body where each state had one vote. Before any important measure could be passed, nine of the thirteen states had to give their approval. Moreover, only a unanimous vote by the states would allow the ratification and amending of the Articles of Confederation.

Both the Second Continental Congress and the Articles of Confederation government had to deal with major economic problems. Independence had broken the Americans' ties with Great Britain's imperial system and left the United States to deal with the economic consequences. Indeed, the Revolutionary War was more economically disruptive than any other conflict in American history. In particular, the Anglo-American war halted most of America's waterborne commerce, which was the lifeblood of the American economy. The British fleet blockaded the American coast and swept many of the American merchant ships from the sea. Furthermore, with slaves escaping and white males entering the military, the cost of agricultural labor escalated, and thus crop acreage decreased. Food shortages also resulted from the disruption of trade and farmers' unwillingness to sell their product for depreciated currency. This forced the civilian population to make food substitutes, including maple syrup for sugar, salt produced from lye in walnut ashes, and "tea" made from checkerberries.

In addition, to pay for the war, the Congress and the state governments issued paper currency and bonds and imposed various taxes. The paper money remained in the United States, but the Continental money soon rapidly depreciated in value because of repeated issuings of the currency, which eventually totaled $200 million. In March 1780 the Continental Congress ordered that the states would receive two dollars in new bills for every forty dollars in old bills that were destroyed. The plan was largely unsuccessful, though, and by December 1780 $100 of old Continental money was worth only one dollar of specie.

Nevertheless, occasionally merchants and ship captains were able to turn a profit through privateering, which involved state governments or Congress chartering private vessels to seize British merchant ships. Moreover, the war led to the production of some manufactures to make up for the loss of imported goods. It was difficult, however, to increase production, since nearly all goods were hand-made by artisans and craftsmen. The largest profits came from government contracts for merchants with the right government connections.

Price-gouging, the hoarding of necessary goods, and refusing to accept paper currency for purchases quickly led to mob action. In 1779, Philadelphia experienced social unrest. In January soldiers were called in to end a strike by 150 merchant seamen who were demanding higher wages. In May gangs intimidated merchants and imprisoned several of them. Then in early October the tension climaxed during the "Fort Wilson" riot. Between 150 and 200 militiamen who supported price controls moved toward the home of James Wilson, where several dozen prominent free-market men had gathered. Someone inside the house shot at the militiamen, who returned the fire. During the ten-minute skirmish, six people were killed and fourteen were wounded. Eventually, a number of Philadelphia's elite militia, known as the "silver stocking" cavalry, and some Continental dragoons arrived at Wilson's home, and arrested fifteen militia protestors. After the "Fort Wilson" riot, the effort in Pennsylvania and elsewhere in the United States to control prices by popular action started to decline. However, the mob action did compel the government in Philadelphia to distribute food to the poor.

While dealing with the economic consequences of the war, the state governments also passed laws to punish the Loyalists, those Americans who remained loyal to the British government, by depriving them of property, voting rights, and other liberties. Many Loyalists fled to the protection of British-controlled locations, and subsequently the Loyalists often went with the British forces when they evacuated an area. During and after the war, approximately 100,000 Loyalists left the United States and relocated in England or some part of the British Empire. Some, however, returned to the United States, especially after most states repealed the anti-Loyalist legislation.

Women, whether they were Loyalists or Rebels, were forced to adjust to new roles during the Revolutionary War. With so many men serving in the military, many women had to manage farms or businesses during a time of significant economic problems. Some women also formed volunteer groups to provide supplies to the soldiers. For example, the Ladies Association of Philadelphia, founded in 1780, solicited funds totaling $300,000 that were used to acquire supplies for the American troops. The success of this organization led to the formation of similar groups in other states. As these organizations developed on the home front, other women went to the army camps to join their male relatives and to provide nursing and cooking services. A few women even served as spies or disguised themselves as men to participate in battles.

In the decades after the war, there would emerge a new role for women within America's republican society. In particular, women would embrace republican motherhood, which meant that women were to act as educators by raising children to be virtuous citizens of the republic. As a consequence, there developed a new emphasis on female education to provide women with better preparation for republican motherhood. This did not, however, lead to suffrage rights or other direct political participation for women.

As women adjusted to their new wartime roles, African Americans often experienced the effects of the war. Although protecting freedom and avoiding political enslavement were basic ideas of the American Revolution, in 1776 some 500,000 African Americans were held in slavery. As a result, many African Americans opposed the revolution. Approximately 50,000 slaves won their liberty during the war. One-half escaped to the British army or navy, while most of the rest fled to the cities, where they lived as free individuals; some even joined the Indian tribes on the frontier. Initially the Continental Congress excluded African Americans from military service, but this policy was reversed at the end of 1775. Eventually about 5,000 blacks, primarily free individuals living in the North, served for the United States during the Revolutionary War. Slaves who served in the war received their freedom and occasionally some land. African American troops usually served in largely white units. However, Massachusetts and Rhode Island organized a few all-black companies.

In the northern states, manumission, or the voluntary freeing of slaves, increased during the 1770s. And in 1780 Pennsylvania became the first state to pass an emancipation statute that called for the gradual end of slavery for those slaves born after the enactment of the law. Over the next twenty-five years all northern states, except Delaware, passed laws to bring about the gradual end of slavery. Furthermore, by 1790 every state except South Carolina and Georgia had outlawed the slave trade. This resulted from adherence to revolutionary ideas, a decrease in the need for slaves because of a declining tobacco market, an increase in the slave population in the United States, and southern fears about possible slave revolts. In addition, some slaveowners in the upper South, affected by changing economic conditions or revolutionary principles, supported individual manumission. In the lower South, however, the slaveowners moved to maintain the slave system without any manumission or decline in control.

The Second Continental Congress and the Articles of Confederation government also sought foreign assistance. The Revolutionary leaders especially pursued a military alliance with France. Initially, the French government gave supplies to the United States but refused an alliance. As the primary American representative in France, Benjamin Franklin continued to lobby for diplomatic relations. When news arrived in France and England in December 1777 concerning the British defeat at Saratoga, Lord North, the British prime minister, offered the Americans complete home rule within the empire if they would end the war. Concerned by this offer, the French government, which wanted to weaken Great Britain even further, agreed in February 1778 to two treaties with the United States.

According to the Treaty of Amity and Commerce, the United States gained most-favored-nation status in its trade with France. As a result of the Treaty of Alliance, France formally recognized the United States and guaranteed in perpetuity American "liberty, sovereignty and independence." Eventually the French would contribute about 12,000 troops and a fleet to the American cause. In addition, the French government rejected any claim to Canada but continued to assert its claim to the important Newfoundland fishing area. Moreover, France promised it would not make peace until Great Britain recognized American independence, and a secret addendum to the treaty invited Spain to join the Franco-American alliance, which the Spanish government did in April 1779. The intervention by France and Spain thus made the Anglo-American conflict an international war. This significantly complicated

Great Britain's effort to end the Revolutionary War and substantially helped America to achieve its eventual victory over England.

The war that started in New England in 1775 and shifted the next year to the middle states moved into a southern phase in 1778. Great Britain adopted a southern strategy because its leaders believed that the South was overwhelmingly populated by Loyalists. Since Britain now faced a worldwide war against France, the London planners recognized that fewer British troops could be used in the American colonies. Thus there was a need to rely more on the Loyalists. In addition, if Britain could retain control of only some of the rebellious North American colonies, the London government preferred the southern region because of its important raw materials.

British leaders, however, had overestimated Loyalist strength in the South. Indeed, brutal civil war occurred between the Loyalists and the Revolutionaries, with the former suffering a crushing defeat at King's Mountain, North Carolina in October 1780. Furthermore, as the British forces moved northward through the Carolinas, they suffered significant casualties at the Battle of the Cowpens and the Battle of Guilford Courthouse. After these setbacks, General Charles Cornwallis led Britain's primary southern army into Virginia to cut off the rebel supply lines into the Carolinas.

In 1781, as the war entered its seventh year, the main Continental army, under the command of George Washington, faced a mutiny. More than a thousand Pennsylvania troops marched off for Philadelphia to force the Continental Congress to provide back pay. An agreement was reached by the end of January, but by then New Jersey troops had also mutinied. This time there was no settlement, and several of the leaders of the New Jersey force were executed before the affair was ended. Moreover, despite the French entrance into the war in 1778, the United States had failed to win a decisive battle. But on October 17, 1781, a Franco-American naval and land operation forced British General Cornwallis to surrender his entire army at Yorktown, Virginia.

After the surrender of Lord Cornwallis's army, a new British government took office in March 1782, under the Marquis of Rockingham, who died on July 1, and then under the Earl of Shelburne. The new ministry sent Richard Oswald to Paris to open peace negotiations with an American delegation that eventually included Benjamin Franklin, John Adams, and John Jay. The Continental Congress also appointed Thomas Jefferson and Henry Laurens as negotiators, but neither played a substantive role in the negotiations.

The final Anglo-American treaty, which ended the Revolutionary War, was signed in Paris on September 3, 1783. It was remarkably favorable to the United States. Great Britain recognized American independence and provided a very generous cession of territory. Unable to control the area west of the Appalachian Mountains and unwilling to see the French or the Spanish seize control, the British government not only recognized the independence of the thirteen rebelling colonies, but also ceded to the United States all the territory south of Canada from the Appalachian Mountains to the Mississippi River. The southern boundary would be the frontier of Spanish-controlled East and West Florida. Moreover, the British government included no provisions in the treaty to guarantee the lands of their Indian allies.

Another article of the treaty secured for Americans all the privileges of fishing off Newfoundland's Grand Banks and in the Gulf of the St. Lawrence. The Americans also could dry and cure fish on the unsettled shores of Magdalen Island, Nova Scotia, and Labrador. But the British inserted the "liberty" to fish for the "right" to fish, which would create a long-standing controversy in Anglo-American relations.

The treaty further asserted that British creditors should "meet with no lawful impediment" in recovering their prewar debts. In addition, all prosecutions of Loyalists should cease, and the Articles of Confederation Congress was to recommend strongly that the Loyalists' property be restored by the states. And the British pledged to evacuate their remaining forces "with all convenient speed" from United States territory. Actually the British would remain in forts in the Old Northwest until the signing of Jay's Treaty in 1795.

During the Revolutionary era, Americans emphasized the interconnection between culture and liberty. The nation's public symbols demonstrated America's reliance on those virtues espoused by ancient republics, including simplicity, industry, morality, patriotism, and civic spirit. Indeed, many felt that art could promote these virtues and inspire the citizenry. As patronization of the arts occurred after the Revolutionary War, the number of artists more than tripled in America. John Trumbull spent his career portraying the great events from America's past. His works include four panels in the Capitol rotunda in Washington, D.C., depicting the signing of the Declaration of Independence, the surrender of General Burgoyne at Saratoga, the surrender of General Cornwallis at Yorktown, and the resignation of General Washington. Charles Willson Peale, who had fought at the Battles of Trenton and Princeton and endured the harsh winter at Valley Forge, depicted the Revolutionary leaders with extraordinary realism. During a twenty-three-year period, he painted George Washington seven times from life. John Singleton Copley, perhaps the best American artist of the early republic, painted famous historical scenes and created portraits that have almost a three-dimensional effect. Moreover, Gilbert Stuart's paintings, including three portraits of George Washington, showed an incredible accuracy, and Stuart later foreshadowed Impressionistic art by working with pigment dots.

At the same time, American architecture was greatly influenced by the Federal style, which synthesized Roman classicism and eighteenth-century English concepts. Examples of this were the Virginia state capitol, finished in 1789, and Federal Hall in New York City, which was the first seat of Congress under the Constitution.

In addition, music was used to induce people to place the public good above self-interest. As singing schools multiplied, American composers published numerous tunes to inspire the public. The two leading composers were Francis Hopkinson, a signer of the Declaration of Independence, and William Billings, trained as a tanner. Hopkinson's most important work was a cantata, "The Temple of Minerva," that praised America's alliance with France. And Billings' marching song, "Chester," became the war hymn of the American Revolutionaries.

Once the Revolutionary War ended, there also occurred a major revival of interest in the theater. Though largely writing in imitation of English farces, American playwrights stressed the theme of a contrast between American virtue and European corruption. Leading playwrights were Mercy Otis Warren, Robert Munford, William Dunlap, and Royall Tyler.

By 1776 private academies and charity schools were widespread. Yet a public school system existed only in New England. The Revolutionaries' republican ideology, however, asserted that education was needed to promote civic virtue and to maintain the republic. Thus most state constitutions called for public schools. But progress was slow, especially in the South, where the southern gentry believed that universal education would be financially wasteful and could be potentially dangerous if the poor became too ambitious.

During the Revolutionary War, higher education experienced reduced enrollments and generally difficult times. But in the postwar period, American colleges significantly expanded. In addition, schools changed their primarily classical curriculums to a more "practical" education, though classics were still covered. Moreover, higher education became considerably more nonsectarian. Of the nine colleges established before the Revolutionary War, eight were associated with a particular religious sect. Of the fourteen colleges founded from 1776 to 1796, however, ten were nonsectarian. The University of Georgia, chartered in 1785, became the first state university, but in 1795 the University of North Carolina, chartered in 1789, was the first to open.

Certainly education in the United States promoted cultural nationalism. Noah Webster published a spelling book in 1782 titled *The American Spelling Book*, but among several generations of Americans it was commonly known as "the Blue-backed Speller." This work standardized spelling often different from the British usage. Combined with a grammar book and a reader that Webster published in 1784–1785, the spelling book helped forge a common language for the American people. In 1789 Webster asserted that "As an independent nation our honor requires us to have a system of our own, in language as well as government." Also in the 1780s, Jedidiah Morse published two geography textbooks to provide "a description of our own country."

The expansion of education created a society with the world's highest literacy rate, and America's literate citizens wanted additional publications to read. Between 1775 and 1790 the number of newspapers increased from thirty-seven to ninety. Between 1775 and 1795, twenty-seven new magazines were published. In addition, the number of books published in America significantly increased.

Readers wanted an American literature that emphasized American themes. Though few people wrote American history, almanacs started to include articles on historical topics, especially the Revolutionary War. Moreover, David Ramsay, a Charleston physician, wrote *History of the American Revolution* (1789) that stressed the rise of America's republican nationalism. In 1788 Mercy Otis Warren finished a history of the Revolution, but she did not publish it until 1805. The most popular account of the American Revolution was published in 1789 by William Gordon, who had plagiarized much of it from British sources.

Works of fiction were also very popular in America. The most prominent poets were the Connecticut Wits, including John Trumbull, cousin of the painter, Timothy Dwight, David Humphreys, Joel Barlow, and Lemuel Hopkins. Often using mock heroic satire, these Yale graduates glorified the union of the states.

Many American leaders opposed the reading of novels, however, because they believed it induced readers to neglect republican simplicity and exposed them to corrupting ideas. Nevertheless, novel-writing, which often promoted civic virtue, prospered in the United States. Indeed, Charles Brockden Brown in 1798 published *Wieland* and thus established the Gothic romance in America.

Cultural nationalism and increased education also helped to advance scientific studies in the United States. Though Americans had little interest in pure science, they made advancements in surveying, navigation, cartography, instrument-making, natural history, and other fields. Moreover, learned societies increased in number and often promoted agricultural changes. And various types of museums were established, including Charles Willson Peale's museum of natural history in 1787.

The law also changed in America during the Revolutionary era. The Revolution in some ways freed American law from a dependence on English precedent. In particular, the American Revolution clearly had an immediate impact on laws concerning slavery, criminal punishment, and inheritance. For example, by the end of the eighteenth century nearly every state had established partible inheritance by which all children, not just the eldest son, would inherit property from their father. Most legal reform, however, involved processes that started before the Revolution had begun. The Revolution in some cases interrupted or accelerated these reforms, but it did not transform them.

At the same time, church-state relations changed in a number of the former colonies. Though the Congregational church retained its legal establishment in Massachusetts and Connecticut, the Anglican church was disestablished in five southern states and in several counties in New York. But the Revolution also provided a new world view that was conducive to creating a reorganization of the churches. This resulted in a nationalization of denominations. The Baptist and Methodist sects dramatically increased their memberships. The Methodists, led by Francis Asbury, formed a united organization in 1784 and expanded southward and westward, especially through the work of itinerant preachers.

As a result of the American Revolution, the destiny of the American people had been changed. The Revolution altered the nature of American society in important ways and created a new nation based on the idea of republican liberty. Furthermore, the American Revolutionaries hoped that their new nation would be an example for the illumination and emancipation of the rest of the world. Indeed, many believed, as Thomas Jefferson asserted, that the United States was "the last best hope of mankind."

SELECTED BIBLIOGRAPHY

Adams, Willi P. *The First American Constitutions: Republican Ideology and the Making of the State Constitutions in the Revolutionary Era*. Chapel Hill: University of North Carolina Press, 1980. A comprehensive discussion of the political effects of the American Revolution in the states.

Brown, Wallace. *The King's Friends: The Composition and Motives of the American Loyalist Claimants*. Providence, RI: Brown University Press, 1965. This work demonstrates that the Loyalists came from all classes of colonial society.

Calhoun, Robert M. *The Loyalists in Revolutionary America, 1760–1781*. New York: Harcourt Brace Jovanovich, 1973. (Originally published in 1963.) This study emphasizes the Loyalists' views, which were generally similar to those of other colonists prior to 1774, and the Loyalists' subsequent reaction against the direction of the Revolutionary movement.

Carp, E. Wayne. *To Starve the Army at Pleasure: Continental Army Administration as American Political Culture, 1775–1783*. Chapel Hill: University of North Carolina Press, 1984. An analysis of how Americans' political ideals contributed to the Continental army's logistical problems and thus prolonged the war.

Davis, David B. *The Problem of Slavery in the Age of Revolution, 1770–1783*. Ithaca, NY: Cornell University Press, 1975. A study of how Americans dealt with the issue of slavery during a Revolution based on the idea of liberty.

Dull, Jonathan R. *A Diplomatic History of the American Revolution*. New Haven, CT: Yale University Press, 1985. The most recent comprehensive study of American foreign policy during the Revolution.

Greene, Jack P. *Peripheries and Center: Constitutional Development in the Extended Politics of the British Empire and the United States, 1607–1788*. Athens: University of Georgia Press, 1986. This work covers the constant conflict between local and centralized power during the Revolutionary era.

Greene, Jack P., and J. R. Pole, eds. *The Blackwell Encyclopedia of the American Revolution*. Cambridge, MA: Blackwell Publishers, 1991. A comprehensive account of the events, people, and ideas involved in the Revolutionary movement.

Henderson, H. James. *Party Politics in the Continental Congress*. New York: McGraw-Hill, 1974. An analysis of the increasing sectionalism in the voting in the national government.

Higginbotham, Don. *The War of American Independence: Military Attitudes, Policies, and Practices, 1763–1789*. New York: Macmillan, 1971. An outstanding survey from the Macmillan Wars of the United States series.

Jameson, J. Franklin. *The American Revolution Considered as a Social Movement*. Princeton, NJ: Princeton University Press, 1926. A study of the social change of the Revolutionary era and the internal conflict connected with it.

Jensen, Merrill. *The New Nation: A History of the United States During the Confederation, 1781–1789*. New York: Vintage, 1950. This work contends that a group of radical democrats created the American Revolution but that conservative aristocrats regained control with the adoption of the Constitution.

Kerber, Linda. *Women of the Republic: Intellect and Ideology in Revolutionary America*. Chapel Hill: University of North Carolina Press, 1980. An analysis of the Revolution's effects on the status of American women.

Main, Jackson Turner. *The Social Structure of Revolutionary America*. Princeton, NJ: Princeton University Press, 1965. This work demonstrates that there was a significant amount of social mobility in the Revolutionary era.

Morgan, Edmund S. *The Birth of the Republic, 1763–89*. 3d ed. Chicago: University of Chicago Press, 1992. A balanced account of the Americans' search during the Revolutionary era for principles on which they could take a common stand.

Nelson, William H. *The American Tory*. New York: Oxford University Press, 1961. The author characterizes the Loyalists as "cultural minorities."

Norton, Mary Beth. *Liberty's Daughters: The Revolutionary Experience of American Women, 1750–1800*. Boston: Little, Brown, 1980. A study of how the Revolution affected American women.

Quarles, Benjamin. *The Negro in the American Revolution*. Chapel Hill: University of North Carolina Press, 1961. This work contains information on the African Americans' military involvement in the Revolutionary War.

Rakove, Jack N. *The Beginnings of National Politics: An Interpretive History of the Continental Congress*. Baltimore: Johns Hopkins University Press, 1979. The author analyzes the creation of an effective national government.

Royster, Charles. *A Revolutionary People at War: The Continental Army and American Character, 1775–1783*. New York: W. W. Norton, 1981. In this important book, the author attempts to integrate the history of the Continental army with the social context of the Revolutionary era.

Shy, John. *A People Numerous and Armed: Reflections on the Military Struggle for American Independence*. New York: Oxford University Press, 1976. This study provides insights on various social and political aspects of the war.

Silverman, Kenneth. *A Cultural History of the American Revolution*. New York: Columbia University Press, 1976. An extensive study of painting, music, literature, and the theater from 1763 to 1789.

Ward, Christopher. *The War of the Revolution*. 2 vols. New York: Macmillan, 1951. A very detailed account of the military campaigns.

Ward, Harry. *The American Revolutionary: Nationhood Achieved, 1763–1788*. New York: St. Martin's Press, 1995. A comprehensive overview of America's Revolutionary experience.

Wood, Gordon. *The Creation of the American Republic, 1776–1787*. Chapel Hill: University of North Carolina Press, 1969. This study argues that the Revolutionaries were more radical and democratic than most previous historians had believed.

———. *The Radicalism of the American Revolution*. New York: Alfred A. Knopf, 1992. The author contends that the Revolution was "the most radical and far-reaching event in American history."

Young, Alfred F., ed. *The American Revolution: Explorations in the History of American Radicalism*. DeKalb: Northern Illinois University Press, 1976. Some of the essays assert that there existed a lower-class ideology calling for more democratic reform than the Revolution's political leaders were seeking.

Zilversmit, Arthur. *The First Emancipation: The Abolition of Slavery in the North.* Chicago: University of Chicago Press, 1967. This work covers the American Revolution's impact on African Americans in the northern states.

8

The Constitutional Convention, 1787

INTRODUCTION

During the Revolutionary War, there was much discussion about how the new United States should govern itself; that is, what form of central government should be established to replace royal authority. By 1777, all of the former colonies had replaced their governments, and in eleven, new constitutions were approved. In general, format of these governments was similar to that of the colonial government, with an executive and a two-house legislature, with at least one house elected by the people. Most states considered two fundamental reforms: the strict limitation of executive authority, which stemmed from colonists' experience with Great Britain, and the inclusion of bills of rights in constitutions, in order to guarantee the kinds of fundamental liberties expressed in the Declaration of Independence. These included such things as freedom of religion, speech, assembly, and the press; certain procedural rights within the legal system; and protection against arbitrary treatment or seizure.

Replacing the central government was a harder task because there was nothing to build upon, as there had been with the states. No one wanted to build on the example of the British monarchy, and the Second Continental Congress was an extralegal legislative body in which each state had one vote; it was inefficient, dependent on the voluntary cooperation of the delegates and their states, and lacking in authority and prestige.

Howard Chandler Christy's anniversary poster of the Bill of Rights is a reminder that many people voted to ratify the Constitution on the promise that such a bill of rights would be added. (Reproduced from the Collections of the Library of Congress)

It was just the kind of government one would expect from a nation breaking away from a strong central government.

In 1777, therefore, John Dickinson of Pennsylvania drew up a plan of union that came to be known as the Articles of Confederation. Though Dickinson's original plan called for a fairly strong central government, the Congress weakened it considerably by the final draft, and it was sent to the states for ratification, which was completed by 1781.

The Articles created what amounted to a perpetual league between independent nations. It was a confederation in the true sense of the word, a legalization of the Second Continental Congress. The Articles clearly stated that each state retained its sovereignty, and Congress could act only in those areas specifically assigned to it. Like the Congress, there was a unicameral legislature, with delegates selected by state governments, and each state had one vote. Congress was given authority to control foreign affairs, declare war and make peace, coin money, borrow money, requisition states for money, settle interstate disputes, govern the western territory and admit new states, run the postal service, and handle Indian affairs. However, to act in any of these areas, the consent of at least nine of the thirteen states was necessary rather than a simple majority. In addition, Congress was not authorized to levy taxes or regulate interstate commerce, two features that plagued the government during the 1780s. Finally, Congress had no powers of enforcement; it had to rely on the voluntary cooperation of the states. While the Articles of Confederation were a clear reaction against the authoritative British government, the reaction was overdone—the Articles of Confederation government was impotent to deal with the serious problems of the postwar era.

There was a severe depression between 1784 and 1787, a not unusual occurrence after a war. Loss of trade with Britain was one problem, but another was the Confederation Congress's inability to do anything about interstate trade barriers that various states erected against their neighbors. In addition, the government showed diplomatic weakness by its inability to force the British to vacate forts in the northwest or cease selling arms to the Indians who were using them to kill settlers. Finally, the financial distress of the government continued because the states refused requests for money and refused to approve an amendment that would have allowed Congress to impose a tax on imports.

During this period, many public figures in America saw these weaknesses in the Confederation and supported movements to make changes in the Articles to bring about a stronger central government. George Washington said in 1786, "I predict the worst consequences from a half-starved limping government, always moving upon crutches and tottering at every step," and in early 1787, Alexander Hamilton decided that the country had reached "almost the last stage of national humiliation."

Despite these well-founded concerns, the Constitutional Convention came about somewhat inadvertently; it was a spin-off from a 1785 conference at Mount Vernon, called to discuss navigation on the Potomac River, and a subsequent conference the following year in Annapolis, at which delegates realized that problems other than navigation and commerce needed to be dealt with. The Confederation Congress authorized a new conference, therefore, and it convened at the State House in Philadelphia in the summer of 1787. Technically, the fifty-five delegates were there to devise amendments to the Articles of Confederation, but most were thinking in terms of a completely new document.

Jefferson called the delegates "an assembly of demi-gods." While they were not quite that, they were a distinguished group which included two future presidents, two future chief justices, and six future state governors. Thirty were college graduates, many had served in the army, and most had served either in Congress or in their state legislatures. And many were very young—James Madison was 36, Hamilton just 32, and Jefferson 44—although Benjamin Franklin, at 81, was also an active participant. Washington led the Virginia delegation and was chosen the presiding officer, where he lent inspiration and dignity but added little to the debate.

The most important decisions of the Constitutional Convention centered around three major areas: representation in Congress, separation of powers, and division of power between the states and the national government.

With respect to representation in Congress, delegates asked whether all states should have equal representation (as the smaller states wanted) or whether representation should be apportioned on the basis of population (as the larger states wanted). And if representation was to be based on population, how would slaves be counted? Finally, would members of Congress be chosen by state legislatures or by a vote of the people? The key to this issue was to establish a two-house legislature, in which the states would be equally represented in the upper house (the Senate), while population would determine how many representatives each state had in the lower house (the House of Representatives). In that way, each faction was satisfied. As for slaves, a compromise was made in which five slaves counted as three people in the determination of congressional representation (as well as in the amount of direct taxation Congress could impose). State legislatures would select Senators (and continued to do so until 1912), while the people would elect the members of the House of Representatives.

The second issue, separation of powers, concerned the amount of power Congress (the legislative branch) should have over the executive and judicial branches of the government. Some thought Congress should retain considerable authority over the other branches, while others argued that there should be divided authority among the branches, which then might be able to check and balance each other to reduce the possibility of oppression. In this argument, those who favored separating power among the branches of the government won out. The Constitution provided for an elaborate set of checks and balances, including such things as the presidential veto, Congressional authority over money matters, and lifetime tenure for judges, to assure a government in which no single branch could predominate.

The third major issue, that of federalism, or the division of power between the states and the national government, revolved around differences of opinion as to how much power to give to the new government and how much to leave to the states. When the dust settled, the federal government was assumed to have no powers other than those granted to it by the Constitution. These included many of the same powers the Articles of Confederation government nominally enjoyed, as well as the power to levy taxes, the power to regulate foreign and interstate commerce, and the power to pass laws "necessary and proper" for implementing its other powers. These were clearly responses to perceived problems of the Articles of Confederation government. In addition, certain restrictions were placed on the states, principally in areas where they might come into competition with the federal government. States were thus forbidden to issue paper money or levy taxes on foreign or interstate commerce.

Those who wrote the Constitution hoped to create a government that, in Madison's words, was "for the ages." For this reason, they wrote in very general terms so that the federal government could adjust its powers in various ways as changing times demanded.

When the deliberations ended in September 1787, the document was submitted to the people and the states for ratification. The framers of the Constitution had wisely declared that it would go into effect once nine states had ratified it, knowing that it might be impossible to obtain ratifications from all thirteen states. Two factions quickly arose: those supporting the Constitution, who were called Federalists, and those against it, generally known as Anti-Federalists. These were not political parties in any but the vaguest sense, but rather groups of people divided over a certain issue. Still, there is a considerable amount of correlation between these groups and the parties that formed around Hamilton and Jefferson in the 1790s.

The ratification debate captured national attention and was often bitter and uncompromising. The objections of the Anti-Federalists ranged around two areas. Some deplored the absence of a guarantee of fundamental liberties in the Constitution and feared that the strong federal government would deny these liberties to the people, while others were upset about the limitations on states' rights, reflecting the chronic fear of an authoritarian central government. For many, it was hard to accept such a drastically different form of government when they had no idea how it would work in practice.

Each state held its own ratification convention, and some states ratified quickly and by overwhelming margins, especially the smaller states, who feared that if the Constitution were not ratified, the nation would break apart and their chances for survival would be minimal. In other states, there were considerable numbers of opponents, and the vote in the conventions was very close. In Massachusetts, the promise of a bill of rights added to the Constitution changed enough votes to win ratification by a margin of 19 out of 355. In June 1788, New Hampshire was the ninth state to ratify, which assured the implementation of the Constitution, but it was problematical because the two largest states, New York and Virginia, still were outside the fold. Finally, in Virginia, Washington exerted his influence, and the ratification forces won, 89 to 79. In New York, the convention was almost equally divided between Federalists, led by Alexander Hamilton, and Anti-Federalists, led by the popular governor, George Clinton. To counter Clinton's strength, Hamilton lined up James Madison and John Jay, and together they wrote a series of essays arguing in favor of the Constitution. Published together later, they are known as "The Federalist" and represent a very thorough contemporary commentary on the Constitution. Their essays, along with news of ratification in New Hampshire and Virginia, finally allowed the Federalists to prevail by a vote of 30 to 27. Significantly, in the first session of Congress, twelve amendments were agreed upon, of which ten were rather quickly ratified by the states and became known collectively as the Bill of Rights.

INTERPRETIVE ESSAY
Julia A. Woods

On May 25, 1787, a group of men met at Independence Hall, in Phila-delphia. They were acutely aware of the historical importance of their meeting. Eight of the men at this gathering had been present before in the same room for an equally important task: the fearful prospect of war with England—if they had failed then, they would have expected to be hanged for treason. Now their problems were no less serious, though more complex. The delegates to the Constitutional Convention believed that their presence was the best chance they had of saving all that their new nation had gained since the signing of the Declaration of Independence eleven years before.

The Constitutional Convention represents an extraordinary event in the history of governments. Before the Convention, structures of govern-ment were formed in entirely different ways, either by evolving over long periods of time, as in the case of the British and French govern-ments, or by imposition of government by military commanders after a successful invasion or coup d'etat. The U.S. Constitution represented a new, rational, and peaceful way of changing forms of government. A group of prominent men, chosen by popularly elected legislatures, as-sembled to create a new form of central government, which was then ratified by specially elected assemblies in each state amid free and oc-casionally furious debate. After the states ratified the Constitution, voters peacefully elected the political leaders of the new nation, who then set about the business of establishing the day-to-day functions of a national government. Such a thing had never before been accomplished. Euro-pean observers watched in wonderment, marveling at the absence of violence, the freedom of debate, and the orderliness of it all.

Americans themselves were acutely aware that they were attempting to create a government in an entirely new way. The Continental Con-gress had started out as an organized means of communicating among the colonies and presenting their collective demands to the British gov-ernment. In 1777, the Continental Congress adopted the Articles of Con-federation, which would have created a central government to coordinate wartime needs among the former colonies during the Revo-lution, but the states did not ratify the Articles until 1781. Waging a war on several fronts presented a different set of problems than governing a large territory in peacetime. The Baron de Montesquieu, a French political theorist, had written that republics could exist only in tiny countries, not in the vast region included in the new American states. The drafters of the Constitution, many of whom had either read Montesquieu or were familiar with his views, were in a difficult position. Should they defy the wisdom of one of the most respected political theorists of the century? Could they create a government that united the states without destroying their independence? They believed that they had no alternative and so chose to act boldly; their success was proof of their determination to create a unified whole with the same sense of purpose that had united them against Britain in defense of their rights.

The Articles of Confederation, which created a loose confederation among the states, proved inadequate. The authors of the Articles had been railing at the British government for years about its overbearing and unfair impositions and were determined not to re-create such a despotic government among themselves. Furthermore, none of the newly formed governments of the former colonies was disposed to trust the others, nor a central government. From their founding, the various colonies had varying interests, with their economies based on different crops, trade goods, and businesses. New York and Massachusetts, for example, shared similar trading interests but also had hostile boundary disputes. Southern and northern colonies had different climates, cultures, and interests, and travel between them was so slow that many colonists had traveled to England and yet had never visited a colony a few hundred miles to the north or south. Most people's loyalty was to their local and their state governments, not a distant central authority.

As a result, the Articles were carefully designed to ensure that no one state could dominate the others. Any state could veto an enactment of the central government, and so agreement on most matters was difficult, if not impossible. The fundamental flaw in the Articles was that they merely created an alliance among the states and had no power to compel state governments to balance their individual interests with the collective interests of all the states. The result was a weak central government. The Constitution of 1787 created a central government with the power to act against individuals rather than just the states, thus creating a much stronger government.

After the war, some leaders in the newly independent states were convinced that a stronger central government was needed. These men had a continental, rather than a regional, perspective. Some of these men had served in the Continental army or the Continental Congress and were impatiently waiting for the states to pay long-overdue assessments necessary to pay off the remaining war debt. Others were men who wanted to do business in more than one state but were frustrated by the confusion of different state currencies, the value of which fluctuated wildly. Merchants who wished to trade with other countries were discouraged by Congress' inability to pass and enforce trade regulations; European countries, seeing the weakness of American government, had passed high taxes on American goods without fear of similar tariffs on their own goods sold in America. Citizens of states that had paid their share of the Continental war assessments were unhappy with states that clearly had no intention of doing so. The chaos in trade and currency made it difficult for many merchants and shopkeepers to do business. Many people hoped that a stronger government would bring order.

Trade regulation was to be the topic of discussion for a group of men who met in Annapolis, Maryland, in August 1786. With only five states represented, the delegates decided that a later convention was necessary with representatives from all the states and with an agenda that included more than trade. They issued a call for a convention to be held the following summer and urged the state legislatures to select delegates to go to Philadelphia to discuss a revision of the Articles of Confederation. Not long after, a group of disgruntled farmers and war veterans in western Massachusetts led by Daniel Shays forced the closure of local courts in order to prevent foreclosures on their land. Many war veterans had been unable to pay their mortgages or taxes because of the economic chaos and currency fluctuations. The rebels were defeated by the local militia before they could seize a local arsenal, but when the news of Shays' Rebellion spread, lawmakers were alarmed. The Annapolis Convention's recommendation of a convention to revise the Articles made a lot of sense, as a strong central government would help prevent such rebellions in the future. George Washington himself urged the Virginia legislature to send a delegation. Washington's support was particularly important because, as the general who led the new nation to victory in the Revolution, he was regarded in all the states as the war's greatest hero. So great was his influence and prestige that no one believed that he would involve himself in a disreputable enterprise; his support established the credibility of the Convention. By the middle of October, seven state legislatures had selected delegates for the Convention and Congress issued a call for the remaining states to choose their delegates.

The plan was for the Convention to meet on May 14 in Philadelphia. The Virginia delegation arrived early, forcing the delegates to wait for a majority of the other states' representatives to arrive. The states had selected seventy-four delegates in all, although no more than fifty-five would actually attend the debates, and the delegates arrived and departed according to the difficulties of travel, their business or governmental responsibilities at home, or their dissatisfaction with the decisions of the Convention. Two of the most eminent men of the country were missing: Thomas Jefferson and John Adams, both serving as ambassadors in Europe. Others did not attend because they distrusted the Convention's agenda: John Jay of New York thought the Convention had little chance of success in revising the Articles, Samuel Adams disliked the idea of a general revision of the Confederation, and Patrick Henry was suspicious, stating later that he had refused his appointment as a delegate because "I smelt a Rat" (quoted in Peters, *A More Perfect Union*, p. 23). Because many of those who disagreed with the business of the Convention excused themselves from attending, the men who met in Philadelphia tended to support a strong central government.

The delegates were a respectable, though young, group. Their ages ranged from 27 to 81. Benjamin Franklin, the oldest delegate and a highly respected veteran of the Revolutionary cause, was so hobbled from gout that he had to be carried into the chamber in a sedan chair he had brought back from France. The average age was 43. They were substantial farmers, lawyers, merchants, and state officeholders, typically occupying a combination of these roles. Six had signed the Articles of Confederation. Forty-two had served in Congress, eight had helped draft their states' constitutions, and twenty-one had fought in the Revolutionary War. Most came from well-to-do families. Half were college educated, at a time when few men, even the sons of wealthy men, went to college. They came from long-settled regions of their home states, rather than the frontier. Many had traveled, both in America and in Europe. Most of these men knew or knew of each other, so the Convention met in an air of familiarity and mutual respect. The only state not to send delegates was Rhode Island.

Since Virginia had led the way by selecting delegates first, the Virginia delegation took a leadership role. James Madison, a 35-year-old former Virginia legislator and Confederation Congressman, had spent a great deal of time pondering the problem of the structures of government. He had been troubled about the state of government under the Confederation and had read a great deal about government, including books suggested by his friend Thomas Jefferson. Despite his youth, he exercised a great deal of influence in the drafting of the Constitution, and much of what we know of the debates during the Convention comes from his notes.

The first order of business was to vote for a presiding officer, and the delegates elected George Washington. The delegates agreed on the rules of procedure, with an especially important and unusual provision: they agreed to keep the proceedings entirely secret. None of the delegates was permitted to take notes from the official journal of the Convention without permission. Only members of the Convention would be permitted to look at the journal. The proceedings were not to be printed or even discussed outside the Convention room. The reason for this rule was that no member wished to have his own views published; a member could thus feel free to change his views as the discussion proceeded. These men were all politicians, and politicians are expected to maintain some consistency in their opinions; having one's opinions published tends to make it hard to change them later. No delegate wanted to be obligated to explain to his supporters back home why he was so positively on one side of a debate only to change sides later. The delegates typically held strong views about the nature and duties of government, but they were not sure about how to put such ideas into practice. The secrecy rule was intended to allow free and vigorous debate, and to make compromise as easy as possible. Not everyone approved of this rule. Jefferson, writing letters from Paris, disapproved of secrecy but nevertheless hoped for the best from the Convention. The delegates obeyed this rule faithfully: even Franklin, a famously talkative man, followed the rule, though he had to be reminded on occasion.

The delegates agreed to another important procedural rule. The standard procedure for such deliberative bodies was to debate matters one at a time, voting on each issue in turn and then moving on to the next item; once an item was voted on it would not be reopened. The delegates to the Constitutional Convention agreed instead to form a Committee of the Whole. This decision allowed for debate in which no provision would be formally adopted until the entire Constitution was complete. After the Committee of the Whole completed its work, the Convention would vote to adopt or reject the document entirely. The result was that the majority of debate on the Constitution took place in the Committee of the Whole or in different subcommittees. As discussion of a provision clarified delegates' views of previous issues, the prior matters could be freely reopened and revised. The result was that each delegate knew that if he was unsure about an issue or disliked a provision, he could postpone argument on the matter while debate continued and hope to raise the issue again, perhaps after other delegates had thought about the matter more thoroughly in the context of subsequent debates. For example, the delegates discussed representation in Congress repeatedly, discussing the problem for a while, then turning to other matters while tempers cooled, then raising the issue again for further debate until a compromise was finally reached. The Convention was operating under rules designed to ensure a maximum of flexibility and compromise, with every delegate given ample opportunity to reconsider matters and make his views known.

After agreeing on procedure, the Convention was ready to get to the work at hand. Edmund Randolph, the governor of Virginia and leader of the Virginia delegation, presented what came to be known as the Virginia Plan. Madison had drafted this plan soon after the Annapolis Convention, and the Virginia delegation had been discussing it since their arrival in Philadelphia while they waited for delegations to arrive from other states. Virginia was then one of the largest and most populous states, and no one was surprised that the Virginia Plan reflected the concerns of the larger states. The Virginia Plan proposed to eliminate the Confederation mechanism of one vote in Congress for each state, instead apportioning representation in a two-part legislative body by the population. This legislature would be dominated by the larger, more populous states. The central government would also have executive and judicial branches, both of which would have the power to override state action in matters of particular national interest. The Virginia delegation clearly proposed to scrap the Confederation government altogether and create a strong central government.

The reaction to the Virginia Plan varied. Some delegates were concerned about exceeding their authority to revise the Articles of Confederation, but they were so unhappy with the state of government under the Articles that they were willing to stay in the Convention to find a solution, regardless of the form it took. Other delegates were interested in the proposal but not happy with specific provisions. Alexander Hamilton, representing New York, was pleased that the Convention was considering abandoning the Articles. He recommended abolishing state governments entirely and creating a new national government without individual state governments to interfere. Hamilton's views were the most strongly nationalistic of those of the delegates, and few of the delegates liked the idea of abolishing the state governments, to which they had strong loyalties. If the delegates would not accept Hamilton's extreme views then they might have been persuaded that bold action was necessary if only to prevent radicals like Hamilton from winning later.

Opposition to the Virginia Plan was based primarily on two issues. The first was that the plan proposed to give too much power to the central government. Not only did the delegates not want to create a central government with the power to oppress them as the British government had, but they also were practical politicians who doubted that such a plan would ever be ratified by the states. The states, they argued, would never agree to a government with the power to veto state laws. The second objection to the Virginia Plan was that it gave too much power to the larger states: the proposed legislature would be dominated by large states, and so getting smaller states to ratify the amendments would be impossible. A more powerful legislative branch, as envisioned in the Virginia Plan, was needed, but the representatives from the smaller states wanted a stronger voice in this government and thought that their states' interests would be ignored in a legislature controlled by larger states.

Despite their differences, the delegates chose to remain and debate specific provisions in order to reach a compromise, rather than give up and go home. Any disgruntled former delegate to the Convention could have created substantial opposition to the Convention, especially had he chosen to reveal the details of the debate, but most of the delegates stayed and all obeyed the secrecy rule.

After two weeks of debate some of the delegates proposed a break. The Convention had postponed discussion on the issue of representation in Congress, turning their attention to other matters. They debated the nature of the executive branch, agreeing on an individual as president rather than an executive council, and they discussed the creation of a Supreme Court. After a few days' break, the delegates returned on June 16 to resume debate. William Paterson, the former governor of New Jersey, presented a plan intended to address the concerns of delegates from smaller states. Paterson was well regarded despite his short stature, which at 5'2" was even shorter than Madison's 5'4", and the delegates respected his views. The New Jersey Plan resembled the Virginia Plan in some respects with important differences regarding the executive branch and representation in the legislature; it expressly retained sovereignty in the states.

The idea of sovereignty, which is the theoretical source of political power, was important to political theory of the time, an age when sovereigns, or monarchs, held all political power in most countries. Without a monarch, where would political authority reside? Contrary to some people's expectations, the delegates at the Constitutional Convention devoted little of their time to discussing the finer points of political theory. But Paterson's proposal to retain sovereignty in the states made one fact clear: by proposing that the states retain ultimate political power, he asserted that the smaller states would rather remain in a loose, even chaotic, confederation than consent to be dominated by the large states in a strong national government. During the debate on the New Jersey Plan, another fact became clear: the small states would consider abandoning the Confederation government if the new form of government would protect their interests.

The Convention rejected the New Jersey Plan, but debate continued with the delegates well aware that they must find a plan acceptable to delegates from both the large and small states. After fruitless debate in the steamy summer heat, the Convention was deadlocked and voted to create a committee charged with resolving the issue of representation. The Convention chose committee members on the basis of their willingness to compromise, which meant that Madison, a strong supporter of the Virginia Plan, was not chosen. The committee reached a compromise, based on a suggestion from Franklin: the lower house would consist of members elected in proportion to the population of the states and the states would be represented equally in the upper house. The committee presented its compromise when the Convention resumed debate on July 5, after a break to celebrate Independence Day. The delegates hated the committee's proposal and after heated debate referred the proposal to another committee. Eventually the second committee created a modified version of Franklin's suggested compromise.

At this point in the debates, one of the most divisive issues arose: slavery. The debate began with a practical problem: how were the slaves to be counted when calculating the number of representatives for each state? Delegates from nonslave states argued that only the free population should be counted, and delegates from slave states wanted all persons, slave and free, to be counted. What about when levying taxes on a per capita basis? Were slaves to be included in that calculation? The delegates did not debate the morality of slavery at this point because they knew such a discussion would only infuriate both sides and make compromise impossible. The compromise that a committee eventually reached was that three out of five slaves would be counted for the purpose of both representation and taxation.

Many observers have wondered how these men who claimed such an interest in freedom could agree to create a government that permitted slavery. Some of the delegates believed, perhaps naively, that slavery would disappear on its own when it ceased to be profitable. Other delegates believed that the right to own other human beings was as important as the right to own land, since both were the source of income that freed a man from domination from an employer and allowed for true independence. Most of the delegates also shared the views of most Europeans and white Americans that Africans and their American descendants were inferior to whites. They did not consider African Americans, whether enslaved or free, to be their political or social equals. Ironically, the presence of slaves in their midst may have made many of these men more aware of the value of freedom and more determined to secure their own political rights. These questions remain a controversial issue among historians, and their full implications merit more consideration than is possible in this essay.

One of the most intense debates at the Convention was about the importation of slaves. Some of the delegates raised the issues of the immorality of slavery and its harmful economic effects. In some of the nastiest debates of the Convention, Southern delegates forcefully reminded the others that the South would never ratify a constitution that endangered slavery. Without ratification by Southern states the Constitution would fail, the states would dissolve into bickering, helpless and isolated governments, and the delegates would have wasted their time entirely. So, once again, compromise was necessary. The compromise reached was that Congress would have the power to ban the importation of slaves, but not before the year 1808. Nearly twenty years after the Convention, President Jefferson signed a law ending the international slave trade as of January 1, 1808, which made importing slaves from Africa illegal. However, the trade continued illegally until the Civil War. Some delegates believed that by closing the international slave trade, slavery would eventually disappear without a struggle. They were wrong; the slavery issue had to be decided in a bloody civil war.

The next extensive debate concerned the presidency. The easiest decision was that the president and vice president would be elected for four-year terms and would be eligible for re-election. A more difficult problem concerned the procedure for these elections. The Committee for Postponed Matters was assigned the task of devising an election procedure. The committee devised the electoral college, a complicated mechanism that would solve two problems: the electoral college guaranteed each state, no matter how small, at least three votes in the election of the president, thus preventing large states from completely dominating the small ones in the selection of the president. Also, if no candidate received a majority of votes in the electoral college, the president was to be elected by the House of Representatives. The procedure was devised such that once the people voted for the president, electors would then vote according to the wishes of the people. Thus the electoral college was to serve essentially as a counting mechanism and an administrative convenience. The candidate with the second largest number of votes was to become the vice president. This provision caused problems when, in the election of 1800, Thomas Jefferson and Aaron Burr received the same number of votes, leading to a bitter fight when the election was decided in the House of Representatives. The procedure was changed in the Twelfth Amendment, which required voting for the president and vice president in separate ballots.

The next issue involved powers of the executive branch. The vice president was given the role of presiding over the Senate, with the power to vote only to break ties, and the result was a vice presidency without any real power. The powers of the president were a more difficult matter. The president was to have the power to make treaties and to appoint ambassadors, Supreme Court justices, and other important public officials with the consent of the Senate. Treaties were to require a two-thirds majority vote in the Senate. As a means of preventing the abuse of power, the Convention created a procedure for the impeachment of the president, vice president, and other federal officials. The House would vote to impeach and the Senate would hold a trial, with a two-thirds vote required for a conviction, which would expel the official from office. The delegates were optimistic that the powers of the presidency, while substantial, would be balanced by those of the House and Senate, and thus neither branch would be able to dominate the other.

By early September, the Convention was nearly through with its work. The Convention had worked all summer, with only occasional breaks, and everyone was relieved to turn the task of drafting a final document over to the Committee of Style. While the Committee worked, delegates struggled with a few last problems concerning ratification and other issues. The delegates worked out a procedure for ratification that required nine of the thirteen states to ratify the Constitution for it to go into effect. Each state would hold elections to select delegates to a convention to ratify the Constitution. This mechanism bypassed the requirement in the Articles that changes be confirmed by unanimous vote, but the delegates by this time were long past caring about that issue. Most of the delegates were eager to get home and start the political maneuvering necessary to ratify the Constitution in their state's convention.

By the time the work on the Constitution was finished, some of the delegates had doubts. Edmund Randolph, who had presented the Virginia Plan to the Constitution, refused to sign, though in the end he recommended ratification to the Virginia convention. George Mason, also from Virginia, refused to sign and wrote a tract opposing ratification. One of the Massachusetts delegates, Elbridge Gerry, refused to sign and later stated his objections publicly, citing in particular the absence of a bill of rights. Approval by the large and commercially dominant states of Virginia and New York would be necessary for a workable government to take effect, and the supporters of the Constitution would follow developments in those states very closely. Madison's energy and Washington's prestige worked together to ensure ratification in the Virginia convention, and other states soon joined in the movement toward ratification. Eventually all of the states ratified, though some conventions called for the passage of a bill of rights. Madison had promised to see personally to the passage of a bill of rights, and did so after his election to the new Congress. At the Philadelphia convention, he and other delegates had not seen a need for a bill of rights and were preoccupied with the other problems in drafting the Constitution.

The addition of the bill of rights to the Constitution points out one of the most ingenious accomplishments of the Constitutional Convention. The delegates were awed by the task before them and struggled with the problems of creating a new government very seriously. In some controversial provisions, they were careful to use general language, knowing that later generations would have to determine exactly what those words meant. They also realized that they could not possibly anticipate all of the problems that the government would encounter and so they devised a means of amending the Constitution. This mechanism requires Congress and the states to approve of such an amendment, thus ensuring that as many people as possible have an opportunity to influence such an important measure.

The greatest insight of the framers was their humility as they realized that they could not possibly foresee the future challenges the Constitution would face. Because of their wisdom, the U.S. Constitution has withstood enormous social upheaval, including the bloody Civil War and its bitter aftermath. Americans knew then that the flexibility of the Constitution is its greatest strength.

SELECTED BIBLIOGRAPHY

Alexander, John K. *Selling of the Constitutional Convention: A History of News Coverage*. Madison, WI: Madison House, 1990. An interesting approach to the subject of the public's view of the Convention.

Anderson, Thornton. *Creating the Constitution, The Convention of 1787 and the First Congress*. University Park: Pennsylvania State University Press, 1993. Looks at the Convention in the context of its immediate political aftermath.

Banning, Lance. *The Sacred Fire of Liberty: James Madison and the Founding of the Federal Republic*. Ithaca, NY: Cornell University Press, 1995. Banning analyzes Madison's thought and argues persuasively that Madison's political principles remained consistent throughout his political career.

Barlow, J. Jackson, Leonard W. Levy, and Ken Masugi, eds. *The American Founding: Essays on the Formation of the Constitution*. Westport, CT: Greenwood Press, 1988. A classic collection of essays on the Convention, with a wide range of interpretations.

Beard, Charles A. *An Economic Interpretation of the Constitution of the United States*. New York: Macmillan, 1913. Beard shocked many by arguing that the Founding Fathers were, in fact, looking out for their own financial interests, a view that provoked a furious debate among historians.

Beeman, Richard R., Stephen Botein, and Edward C. Carter II, eds. *Beyond Confederation: Origins of the Constitution and American National Identity*. Chapel Hill: University of North Carolina Press, 1987. Before anyone would accept a constitution binding the former colonies together, they had to accept the idea that the destiny of the former colonies was a shared one.

Bowen, Catherine Drinker. *Miracle at Philadelphia: The Story of the Constitutional Convention, May to September*. Boston: Little, Brown, 1966. An entertaining narrative of the Convention.

Brookhiser, Richard. *Founding Father: Rediscovering George Washington*. New York: Free Press, 1996. An engaging biography of Washington written from a conservative perspective.

Collier, James L., and Christopher Collier. *Decision in Philadelphia: The Constitutional Convention of 1787*. New York: Random House, 1986. An interesting narrative of the Convention.

Coulter, Ellis Merton. *Abraham Baldwin: Patriot, Educator and Founding Father*. Arlington, VA: Vandamere Press, 1987. An interesting study of a lesser-known delegate.

Cunliff, Marcus. *Washington: Man and Monument*. Boston: Little, Brown, 1958. A classic biography of an enigmatic subject.

Finkelman, Paul. *Slavery and the Founders: Race and Liberty in the Age of Jefferson*. Armonk, NY: Sharpe, 1996. Argues that the Constitution was in essence a pro-slavery document.

Kaminski, John P., and Richard Leffler, eds. *Federalists and Antifederalists*. Madison, WI: Madison House, 1987. An excellent source for those interested in the debate on the Constitution.

Kerber, Linda K. *Women of the Republic: Intellect and Ideology in Revolutionary Amer-

ica. Chapel Hill: University of North Carolina Press, 1980. Presents the women's perspective of the Revolution and its consequences.

Levy, Leonard W., and Dennis J. Mahoney, eds. *The Framing and Ratification of the Constitution.* New York: Macmillan, 1987. A collection of very different views on the Convention and the politics surrounding it.

Madison, James, Alexander Hamilton, and John Jay. *The Federalist Papers.* Isaac Kramnick, ed. 1788; New York: Penguin, 1961. Essential for every serious student of the Constitution and the ratification debates.

Main, Jackson Turner. *Political Parties Before the Constitution.* Chapel Hill: University of North Carolina Press, 1973. Each of the delegates had to consider his political allies at home, and so this book presents an essential background to the Convention.

May, Henry. *The Enlightenment in America.* New York: Oxford University Press, 1976. A classic work that traces the influence of the Enlightenment on the drafting of the Constitution.

McCoy, Drew R. *The Last of the Fathers: James Madison and the Republican Legacy.* Cambridge: Cambridge University Press, 1989. An account of Madison's later life.

McDonald, Forrest. *We the People: The Economic Origins of the Constitution.* Lawrence: University Press of Kansas, 1958. A response to Charles Beard's arguments regarding the economic motives of the delegates.

———. *Novus Ordo Seclorum: The Intellectual Origins of the Constitution.* Lawrence: University Press of Kansas, 1985. By one of the foremost biographers of the Founding Fathers.

Middlekauff, Robert. *Benjamin Franklin and His Enemies.* Berkeley: University of California Press, 1996. This biography takes the unusual approach of describing a man by the nature of his enemies, and Franklin, as always, emerges as charming as ever.

Miller, William L. *The Business of May Next: James Madison and the Founding.* Charlottesville: University Press of Virginia, 1993. An eccentric but accessible account of the Convention.

Paine, Thomas. *The Thomas Paine Reader.* Michael Foot and Isaac Kramnick, eds. New York: Penguin, 1987. A study of the most radical and one of the most engaging political writers of his time.

Peters, William. *A More Perfect Union.* New York: Crown, 1987. Presents an entertaining and detailed account of the substance of the delegates' debates.

Rakove, Jack N. *James Madison and the Creation of the American Republic.* Glenview, IL: Scott, Foresman, 1990. An excellent work from the Library of American Biography, and thus focused on Madison and his role in the Convention and ratification.

———. *Original Meanings: Politics and Ideas in the Making of the Constitution.* New York: Knopf, 1996. Addresses the ideas behind the Constitution in all their complexity.

Wood, Gordon S. *The Creation of the American Republic, 1776–1787.* New York: W. W. Norton, 1969. A massive analysis of the changing American political culture that produced the Constitution.

The XYZ Affair led to a quasi-war with France, in which the U.S. Navy performed very well. Here the U.S.S. *Constellation* is locked in battle with the French ship *L'Insurgent* in February 1799. (Reproduced from the Collections of the Library of Congress)

9

The XYZ Affair, 1798–1800

INTRODUCTION

Probably no one had had as much experience in public affairs as John Adams had when he came to the presidency in 1797. He was 62 years old, had graduated from Harvard, defended the British soldiers involved in the Boston Massacre, and served as a delegate to both the First and Second Continental Congresses. He was a member of the peace commission that negotiated the Treaty of Paris (1783), had been minister to Great Britain from 1785 to 1788, and finally, was vice president under George Washington for eight years. He was honest, intelligent, and devoted to his country. What faults he had, however, lay in his personality and were enough to keep him from being a truly great president.

Adams was seriously impressed with his own importance, and in the early days of the government he had favored ornate titles and decorum for high officials, which offended those who thought that titles and decorum seemed a little too British. Physically, Adams was short and rather fat, and this made his appeal to dignity appear even more ridiculous, especially when he was compared to the tall, lean figure of Washington. It was no surprise that Adams's political foes referred to him as "His Rotundity."

Also, Adams lacked tact and the politician's touch to conciliate party dissension and maintain party harmony. At this time, the Federalist party was divided between those loyal to Adams and those who saw Alexander Hamilton as the rightful political heir to Washington, despite the fact that the young former Treasury secretary held no official post in the Adams administration. In this circumstance, Adams needed the skill of a master politician to hold the Federalists together while he was president, since many, if not most, of the party regulars looked to Hamilton for leadership. Adams lacked this ability and spent an often lonely and frustrating four years in office, his miseries compounded by the necessity of spending long periods of time in Massachusetts attending his ailing wife, Abigail.

Foreign affairs dominated Adams's administration. The principal issue was a dangerous breakdown in relations with France, and its domestic consequences. While many Americans had appreciated the help of France during the Revolutionary War and had applauded the outbreak of the French Revolution, their ardor for the French had been cooled somewhat by news of the excessive violence of the early 1790s. France, meanwhile, had been quite upset when the United States had signed Jay's Treaty with Great Britain in 1795. Although unpopular in the United States, this treaty had settled a variety of grievances left over from the Revolution and improved trade relations between the two countries. This state of better Anglo-American relations left Britain ready to be more of a threat to its traditional rival, France, and the French thought the Americans quite ungrateful for signing and ratifying the treaty. They read more into Jay's Treaty than was actually there, seeing it as an alliance between the two countries and therefore as a repudiation of the Franco-American alliance of 1778.

At this time France was ruled by a five-man committee called the Directory, and the wise and shrewd Charles Maurice de Talleyrand was the foreign minister. He issued an order confiscating all foreign ships engaged in trade with the British, and in a very short time some 300 U.S. ships were seized and sold to the highest bidder. Furthermore, the French refused to accept the credentials of Charles Coatesworth Pinckney, the new American minister to France, and told him that he would be arrested if he stayed in the country. The angry Pinckney went to Amsterdam, where he was joined by John Marshall and Elbridge Gerry. The three Americans constituted a commission that returned to France to negotiate a settlement in the matter of the confiscated ships. In Philadelphia, Congress approved Adams's request for increased military spending.

When Pinckney, Marshall, and Gerry reached Paris, they were ill-received. Three of Talleyrand's agents met them and demanded a payment of $250,000 as a bribe and $10 million as a loan to France to be paid before negotiations would begin. The outraged commissioners reported the incident to Adams, who sent a short note to Congress, denouncing the French for their insulting treatment and urging readiness for war.

Republicans in Congress, still somewhat sympathetic to the French, doubted that Talleyrand's agents had done what Adams said they had done and demanded that the president make public the diplomatic correspondence concerning the incident. Adams complied and sent the report of the commissioners to Congress, deleting the actual names of the Frenchmen and substituting for them the letters X, Y, and Z, thus giving the affair its name.

The publication caused a great sensation; the country was swept with nationalistic pride and Adams was genuinely popular for perhaps the only time in his life. The army and navy were quickly expanded, and old General Washington was called out of retirement to be commander-in-chief, agreeing only on condition that Hamilton be named his second-in-command.

Americans became outspokenly anti-French all over the country. Those wearing the tricolor in sympathy with the French Revolution suddenly ran the risk of being mobbed, and 1,200 young men of Philadelphia marched to the president's home to offer their services in the fight against France. Everyone took to wearing a black cockade—a rose of black ribbon about four inches in diameter—as a symbol of Federalism and patriotism. There were wild rumors of invasions and French-inspired slave insurrections, and known French immigrants were harassed. Harvard dropped the French oration from its commencement program, and July 4 speakers universally praised Adams and damned the French; the Federalist president of Yale went so far as to say that if French ways prevailed, "we may see our wives and daughters the victims of legal prostitution; soberly dishonored; speciously polluted."

Along with enlarging the army and navy, Adams and Congress cut off all trade with France, abrogated the treaty of 1778, and authorized public and private American ships to capture French vessels. But Adams refused to request that Congress make a formal declaration of war, much to the disgust of Hamilton, who was itching for military glory, and to the Hamiltonian Federalists, who thought a war would entrench them in control of the federal government. As a result, an undeclared naval war (sometimes called a "Quasi-War") took place in 1798 and 1799, in which the American navy, new as it was, fought with considerable credit, capturing some eighty-five prizes and taking advantage of France's preoccupation with European problems.

At the height of the hysteria, and in an effort to maintain authority and weaken the political opposition, the Federalists in Congress came up with the Alien and Sedition Acts. These were passed for the stated purpose of protecting the country from subversion or dangerous foreign influence in the midst of the hostility with France. Since it was the Republican party that traditionally favored France, and since many Republicans were foreigners by birth, French or Irish for the most part, the Alien and Sedition Acts were quite clearly aimed at them. There were four acts in all:

1. The Naturalization Act lengthened from five to fourteen years the length of residence required for citizenship.
2. The Alien Act gave the president power to deport any foreigner considered dangerous.
3. The Alien Enemies Act threatened all foreigners with imprisonment if war were declared with or invasion threatened by their native country.
4. The Sedition Act was the most extreme of all. It laid fines of up to $2,000 and prison sentences of up to two years for anyone speaking, writing, or publishing antigovernment material.

Though the Naturalization and Alien Acts were never enforced, they probably had the desired effect of discouraging immigration and encouraging some resident foreigners to leave. The Sedition Act was enforced, and some ten newspaper editors were convicted, one for hoping that when a salute was fired in honor of the president, the wadding of the cannon would strike "him in the rear bulge of his breeches."

More serious was the imprisonment for four months of Matthew Lyon, a Republican congressman and publisher from Vermont, who wrote that he saw in the president "every consideration of public welfare swallowed up in a continual grasp for power, an unbounded thirst for ridiculous pomp, foolish adulation, and selfless avarice." In addition to his four-month prison term, Lyon also had to pay a fine of $1,000. On the other hand, he became a martyr to his constituents—he was overwhelmingly re-elected to Congress, and his conviction convinced Republicans everywhere that the Federalists were denying constitutional liberties by means of these acts.

In order to dramatize their determination not to submit to what they viewed as a clear violation of the Constitution, Jefferson and Madison each wrote a set of resolutions that were then passed by the legislatures of Kentucky and Virginia. The Kentucky and Virginia Resolutions, as they are commonly known, set forth an explicit states' rights interpretation of the Constitution, declaring it to be a contract with the people, who retained the right to judge infractions of that contract (at this time the Supreme Court had never acted on the constitutionality of an act of Congress). The resolutions went on to say that Congress had violated the Constitution, and each author delineated a specific remedy. The more cautious Madison spoke of states interposing between the federal government and the people and suggested that a convention of the states might more clearly define the powers of the federal government. The more radical Jefferson suggested the idea of nullification—that a state could nullify or abrogate federal laws that it felt violated the Constitution. Neither Kentucky nor Virginia ever acted on the remedies suggested in the resolutions their legislatures had passed, but they were circulated to other state legislatures, some of which rejected the ideas in them. State sovereignty as a political concept had little appeal then, and it is probable that the Kentucky and Virginia Resolutions were written more for their political effect; in a sense they were part of the Republican platform for the 1800 election.

Meanwhile, it was becoming apparent that there would be no declared war between the United States and France. Talleyrand finally saw the wisdom of accommodation and let Adams know that France was now ready to accept his diplomatic representatives. After a further break with Hamiltonian Federalists, who did not want to reestablish relations with France so readily, Adams fired his secretary of state, Thomas Pickering, an ally of Hamilton's, and sent a new commission of three to France in 1800. There Napoleon Bonaparte, who had recently assumed authority in France, greeted them cordially. In the negotiations, France refused to pay indemnity (for damages to American interests) unless the treaty of 1778 were reactivated. But the U.S. commissioners were not authorized to do that, so a kind of honorable forgive-and-forget agreement was signed. Called the Convention of 1800, it was important because it formally released the United States from the treaty of 1778, included a mutual understanding about neutral rights, and secured the goodwill of Napoleon, which quite likely made possible the purchase of Louisiana in 1803. President Adams thought the Convention of 1800 was important. Years later he said, "I desire no other inscription over my gravestone than: Here lies John Adams, who took upon himself the responsibility of the peace with France in the year 1800."

INTERPRETIVE ESSAY
Donald A. Rakestraw

"Are our commissioners guillotined," inquired the venerable George Washington, "or what else is the occasion of their silence?" The silence of Charles C. Pinckney, John Marshall, and Elbridge Gerry, the special mission sent by President John Adams to resolve differences with the French Republic, was indeed, by the close of 1797, ominous. The success or failure of the envoys would likely spell the difference in peace and war. The longer they kept the Adams administration waiting, the greater the anxiety became. Adams was right to fret. He presided over a nation far from prepared for an altercation with a major European power. The American republic had achieved much in its brief life—a peaceful transfer of power from George Washington to John Adams, the implementation of a federal constitution, the establishment of a national financial system, and the completion of significant treaty arrangements with Britain and Spain. Despite the noteworthy successes, however, the nation remained young and vulnerable. To be drawn into the squabble between Britain and France could threaten not only the security but also the independence of the United States.

As the close of the eighteenth century approached, the United States was still in the early stages of its republican experiment with newly formed political parties distinguished most by their opinion on the limits of republican liberty and the role of government in that determination. The natural affinity that many Americans had for libertarian ideals had been complicated by the degradation of a revolution for *liberté* in France into a bloody European war pitting France against Great Britain. The conflict increased the skepticism in the United States of the Federalist party by confirming its worst nightmares of unchecked republicanism. The Republican party, however, strained to remain sympathetic to fellow libertarians. As the conflict increased between Britain and France, the two American parties chose sides. Always dangerous for domestic policy to be too closely associated with foreign controversies, it was particularly perilous for a nation susceptible to exploitation by one or both of the belligerents. In this context the interplay of domestic and foreign policy required careful management. Even a minor incident might tempt the astute politico to find domestic capital in foreign adventure.

The Adams administration, reflecting that fragile balance, was precariously perched atop a dysfunctional Federalist party with a Republican serving as vice president. Having won the election of 1796 by a meager three electoral votes, Adams could not wield authority with absolute confidence. He had been opposed by the powerful Federalist leader Alexander Hamilton, whose machinations to secure the presidency for the more malleable Thomas Pinckney had so fouled the outcome as to make opposition leader Thomas Jefferson vice president. In addition, Adams's decision to retain Washington's cabinet permitted Hamilton, though a private citizen, considerable influence over the formulation of national policy. Joseph McHenry at the War Department, Oliver Wolcott at Treasury, and Timothy Pickering at State were more inclined to follow Hamilton than their president. Adams was a president with a delicate popular base surrounded by dubious advisers. Under these circumstances, pressed from both sides, Adams had much at risk with the diplomatic mission of Pinckney, Marshall, and Gerry: the High Federalists (the more extremist wing of the Party) wanted war but had acquiesced to this one good-faith effort to negotiate restitution from the French Directory.

It is perhaps because of the general apprehension of a young nation and an intense desire to win its due respect that the so-called XYZ Affair had such astounding repercussions. Indeed, a seemingly inconsequential occurrence to the seasoned European diplomats would explode into an incident that came to dominate the attention of the Adams administration and much of the nation. In the two years following the affair, reactions altered the American political landscape with a near-fatal blow first to one party, then to the other; prompted the restructuring of the U.S. military and revival of the debate over the need for and danger of a standing army in peacetime; undermined the constitutional rights of U.S. citizens; affected the course of America's future both hemispherically and internationally; and introduced the United States to the paradox of limited war.

In March 1798 news of the U.S.-French negotiations finally arrived in Philadelphia to the eager ears of the Adams administration. As if to heighten the drama, a painstakingly slow process of deciphering the despatches was required before the full extent of the debacle could be understood. The only thing known immediately was that the mission had not been a success. Rumors circulated from Europe about the mission's failure. Adams's insecurity had been evident in his queries to his cabinet in January as to what course he should pursue if the news was bad: Should he call for war? Should he issue an embargo? Hamilton had earlier supported a limited war that retained diplomacy as an option, but it was apparent that Adams was uncertain.

When the alleged affront was finally made known, Adams was more inclined toward a formal declaration of war than Hamilton's faction had been. The president believed full-scale war to be an economic imperative. Without it there would be no way to sustain national honor and the U.S. economy. It should be noted that the suspected insult was no more than what diplomats had come to expect in Europe. Bribes were customary. In fact, the United States had recently paid the Barbary states tribute to secure American trade in the Mediterranean. The actual problem faced by the envoys had been more a technical one than one of honor: they had not been authorized to disburse such a sum, and to do so would have violated neutrality and perhaps provoked the British.

The reaction to news of the failed mission was immediate. Federalists called for war in the name of honor while Republicans chastised them for overreacting in an attempt to rationalize an unnecessary war waged for political advantage. Suspicious Republicans demanded to see all the correspondence from the mission. Only too glad to comply, Adams transmitted the entire deciphered record to Congress, the only alteration being the substitution of the letters X, Y, and Z for the names of the three offending French commissioners. (A fourth commissioner, code-named "W," was also part of the affair, but he played a lesser role, and the appellation "XYZ Affair" soon became popular.) Stunned Republicans hastily reconsidered their position on public disclosure of the documents and insisted that they be held from public view. It was too late, however; the genie had escaped the bottle. The Federalists seized upon the failed mission as a golden opportunity to solidify their political base at the expense of the now-embarrassed Republicans. Not only would the XYZ correspondence be made public but also, within short order, the Federalists saw to the dissemination of thousands of free copies throughout the nation. The offense that had in fact been a technicality was now obscured by the lurid description of the humiliating treatment of official representatives of a sovereign nation required to pay a bribe merely to be recognized. Pinckney's rejection of the French demand with "No, no; not a sixpence" would soon be heralded as a heroic rebuff of an improper advance. National hackles were up. Honor had been maligned. Merchants in a number of cities volunteered to subscribe warships to lend to the government for retaliation against the now-hated French.

As word circulated, a contagious war fever spread in the name of national honor and a determination to redress the disrespectful treatment of America's envoys. Addresses were delivered from lectern, stump, and pulpit across the United States. The mantra erroneously attributed to Charles Pinckney, "Millions for defense but not a penny for tribute," quickly became the favorite refrain in public gatherings and rallies. The song "Hail Columbia" was composed to sound out the patriotic theme of American national honor. Many of the addresses were directed to Adams, who was delighted with his sudden and unaccustomed popularity. The best way to retain it and the political rewards that should accrue to the party was to feed the patriotic zeal and capture it as exclusively Federalist. Adams devoted considerable time and attention to responding to the addresses, denouncing the godless French, questioning the patriotism of the Republicans, and calling for war to preserve "the national character when its existence as an independent nation is at stake." In the second week of May he proposed a day of "humiliation, fasting, and prayer" and, in one particularly exuberant moment, admonished a crowd that the "finger of destiny writes on the wall the word: War."

The correspondence addressed to Adams indicated a public consensus forming around common themes. The nation was willing to unite in a rare show of support for the government in Philadelphia and to invert its former fondness for revolutionary France to resentment and disgust; honor demanded a firm and concerted response. Americans were finally casting an objective and critical eye on their recent friend and ally. Hamilton published a series of newspaper articles collectively entitled "The Stand," in which he argued that France was bent on the domination of mankind. In the process the Gallic aggressors would cripple the power balance in Europe—a change portending grave consequences for the United States. "Standing, as it were," Hamilton warned, "in the midst of falling empires, it should be our aim to assume a station and attitude which will preserve us from being overwhelmed in their ruin."

It soon became not only unpopular but also downright dangerous to express a sympathetic word for the French. Children of Federalists squared off against their "Republican" peers in street fights as the parents of each held the fate of the nation in their hands. Prominent Republicans, including the vice president himself, were placed under surveillance for fear that they, in collusion with subversive French and Irish aliens, would bring down the government. Even fashion was affected: anything associated with France was called into question, especially the tricolor cockades or rosettes that had been sported by citizens as a not-too-subtle indication of support for the French. The Federalists saw to their substitution with a black rosette that, perhaps remotely co-incidental, was also the formal cockade of Britain. To be observed sporting the tricolor in the aftermath of the XYZ disclosures was not the surest way to win friends or invite polite gestures. Any American concerned with continued good health was careful not to display the tricolor on July 4, 1798, when perhaps the most frequently repeated holiday ritual was the burning of the French Foreign Minister, Charles Maurice de Talleyrand, in effigy.

The XYZ Affair had given the Federalist party an issue—a face-saving foreign war—to serve their political purposes. Most important, it could be used as a lever to force the Francophile Republicans from national prominence. Some Federalists also believed that war with France would permit the government to move beyond unprofitable defensive measures toward offensive action that would profit American producers and shippers and bring about increased American influence in the Western Hemisphere. If properly maintained, the frenzy for war also could be exploited to justify the collection of taxes, hasten a military buildup, and sever communication between Republicans and their fellow French "radicals." To draw southerners into the fracas, rumors were spread in collusion with the secretary of state that reported a French plan to incite a slave rebellion in the South to be orchestrated from Santo Domingo. Saboteurs, the rumors contended, were already at work distributing arms among the American slave population.

In their overzealous determination to hold the advantage over Republicans and republicanism, the Federalists pushed through legislation that jeopardized constitutional rights and illustrated the extreme lengths to which they were willing to go. On June 18, Adams signed into law the Naturalization Act—the first of four laws that would jointly be called the Alien and Sedition Acts. These more than any laws since colonial times deserved the label "intolerable." The acts were thinly veiled attempts by Federalists to put an end to republicanism and to drive dissent out of public discourse and dissenters out of the country. Under the Naturalization Act the period required for U.S. citizenship was raised from five to fourteen years with an addendum that required registration with and surveillance by the government. Since most immigrants identified with the Republican party, this law offered the bonus of depleting the ranks of the opposition. Two alien acts were passed that authorized the president to deport any noncitizen believed to be a threat to the security of the nation. This subjected all aliens to harassment by American zealots stirred by the XYZ agitation. The Sedition Act imperiled the rights of citizens most. In its initial form anyone convicted of offering aid to the French could face execution. In its slightly tamer final form, passed in mid-July, the act held that anyone conspiring or criticizing the government would be subject to fine or imprisonment. Twenty-five Republican newspapermen were indicted and ten were convicted under this law for articulating what most Republicans believed.

Republicans howled in protest at this patently unconstitutional assault that posed more of a threat to Americans, many said, than the French ever had. Albert Gallatin, who had emerged as the leader of the congressional Republicans, reminded his colleagues that in such a crisis the only satisfactory method of opposing political enemies was by the device of counterargument. To eliminate that device was to hazard dire consequences. Dire indeed were the consequences imbedded in the most significant and, as it turned out, most far-reaching response to the Alien and Sedition Acts. Thomas Jefferson and James Madison secretly penned two resolutions channeled through the state legislatures of Kentucky and Virginia, respectively. Although Jefferson's Kentucky Resolution was the harsher of the two, Madison's Virginia Resolution concurred that the Alien and Sedition laws were blatant assaults on freedom. Pointing to the Tenth Amendment to the U.S. Constitution, the resolutions contended that the states stood between the people and the central government as guarantor of liberty. To have Philadelphia impose on the people such rigid constraints could well necessitate, in Jefferson's view, a drastic and perhaps violent reaction. Jefferson called on the states to nullify the laws by declining to respect or enforce them within their boundaries. He argued that the central government owed its existence to a compact of the several states. If, in the eyes of those states, the federal government attempted to exercise power not expressly delegated by the Constitution, the states were obligated to oppose it. The dangerous nature of these notions would be felt within a matter of decades as a future generation put the theory of nullification and interposition to the test.

The suggestion of possible insurrection became entangled with an institution that, some feared, the Federalists might be tempted to use to press the United States toward monarchical government—a standing army. Hamilton felt Jefferson's subtle threat of insurrection added justification for a standing army. It might be necessary to force compliance with federal law. Hearing that Virginians were preparing for armed defense against the encroachment of the central government on their rights,

Hamilton proposed dispatching a "clever force" to "put Virginia to the Test of resistance." Hamilton was one of the most vocal advocates of an enhanced military.

The call to arms by Adams after the XYZ disclosures was met in Congress by a number of significant changes in U.S. military capabilities and structure. Prior to the public exposure to the XYZ correspondence, Adams had called for such measures as the production of armaments, defense of American shipping, and stepped-up security along the coast. In April, immediately following the broadcast of the XYZ despatches, Congress established the Department of Navy and authorized the president to increase the fleet from three to twenty-seven vessels, to arm merchant ships, and to commission privateers. As with the establishment of the navy as a separate service, also important to the long-term structure of the U.S. military was the establishment of a separate branch for the Marine Corps. To safeguard the republic on land, Adams was to commission officers to command an army of 10,000 to augment the 3,500 troops currently in service on the frontier. Further, plans were made for a provisional army of 50,000 to be formed in the event of all-out war. The seriousness of the crisis could be felt in every community, since the president was directed to activate 80,000 militia. The buildup would be financed by a direct tax on houses and slaves of $2 million.

Hamilton had aspirations to lead the new army, but Adams felt that the focus of the conflict with France should be on the seas. In early July 1798 the newly constituted navy captured its first prize and by the end of the year had been so successful that the French had practically conceded U.S. dominance in the Caribbean. Finally the United States had gained some respect from the European powers. Early the following year one of the navy's new ships, the *Constellation*, engaged the French frigate *L'Insurgente*. Although the United States lauded the victory, the French captain seemed confused by the exchange. He was sailing under orders to avoid engagement with U.S. ships. France had refused to declare war and, as far as France knew, so had the United States. "Why," the French captain queried, "have you fired on the national flag of a people with whom you are at peace?" This was indeed an appropriate question. The nearest Adams had come to a formal pronouncement of hostilities was the abrogation of all treaties with France in early July and his eviction of the French consuls in the United States shortly afterward.

The Adams administration had faced a dilemma after the furor of the XYZ Affair. The heated rhetoric that benefited the president's party demanded a declared war. How could the popularity of the president and his party be sustained short of all-out war? Further complicating the president's position was the problem of funding. The people would submit to the so-called "window tax" (a tax assessed on houses calculated by the number of windows) and taxes on slaves if indeed the proceeds were dedicated to public defense. But this had become a limited war. The so-called Quasi-War of 1798–1800 had the president questioning his executive prerogative. How far could he go short of a formal declaration of war? The president vacillated on the decision of declared war for several reasons. First, despite his public pronouncements, he knew that a war with a European power would be potentially devastating for the ill-prepared United States. Second, he understood that the chances were great that a declared war on France would force the United States into a closer relationship with Britain, a prospect that could make America too beholden to the British navy for security. Third, and perhaps most significant, Adams shuddered at the specter of a standing army controlled by his nemesis Hamilton. General Washington had let it be known that he would only lend his essential name as titular commander of the army if Hamilton was named Inspector General and served as the actual commander. When Adams, under duress, conceded and called Hamilton to lead the prospective army, he determined that the safest option was to keep it a paper army, effectively neutralizing Hamilton's warrior ambitions. At the same time that he appointed Hamilton as Inspector General, he made public his fateful decision to keep to a limited naval war against France.

It was during the deliberation over the selection of Hamilton that Adams finally faced the fact that his cabinet was less than fully committed to him and that many had fallen in with Hamilton's grand designs. The Inspector General intended to direct American foreign policy and to use the army, when called into existence, to conquer western territories for the United States. The ambitious New Yorker schemed to place Louisiana and the Floridas under American control. Such an accomplishment would not only add valuable land to the nation but would also block the French in the West and squelch republicanism and secessionist talk in that quarter.

The breach between the United States and France created by the XYZ Affair encouraged renewed interest in the political shape of the Western Hemisphere. Some Americans wanted to assist the people of Santo Domingo in their challenge to French rule. A Venezuelan hatched a scheme whereby the United States would join Britain and the Spanish colonies in the Americas against Spain and France. In return for the effort, the

United States would receive the Floridas and Louisiana. Hamilton, keen on conquest, thought the plan worthy of consideration, but Adams, much as his son would do two decades later, declined on the grounds that the United States should act independently. Besides, Adams thought, at this juncture it was best to have Spain neutral.

The increasingly irreconcilable differences of Hamilton and Adams portended serious problems for the Federalist party. When Adams made up his mind to avoid full-scale war with France, his decision exposed to attack Federalists who had implemented taxation to produce an army for a war that apparently would not occur. The outrage at the thought of supplying funds to a government that would use those funds to field an army to collect those funds began to rival the animus directed at the French. Although the provisional army remained provisional, the force that had been produced took on the appearance of a threat to American liberty. In Pennsylvania, for example, farmers who protested the property tax followed John Fries in outright anti-Federalist defiance, providing Congress with the excuse to dispatch the army against the quasi-insurrection in the name of putting down a Jacobin uprising. The Federalists had fallen into a trap. The taxation had been used to activate a military that, by taking the field against the citizens, had proved itself to be the very danger the Republicans had described. Fortunately, Adams in the end was able to put rational behavior ahead of partisan politics and pardoned the rebels.

The Adams administration was such a disappointment to the High Federalists that Hamilton in June 1799 encouraged his devotees to seize control of policy from Adams, who, he argued, was no longer fit to lead. If necessary, Hamilton would come to Philadelphia to aid in what some have described as a threatened palace revolt.

Meanwhile, there was renewed activity on the diplomatic front. Talleyrand had been stunned by the U.S. reaction to the XYZ Affair and, in his typically shrewd fashion, feigned ignorance of the despicable actions of Messieurs X, Y and Z. He denounced them publicly and demanded to know who the troublemakers were. Gerry, who had, to the disdain of the Federalists, remained in Paris, revealed the names. They had not, Talleyrand asserted, acted in his name or that of the Directory. Talleyrand, of course, secretly reveled in the thought of the stress that he had brought on the American political system, especially on the pro-British Federalists. "We have succeeded," he quietly boasted, "in dividing the party of Mr. Adams himself." In addition, he continued, French diplomatic moves had paralyzed "all the efforts of the English faction to start war and force[d] the president to start negotiations again." Appreciating the gravity of the situation, the French government backed away from its previous position and agreed to end privateering, ease the embargoes on American ships, release captured U.S. sailors, and, perhaps most importantly, welcome unequivocally a new minister from the United States.

Adams had Talleyrand's change of attitude confirmed by two other sources. His son, John Quincy, wrote him from Berlin that the French wanted to talk, and the U.S. minister to The Hague, William Vans Murray, assured Adams that the French would receive a new mission without preconditions. Adams, who saw this as the only possible means of extraction from the crisis, decided to send Murray to Paris to negotiate.

Murray's appointment left no doubt that war with France was unlikely and that Adams had chosen peace at the expense of his party's welfare. High Federalists would not be permitted to take the country into the caldron of European war. Hamilton knew that Adams's decision would be a deadly blow to the party. Not only would Federalists lose the issue, but also the people would blame them for the unnecessary panic. Hamilton thus attempted to block the Murray mission, and Secretary of State Thomas Pickering, glad to do Hamilton's bidding, delayed preparing Murray's instructions for his mission. Hamilton warned Adams that the British would consider negotiations with France a betrayal and would declare war. The Adams government now fractured completely. The Hamilton faction determined in the summer of 1799 that Adams should be dropped and another standard bearer found for the upcoming presidential campaign. The split was irreversible when Adams denounced the Hamiltonians as warmongers subservient to the directives of London rather than Philadelphia.

Republicans seized the opportunity to recover lost ground. By placing taxes, the national debt, and arguably exorbitant war expenditures at the feet of the Federalists, they could credibly contend that it had all been a political ploy to muzzle open discourse and to force upon the people a military government. Ironically, the Federalists, with the Alien and Sedition laws, had supplied Republicans with the means of their own undoing. Even though the Federalists, using thousands of copies of the XYZ correspondence, had ridden the war scare to a majority in both houses of Congress in the elections of 1798–1799 (election dates differed by state), the victory had been a Pyrrhic one. Many of the Federalists who came in with the Sixth Congress were moderates—like those in the South who supported candidates such as the heralded former envoy to France John Marshall—who would push for peace. To the chagrin of Hamilton, the moderate faction in the party rejected his leadership in particular and that of the High Federalists generally. Instead, they coalesced with Republicans to suspend military enlistment and to abort the provisional army.

Republicans, as a result of the Quasi-War experience, were themselves undergoing a reassessment of their commitment to unbridled republicanism. Jefferson, once a staunch advocate of the French, had become disillusioned with their vulgar aggression. Whereas he had once thought their taming of Britain a benefit to the cause of liberty, after the XYZ Affair and the difficulties that it produced, he decided that the United States should not be linked to any nation. Republicans in the United States no longer felt it necessary or desirable to associate French success with the survival or promulgation of republican ideals. During the Quasi-War Jefferson lamented that, although he applauded "the progress of liberty in all nations, and would forever give it the weight of our countenance, yet they are not to be touched without contamination from their other bad principles."

The disruption within the ranks in many ways broke the Federalist majority and sent the party into decline. The internal squabble became more overt during the 1800 campaign when Hamilton issued an attack on Adams in the form of a pamphlet entitled "Letter from Alexander Hamilton, Concerning the Public Conduct and Character of John Adams, Esq., President of the United States." Adams's advocates soon retaliated, publishing letters blasting the arrogant and reckless Hamilton. The Republicans looked on as their opponents did more than they ever could to salvage Republican political fortune. Although Adams in the end championed peace, his vacillation and the party's persistent push for war handed the peace agenda to Jefferson and the Republicans. The hard decision by the Adams administration to dispatch a peace mission to France would achieve his goal, but too late to refurbish his and his estranged party's tarnished image.

Adams belatedly attempted a corrective, ousting the most disloyal of his cabinet and deploying the new diplomatic mission to France. John Marshall replaced Pickering at State and Samuel Dexter took over for McHenry at War. In March, after adding (a concession to Hamilton) Chief Justice Oliver Ellsworth and William R. Davie of North Carolina to the mission, the delegation departed for Paris. Before the envoys' arrival, however, a coup d'état in Paris had brought in a new French government, the Consulate, under the direction of First Consul Napoleon Bonaparte. Napoleon, plotting a grand scheme that necessitated a respite from the French conflict with Britain, worked through the resilient Talleyrand, who had returned to the Foreign Office with the new government, to propose acceptable terms to the new American mission. Circumstances in the European war had convinced Napoleon that he should attempt (unsuccessfully, as it turned out) to draw the United States into a new league of armed neutrals. Also, if an accommodation could be found with the United States, perhaps Spain would find it in her interest to relinquish Louisiana to France. With Louisiana as a granary to feed Santo Domingo and the island a source of sugar for France, the complementary regions might form the nexus of a revived French Empire in the Americas.

Negotiations between the French and the new American mission moved forward in fits and starts for more than six months. The Americans stood firm on their instructions to preserve the integrity of Jay's Treaty with Britain, refuse any discussion of aid or loans, reject anything resembling an alliance, and limit any new arrangement to twelve years. Finally, in the fall, an agreement was reached in which the French conceded to American principles of neutrality, the two nations exchanged most-favored-nation status, ships taken during the Quasi-War were returned, and, most important for the American negotiators, the French accepted Adams's de facto abrogation of the 1778 treaties. The obligations made by the Americans during the struggle for independence had proved a constant source of grief and the pith of international aggravation through two presidential administrations.

The new envoys fared considerably better than their predecessors. For the signing of the Convention of 1800, the new American mission was entertained at Môrtefontaine, the country estate of Napoleon's brother Joseph. As Davie, Ellsworth, and Murray enjoyed the fruits of success with the comforting knowledge that they had officially ended the Quasi-War, freed American commerce from French harassment, and released the United States from its problematic treaty obligations, Napoleon's government was secretly concluding a treaty with Spain at San Ildefonso for the transfer of Louisiana. Napoleon's maneuver would soon have monumental importance for the United States. His clever step would open the way for a new American president to achieve through negotiation and dollars what Hamilton had dreamed of doing by force of arms—the annexation of the vast Louisiana Territory.

The century ended with the outrage of the XYZ Affair waning as Americans looked with a new optimism to a new century. The incident's effects, however, had been astounding. The fallout had produced a limited war with France, a rare national cohesion and passion for the respect of national sovereignty, an assault on the liberties of the people from within, the liberation of U.S. foreign policy from the fetters of European diplomacy, and a substantial contribution to what some have called a political revolution.

When the nineteenth century officially began in 1801, the governance of the republic soon passed to the Republican party. The disillusionment brought on by the Franco-American crisis and the split in the Federalist ranks over the handling of that crisis had played a big role in placing Thomas Jefferson in charge of the new Federal City in Washington, D.C., and his Republican colleagues in charge of Congress. The impact of the crisis with France would be seen in the surprisingly pragmatic approach to foreign policy that the new government exhibited. The Convention of 1800 (or the Treaty of Môrtefontaine) had sealed the end to the first phase of American foreign policy, bequeathing to Jefferson the hard lessons of neutrality and entangling alliances. Sadly, the lessons would be ultimately of little use once the Europeans set their minds again to the exploitation of a neutral America—an exploitation that would, with Republicans at the helm, propel the nation into a second war with Britain.

SELECTED BIBLIOGRAPHY

Bowman, A. H. *The Struggle for Neutrality: Franco-American Diplomacy during the Federalist Era.* Knoxville: University of Tennessee Press, 1974. Describes the anti-French foreign policy under the Federalist administrations of Washington and Adams and assesses the French desire to draw the United States into the European war.

Clarfield, Gerald H. *Timothy Pickering and American Diplomacy, 1795–1800.* Columbia: University of Missouri Press, 1969. Examines Secretary of State Pickering's policies toward France during the Quasi-War.

DeConde, Alexander. *The Quasi-War: The Politics and Diplomacy of the Undeclared War with France.* New York: Scribner's, 1966. Details the slide into the undeclared war by an Adams administration undercut from within by the president's own department heads.

Hill, Peter A. *William Vans Murray, Federalist Diplomat: The Shaping of Peace with France.* Syracuse, NY: Syracuse University Press, 1971. Focuses on Murray's part in resolving the Quasi-War with France.

Kaplan, Lawrence S. *Colonies into Nation: American Diplomacy, 1763–1801.* New York: Macmillan, 1972. A useful survey of early U.S. diplomacy that places the XYZ Affair into a broader historical context.

Kurtz, Stephen G. *The Presidency of John Adams: The Collapse of Federalism, 1795–1800.* Philadelphia: University of Pennsylvania Press, 1957. Study of the

Adams presidency, emphasizing the president's defiance of other Federalist leaders to work for peace with France.

Leiner, Frederick C. "The Subscription of Warships of 1798." *American Neptune* 46:3 (1986): 141–158. Discusses how merchants in various cities volunteered to support the construction of warships for loan to the government after hearing of the XYZ Affair.

Lyon, E. Wilson. "The Franco-American Convention of 1800." *Journal of Modern History* 12:3 (1940): 305–334. Surveys the negotiated settlement at Môrtefontaine between the United States and the French government under Napoleon.

Perkins, Bradford. *The First Rapprochement: England and the United States, 1795–1805*. Philadelphia: University of Pennsylvania Press, 1955. Notes that improved relations with England after Jay's Treaty influenced the foreign policy of the Adams and Jefferson administrations.

Stinchcombe, William C. *The XYZ Affair*. Westport, CT: Greenwood, 1981. A detailed account of the mission of Charles C. Pinckney, John Marshall, and Elbridge Gerry in Paris from their appointment in 1797 to the breakdown of negotiations after the bribe and loan demands.

Tucker, Robert T., and David C. Hendrickson. *Empire of Liberty: The Statecraft of Thomas Jefferson*. New York: Oxford University Press, 1992. Contains an excellent though brief account of Jefferson's perception of the XYZ Affair and his involvement in the subsequent crisis.

Elected president in 1800, Thomas Jefferson brought about what he felt was a revolution within the American political system. (Reproduced from the Collections of the Library of Congress)

10

The Revolution
of 1800

INTRODUCTION

By the election of 1800, a fairly well-defined two-party political system
had developed in the United States, evolving from the differences of
opinion that had surfaced during the campaign to ratify the Constitution
and from the policies of the Washington and Adams administrations,
particularly with regard to foreign policy. In general, the Federalist
party, that of George Washington, John Adams, and Alexander Hamilton, believed in a strong federal government closely tied to the rising
commercial establishment and to Great Britain. The Republican party
(sometimes called the Jefferson-Republican or Democratic-Republican
Party), which had developed out of the old Anti-Federalist faction, was
headed by Thomas Jefferson and James Madison and placed its faith in
an agricultural-based society and close relations with France, whose revolution, it was felt, gave it a kinship with the United States. Rivalry
between Federalists and Republicans could be fierce; during the campaign of 1800, a Federalist minister, Thomas Robbins, wrote in his diary:
"I do not believe that the Most High will permit a howling atheist
[Jefferson] to sit at the head of this nation." Robbins later recorded in
his diary, "In the morning we had news of the death of Mr. Jefferson. It
is to be hoped that it is true."

The rumor was, of course, not true, and in the presidential election of 1800, the Federalists nominated the incumbent John Adams and, as his running mate, Charles Coatesworth Pinckney; the Republicans named Thomas Jefferson and Aaron Burr. The main interest in the election centered around the split in the Federalist party between Adams and Alexander Hamilton. Hamilton, angry with Adams for bringing the Quasi-War with France to a close before he could attain military glory, plotted with certain electors from one Adams state to vote only for Pinckney, thus giving Pinckney more electoral votes than Adams and the presidency. But the ploy failed, and worse still, the Republicans, to Hamilton's surprise, won enough votes to capture the election.

But this was not the end of problems in this election. Jefferson and Burr each received 73 electoral votes (Adams had 66, Pinckney 65). According to the Constitution, the House of Representatives had to decide between the two men, both Republicans, by voting on the basis of states, with nine of the then 16 states needed to win. Burr, who should have known better, plotted with the disappointed Federalists, who controlled six states, to upset Jefferson. The first vote taken was eight for Jefferson, six for Burr, with two state delegations divided and not voting. This went on for 35 ballots, and finally, on the 36th, representatives from three states gave in, and Jefferson was elected. This nonsense brought about the Twelfth Amendment to the Constitution, which provided for separate ballots for president and vice president.

Jefferson liked to refer to his election as the Revolution of 1800, although it is hard in retrospect to see just why. There were no revolutionary or major changes of any kind on the part of the Constitution or the government. Jefferson sought no alteration in the fundamental law; he felt that any political objectives could be accomplished through the correct administration of the existing government. Possibly, the phrase "Revolution of 1800" has significance in Jefferson's belief that the republican triumph was a signal of the people wanting to govern themselves. He viewed the ideal United States as an enlarged agrarian society, a simple society based on the honest, hard-working farmer tilling his own little plot of land. He believed in a limited central government, with a well-defined division of power between the central and local governments. The national (or central) government should deal with foreign concerns, the local government with domestic matters. It is one of the ironies of history that Jefferson, as president, was guilty of all the abuses of power that he had accused the Federalists of and then some.

Pledged to economy, he nevertheless spent more in eight years than had been spent in the previous twelve. Pledged to maintain peace, he nevertheless fought the Barbary pirates and initiated the policies that led to the War of 1812. Pledged to ending the ties between business and government and usher in a laissez-faire policy, he nevertheless implemented an embargo that was a serious infringement on business and the right of an individual to an occupation. Jefferson's inconsistencies are one of his more interesting aspects; he wrote much about freedom, yet owned slaves; he lacked all the attributes of popularity—not very good looking, shy in crowds, a poor public speaker—but he remained popular, at least in his own party, throughout his presidency.

Still, historians who take Jefferson's belief in the idea of a "Revolution of 1800" seriously can marshal some evidence to support the assertion, particularly during Jefferson's first term. Jefferson's second term was plagued with the difficult events preceding the War of 1812 and for that reason does not represent as well his political program; his presidency was driven more by circumstances out of his control.

In the domestic arena, Jefferson and his Congressional leaders tried to undo as much of the Federalist agenda as possible. Although Jefferson had been vice president under the Federalist president John Adams, he was not in a position to influence Adams's policies. After 1801, however, he was president and had a sympathetic Congressional majority. Thus his administration, working with Congress, brought about the repeal of the obnoxious Alien and Sedition Acts passed during the XYZ Affair and pardoned those persons who had been convicted under their provisions. Congress did away with the various internal taxes that had been levied to pay for the Quasi-War with France and began the process of reducing the size of the army and navy and the amount of money appropriated for the armed services. Much of this work fell to Jefferson's Secretary of the Treasury, Albert Gallatin, a Swiss-born Republican who worked well with Congress. Gallatin persuaded Congress to repeal internal taxes to the extent that 90 percent of government revenue came from import taxes; his view was that if the people did not have to pay taxes during peacetime, they would be much less likely to object to them during times of war or other national emergencies.

Along with tax cuts, Gallatin also tried to cut government spending. Republicans felt that this was an easy target, since they believed that the Federalists had spent extravagantly during their years in power. As it turned out, that was not the case. Although Congress did trim military spending substantially, Gallatin found that there was little other waste in federal spending and that bureaucratic fraud was practically nonexistent.

Despite the tax cuts and an unexpected $15 million expenditure for the Louisiana Purchase, the national debt dropped from $80 million to $57 million during Jefferson's years as president. This was due less to Jefferson's policies than to the large profits American shippers earned during the early years of the century as the leading neutral traders in the world, a gift, in a sense, from the British, who allowed the trade to continue while they were embroiled in European conflict, since they were the main beneficiaries of it.

In another area of domestic politics, Jefferson was less successful in winning his way. In literally the last hours of his term, President Adams had appointed a large number of judges under the provision of the recently passed Judiciary Act of 1801. Since the Constitution provided lifetime tenure for well-behaved judges, it appeared that even though Republicans held the presidency and controlled Congress, Federalists would continue to be influential in the judiciary branch for many years to come. Consequently, the Republicans planned to repeal the Judiciary Act and thus abolish the judgeships it had created. But this raised a constitutional question: Was it constitutional to remove a judge by abolishing his job when the Constitution provided lifetime tenure? At this time, moreover, another question was equally relevant. Who decided what was constitutional? While some maintained that it was the responsibility of the courts to make this determination, many people disagreed strenuously, and the federal courts had never dealt with the issue.

The question was finally decided in the landmark Supreme Court decision in *Marbury* v. *Madison*. This case involved one of Adams's midnight appointees, Stephen Marbury, who brought suit against the Jefferson administration to force it to give him a legal document called a writ of mandamus that would allow him to take his seat on the bench as a justice of peace in Washington, D.C. In the decision, which Chief Justice John Marshall, another Adams appointee, wrote, Marbury was denied his writ because the court ruled that the part of the Judiciary Act of 1789 under which Marbury was claiming his writ was unconstitutional. The Jeffersonians had to settle for a Pyrrhic victory; they could keep Adams's midnight judges from their posts, but they had to accept the much larger (and to many, much more offensive) principle that the Supreme Court did indeed have the power to judge the constitutionality of Congressional acts.

The success of the Revolution of 1800 in the area of foreign affairs is harder to see, but certainly the Louisiana Purchase of 1803 represented a major accomplishment on the part of Jefferson, one that a Federalist administration would not have been likely to carry out. Jefferson and his supporters had always been more favorably disposed toward the French than the British, even with the embarrassments of the excesses of the French Revolution and the XYZ Affair. Soon after he became president, Jefferson was able to ingratiate himself with Napoleon by offering support to Napoleon's effort to suppress a revolution on Santo Domingo led by Toussaint L'Ouverture, whose mulatto background won him little sympathy in Virginia. Although Napoleon's efforts in Santo Domingo came to nought, Jefferson's professions of friendship no doubt helped make possible the sale of the entire Louisiana Territory to the United States in 1803, after Napoleon had decided he needed to raise cash for European wars.

The purchase of Louisiana challenged Jefferson's constitutional scruples, since there was no expressed power in the Constitution allowing the president to acquire territory. While some of his advisers said such authority was implicit in the fact of nationhood, Jefferson considered linking the sale with a constitutional amendment. But Napoleon seemed anxious to close the deal quickly, so the president threw caution to the wind and bought the land. Once done, the Louisiana Purchase agreement raised little protest, and much of the land itself was so remote that Americans reacted with indifference. With respect to the Revolution of 1800, however, the Louisiana Purchase represented a bold departure from the cautious and formal diplomacy of the Federalists during the preceding decade and demonstrated the pragmatic, commonsense mindset of Thomas Jefferson.

INTERPRETIVE ESSAY
Peter G. Felten

In 1819, Thomas Jefferson called the election of 1800 "as real a revolution in the principles of our government as that of 1776 was in its form." The former president proudly recalled his triumph in the most hotly contested election in the nation's short history. Jefferson's Republicans ousted the Federalists from power, launching more than two decades of

Jeffersonian domination of national politics. To Jefferson, this signaled the "revolution of 1800."

Despite Jefferson's boasts and his Republicans' achievements, many historians contend that 1800 represented more of an evolution than a revolution. These historians highlight the gradual changes undertaken by Jefferson as president. He maintained key portions of the Federalists' economic policies. Jefferson also, like his predecessors from the opposing party, interpreted the Constitution broadly to give the president substantial power. The election of 1800 changed the nation, but these historians insist that it cannot be compared to the revolution of 1776.

The different perspectives of Jefferson and modern historians explain their contradictory interpretations of the election. Jefferson remembered the fiery words of the opposing parties and the tense days when the election's outcome remained uncertain. Jefferson naturally compared 1776 and 1800, the two most decisive events in his public life. Historians, looking back 200 years, emphasize the long-term trends toward democracy, political party development, and presidential power. They more easily dismiss the outward appearance of change that swept the nation in 1800, focusing instead on the larger forces moving through U.S. history.

America in 1800 still had not fully emerged from the turmoil of rebellion and independence. The Constitution remained a relatively untested experiment; it had survived so far, but the failed Articles of Confederation also had lasted more than a decade before being replaced. Who could say the Constitution would not suffer the same fate? If this attempt at constitutional government collapsed, European powers prepared to exploit conflicts between the states. The success of the American Revolution remained very much in doubt.

Compounding these worries, competing political factions emerged during the 1790s. The Constitution's authors had not expected parties to arise. Many of the Founding Fathers feared that "factions," as they called the new political alliances, would destroy the country. James Madison, for instance, argued, "The violence of faction is the MORTAL disease under which popular governments everywhere perished." Factions represented only the narrow interests of a few people rather than the needs of the whole nation. For a republic like the United States to survive, it was widely agreed, honorable citizens would have to act for the common good. Rival factions had no place in this understanding of American politics. George Washington said as much in his last formal speech to the nation: "The common and continual mischiefs of the spirit of party are sufficient to make it the interest and duty of a wise people to dis-courage and restrain it."

Ironically, during the early 1790s these same men created what became the first national political parties. President Washington's cabinet of top advisers repeatedly divided over important issues, including the creation of a national bank and the funding of debts left over from the Revolutionary War. On one side of this debate stood Alexander Hamilton and John Adams, two leading Federalists. This party was strongest in New England. Federalists championed the cause of the rich and the powerful. Hamilton in particular argued that the national government could not survive without the support of the wealthy. Hamilton's successful effort to shore up the American credit rating directly benefited the rich. His advocacy of a national bank and of tariffs aimed to reward the powerful for backing the Constitution. The Federalists celebrated the wealthy because party members believed an elite ought to manage the country. This party held on to the traditional European view of a strict hierarchy governing society. Those at the top, Federalists contended, merited the respect and the deference of ordinary citizens. They alone should rule.

Thomas Jefferson, James Madison, and their allies led the opposition to the Federalists. This party, strongest in the South, became known as the Republican Party. Its leaders clung to the ideals of the Revolution, including a belief in the equality and rights of all free Americans. While the Federalists saw the need for a strong and active national government, Republicans favored a smaller, less centralized administration. The Jeffersonians, for example, worried that a national bank could dominate the economy, helping the rich but hurting the majority. This party called for policies that aided ordinary farmers. The Jeffersonian faith in regular citizens marked a dramatic difference from the Federalists' trust in the elite. The contrast between these newly forming factions went deeper than policy issues; it centered on their belief in the wisdom and virtues of the majority. Although Jeffersonians still excluded women, slaves, free blacks, and the poor from their definition of citizens, the Republicans advocated the expansion of governing power to include ordinary white men. In other words, the Federalists and the Jeffersonians squabbled over more than just minor policy issues. They disagreed fundamentally over who should control the United States.

The hostility between these groups became so intense that prominent members of each faction begged a reluctant George Washington to accept a second presidential term in 1792. Many politicians feared the nation could not survive an election. Washington acquiesced, but the political debate intensified. The parties became more organized and active during the 1790s. As Washington's retirement neared, tensions again rose over the dangers of competing factions in national politics.

The French Revolution gave Americans a regular dose of what they might expect if their republican experiment failed. Initially public sympathies in the United States supported the French rebels. The former British colonists believed the French would follow the American republican example. By the early 1790s, however, increasing numbers of Americans worried about the radicalism of the French revolutionaries. The rebels executed their king, banned Christianity, and waged a war against Great Britain.

Because of these excesses, Americans allied with the still-forming Federalist political faction that generally opposed the French revolutionaries. A leading Federalist declared: "The French Revolution has been, from the first, hostile to all right and justice." After France and England went to war, many Federalists considered the British to be the champion of order and Christianity in Europe. One Federalist, for instance, wrote that England was "fighting the battle of the civilized." With the stakes so high, Federalists dismissed the American rebellion against the British as ancient history. They demanded the United States resist French radicalism, even if it meant cooperation with, or at least toleration of, the British.

Jefferson and his allies, on the other hand, remembered the pains of British colonial rule and praised the French revolutionaries. The Jeffersonians at times frowned on French excesses, yet they viewed the rebels as the European model of the American Revolution. Across the United States, Republicans drank toasts to French "liberty" and condemned those in Europe and America who favored English-style "despotism." The issue raised such passions because the French rebels had challenged the old social order, replacing elite rule with government by the will of the people. The French conflict highlighted the different visions of the future held by the young political parties in the United States. Jeffersonians paralleled the French Revolution to the American Revolution, while Federalists saw it as a threat to the stability and structure necessary for civilization's survival.

In 1796, despite the bitter divisions in his country, President Washington announced his retirement. The United States then held its first contested presidential election. Federalists and Republicans vied for control of national politics. Under the Constitution, the candidate who finished first in the Electoral College balloting would be president, while the runner-up would be vice president. Each state chose its own electors, often by a vote in the state legislature. The competing parties restrained themselves during the campaign, largely out of respect for President Washington. When the votes were counted, the Federalist candidate John Adams narrowly had won the presidency. The vice president would be the leader of the opposing party, Thomas Jefferson. All was not well within the Federalist party, however. Before the Electoral College counted its votes, Alexander Hamilton had launched a secret plot to have the Federalists' vice presidential candidate, Thomas Pinckney, replace Adams at the top of the ticket. Hamilton's last-minute bid failed, but it angered Adams.

President Adams and Vice President Jefferson squabbled over issues large and small. Both men recognized that their many disputes served as a prelude to the 1800 presidential election. This contest held particular significance because it would be the first real referendum on the course of the nation since Washington's retirement. The 1796 election had been a cautious trial run; 1800 would be the real thing. If Adams won, the Federalists would solidify their control of national politics. If Jefferson triumphed, he and his allies could overturn Federalist policies and lead the nation in a new direction. For both sides the stakes were very high.

As the election neared, the crisis atmosphere became more intense. The 1798 Alien and Sedition Acts symbolized the growing divide between Federalists and Jeffersonians. President Adams and the Federalists in Congress enacted these laws to control what they saw as dangerous revolutionary tendencies. Many Federalists feared the political influence of exiles from recent European rebellions. To minimize the clout of immigrants, the Alien Act extended from five to fourteen years the time a person had to live in America before he or she could become a citizen. The new law also expanded the president's power to expel aliens from the country. This disturbed Jeffersonians because their party included many immigrants, but the Sedition Act troubled them much more. The Sedition Act banned "false, scandalous, and malicious" writing and speech that criticized the government or the president (the vice president, a Republican, could be criticized under this law). The Federalists had seen what rabble-rousers had done in France. They had no intention of letting their critics endanger the country's stability.

Jefferson and the Republicans denounced the Federalists' laws for illegally expanding the government's power and for violating the First Amendment to the Constitution. When zealous Federalist judges began handing out sentences under the Sedition Act, the controversy grew worse. Congressman Matthew Lyon of Vermont was fined and sent to prison for four months because he joked about Adams's "unbounded thirst for ridiculous pomp." Another judge convicted Thomas Cooper for trying "to mislead the ignorant and inflame their minds against the President and influence their votes in the next election." Outraged Republicans responded with the Kentucky and Virginia Resolutions. Critics of Adams in these two state legislatures adopted proclamations secretly written by Jefferson and Madison. The Kentucky and Virginia Resolutions insisted the Constitution was designed to maximize individual rights and to limit the power of the national government. The Alien and Sedition Acts, the resolutions argued, marked an illegal extension of presidential authority. Jeffersonians called for a smaller, decentralized government. They pointed to the Alien and Sedition Acts as evidence of a Federalist plot to destroy the Constitution. The Kentucky and Virginia Resolutions had little immediate impact on the nation, but their extremely strict interpretation of constitutional powers illustrated the anger many Jeffersonians felt about Federalist policies.

George Washington's death in 1799 freed the competing political factions to sharpen their attacks on each other. Respect for the former president had limited the appeal of formal parties, which he repeatedly had condemned. Washington's influence already had declined, but he remained a symbol of revolutionary glory and antiparty sentiment. With his death, politicians felt even less restraint. No matter how far they went, there was no danger Washington would come out of retirement to criticize their behavior. Sensing the new mood, Abigail Adams, the president's wife, predicted there would be enough political mudslinging in 1800 "to ruin & corrupt the minds and morals of the best people in the world."

Politicians attacked each other bitterly during the 1800 presidential campaign. Republicans accused President Adams of being an arrogant fool. Jeffersonians also said the Federalists favored conflict with France: "The friends of war will vote for Adams." Anti-Federalist newspapers even claimed that the president planned to marry one of his sons to the daughter of the British royal family. Taking this story to its logical conclusion, a Jeffersonian writer said the Federalists wanted their own king: "There is a monarchical party in the United States, and . . . Mr. Hamilton and Mr. Adams belong to that party."

When it came to making outrageous political charges, however, the Federalists far exceeded their Republican opponents. Federalists borrowed freely from the horrors of the French Revolution to taint their political enemies. They maintained that Jefferson hated Christianity, favored anarchy, and practiced all sorts of sexual perversities. "Consider the effects [of] the election of any man avowing the principles of Mr. Jefferson," claimed one Federalist. "The effect would be to destroy religion, introduce immorality, and loosen all the bonds of society." A Connecticut Federalist insisted that if Jefferson were to be elected, "There is scarcely a possibility that we shall escape a Civil War. Murder, robbery, rape, adultery, and incest will all be openly taught and practiced." A Federalist placard put it most succinctly: "GOD—AND A RELIGIOUS PRESIDENT" or "JEFFERSON—AND NO GOD!"

The hostility of the political rhetoric was not the only difference between the 1796 and the 1800 presidential elections. The Republicans used these four years to become a much better-organized party. Members caucused in every state, planning strategy and winning votes. At the same time, the Federalists had become weaker internally. Adams and Hamilton had been feuding since the end of Washington's presidency. The young, ambitious Hamilton had been Washington's closest adviser. When Adams became president, Hamilton resented his loss of power. Adams, on the other hand, envied Hamilton's influence over Washington. Even after he was elected president, Adams continued to doubt Hamilton's motives. Privately, Adams called Hamilton "a man devoid of every moral principle." Adams deliberately excluded his rival from an official position of power, yet Hamilton retained his clout as an informal adviser to many Federalists.

In 1799 Adams and Hamilton clashed over taxes, the size of the army, and the value of negotiations with France. Hamilton soon began plotting an independent strategy for the presidential campaign. Hamilton and his allies wanted a Federalist elected. They were determined, however, that President Adams not serve a second term. Hamilton knew his efforts would divide the Federalists. He launched his scheme on the assumption that the possibility of Jefferson's election would terrify Federalists enough to unite the party's internal divisions behind Hamilton's candidate. After surveying the political landscape, he decided to back General Charles Cotesworth Pinckney of South Carolina, whose brother Hamilton had supported in 1796. Hamilton knew he could shape Pinckney's policies, a major consideration for the ambitious schemer. However, Hamilton also chose Pinckney because he seemed to offer the best Federalist hope to unseat Adams while still carrying the majority in the Electoral College. Pinckney did not rank with Jefferson and Adams among the top figures in American politics, but from Hamilton's perspective he had some attractive attributes, including a solid reputation as a patriot based on his military service during the Revolution and his rejection of French extortion in the XYZ Affair. Pinckney's home state also made him appealing, since South Carolina appeared to be the most likely place for Federalists to crack the Jeffersonian hold on the southern states. For all these reasons, Hamilton mobilized his political forces behind Pinckney.

The most public aspect of Hamilton's assault on Adams came in a letter "Concerning the Public Conduct and Character of John Adams, Esq., President of the United States." Hamilton intended the letter only for Federalists, but a copy fell into Aaron Burr's hands. Burr, a leading New York Republican, guaranteed that it received attention across the country. In the letter, Hamilton charged that Adams suffered from "great and intrinsic defects in his character which [make him] unfit for the office of" president. Hamilton accused the president of "undermining" the government to the point where the nation might "totter, if not fall," upon Adams's re-election. Yet Hamilton maintained that despite Adams's faults, "I have finally resolved not to advise the withholding from him of a single vote." Instead, Hamilton urged Federalist electors to support both Adams and Pinckney. Hamilton secretly hoped a few Federalists would not favor Adams, allowing Pinckney to carry the election. Hamilton claimed to have reached his conclusions "reluctantly" after "careful observations" of Adams, but his indictment of the president guaranteed a wide division among Federalists. "We are broken to pieces," one Federalist despaired.

While the Federalists feuded, the Republicans won a crucial victory. Political observers agreed that New York could be decisive in the 1800 presidential contest. The Federalists carried the state in the previous election, gaining the votes necessary to triumph in the Electoral College. Unlike Federalist New England and the Jeffersonian South, however, neither party could be certain of controlling New York. Early in 1800, the ambitious Republican Aaron Burr helped his party win a crucial ballot in New York City. This victory assured the Republicans that they would carry New York's electors. The New York vote had more to do with local than with national concerns, but its impact was felt around the country. Burr's manipulation made the Jeffersonians the leading contenders in the presidential campaign. Burr also secured his party's nomination for the vice presidency.

State elections progressed through the autumn. State legislatures were the main battleground since they chose nearly two-thirds of electors in

1800, a larger number than four years earlier. Although the count in the Electoral College appeared to be close, Jeffersonians were confident that with New York in their column they would win in the end. The divided Federalists hoped Pinckney could bring South Carolina into their camp, but they were disappointed when the state followed its region and favored the Republicans.

When Electoral College votes officially were counted, the Republicans carried the day. Jefferson received 73 electoral votes while Adams tallied just 65. In the heated atmosphere of the election, however, the Jeffersonians made a major mistake. Since the Constitution declared that the candidate with the second most votes in the Electoral College would be the vice president, observers expected one Jeffersonian to cast his ballot for someone other than Aaron Burr. If that had happened, Jefferson would have 73 votes and Burr would have 72. Instead, Jefferson and Burr tied at 73 because no elector wasted his vote.

The Constitution stated that if the Electoral College failed to resolve the presidential election, the House of Representatives would choose the president. This complicated matters considerably. Republicans would dominate Congress after the representatives elected in 1800 took office, but that would not happen until March 1801. Until then, Federalists ran the House. Even though nearly everyone recognized that Jefferson should have won in the Electoral College, the Republicans' error gave the Federalists an opportunity to choose the next president.

Congress met in early 1801 for the next, unprecedented, stage of the 1800 election. Under the rules established in the Constitution, each state could cast just one vote for president in the House. If the majority of House members from a state agreed on a candidate, the state would vote for him. If the state's representatives could not reach a consensus, the state would not vote. To win the presidency in the House, a candidate had to be approved by a majority of the states.

Aaron Burr could have proclaimed his support for Jefferson, graciously accepting the vice presidency and resolving the problem rather easily. Burr, however, sent a letter to a supporter indicating that he would serve if elected president by the House. He later denied having written the letter, but by refusing to withdraw his candidacy, he in effect campaigned for the presidency. Burr apparently hoped Federalists would rally behind him as the best alternative to Jefferson. Federalists were delighted. They had been the divided party throughout 1800. Now, when the stakes were highest, the Republicans had fallen apart.

Federalists could not name just anyone president, however. Jefferson had the strong support of seven states in the House. That made him the leading candidate, yet he needed two more votes to triumph. Federalist schemers expected that if Jefferson failed to win in the early balloting, another candidate could surpass him. Most Federalists doubted they could get a member of their party elected, but they assumed that whomever they chose would owe them. They intended to collect on their political debts after the election. Even if a Republican like Burr were chosen by the House, Federalists assumed he would be a compromised and weakened president.

Jeffersonians reacted with scorn toward the plots hatched by the Federalists. The governors of Virginia and Pennsylvania, both staunch Republicans, threatened to send state troops to the Capitol if the House elected anyone but Jefferson. Republicans viewed the Federalists with contempt for seizing on their mistake to overturn the election's results. They saved their strongest hostility for Aaron Burr. The politician who had been their hero for bringing New York into the Republican camp now became their most hated enemy.

Despite the Jeffersonian outrage, the practical politics of the House meant that Federalists would select the next president. Federalist representatives were reluctant to select Jefferson, even if he deserved to win. The balloting stretched for days. The House voted thirty-five times without a resolution. "It is impossible to determine which of the two candidates will be chosen President," a commentator noted. "Rumors are various and intrigues great." As inauguration day approached, the most serious crisis in the nation's history gripped the Capitol. Huge, restless crowds gathered in Washington. Rumors of death threats against Federalists swept the streets. Mysterious fires burned two government buildings, leading to wild speculation about politically motivated arson. Fights broke out in the House gallery. Chaos seemed imminent.

Under intense pressure, Alexander Hamilton and a few of his Federalist allies made a difficult choice. "If there be a man in the world I ought to hate, it is Jefferson," Hamilton said. "With Burr I have always been personally well, but the public good must be paramount to every private consideration." Hamilton cast his support to Jefferson. In the end, Hamilton concluded Jefferson was an honorable man with dangerous ideas. Burr, on the other hand, was reckless and corrupt. Hamilton called him the "most unfit man in the United States for the office of President." Jefferson might lead the nation down the wrong path, the Hamiltonians decided, but a Burr presidency would endanger the Constitution. On February 17, the logjam in the House finally broke when several Federalists submitted blank ballots. By not voting for Burr, they permitted Jefferson to win previously deadlocked states. Jefferson carried ten states, one more than he needed. Burr won four states, making him vice president. Ironically, after the most bitterly partisan campaign in the nation's short history, Federalist votes secured Jefferson's election. Before the next election the Twelfth Amendment to the Constitution was drafted and ratified, creating separate presidential and vice presidential electoral ballots; never again would running-mates tie in the Electoral College.

Jefferson took the oath of office on March 4, less than two weeks after finally winning the presidency. His inaugural address aimed to heal some of the wounds left from the bruising campaign and the brutal fight in Congress. President Jefferson did not use revolutionary words. He did not chart a bold course for his party's first term in power. Instead, he made a conciliatory gesture to his opponents by saying, "We are all Republicans, we are all Federalists." Jefferson underscored the shared experiences and beliefs of Americans. This not only helped calm his defeated rivals but also reflected Jefferson's understanding of politics in the new nation. He considered the Republicans to be the rightful heirs of the American Revolution. Jefferson felt he was restoring the spirit of 1776, not replacing rule by one legitimate political party with a government led by another party. Shortly after his inauguration, Jefferson privately wrote: "I was always satisfied that the great body of those called federalists were real Democratic Republicans as well as federalists." To Jefferson, the Republicans stood for all Americans, not for the interests of a faction.

President Jefferson's understanding of his party came close to becoming reality. Many people reacted with horror to the crisis surrounding the 1800 election. The Federalists withered under the public's anger because cynical Federalists had ignored the intent of the Electoral College in their bid to defeat Jefferson. Additionally, the Federalists had squabbled among themselves during 1800; they emerged from the campaign both discredited and divided. Reflecting these problems, the Federalists lost roughly one-third of their seats in the House in the 1800 congressional elections. They never regained their majority. When Burr killed Hamilton in a duel in 1804, the Federalists' most effective leader died. The party faded over the next decade. By the presidential election of 1820, the Federalists had ceased to exist. As Jefferson had said in 1801, everyone was a Republican.

Although the Federalists largely destroyed themselves, President Jefferson's popular policies won over many of his old critics. Jefferson maintained the core of the Federalist economic program, including Hamilton's Bank of the United States. With the national economy growing, Jefferson decided to stay the course. Jefferson reduced the size of the military and applied the savings to the national debt, living up to his pledge to be "rigorously frugal and simple." The president also eliminated or let die unpopular laws that lingered from the Adams years, such as the Alien and Sedition Acts. Perhaps most important, Jefferson bought Louisiana from the French in 1803. The president privately worried that the Constitution did not permit the acquisition of new national territory. He considered proposing a constitutional amendment to overcome his legal qualms about the purchase. In the end, however, Jefferson decided he had to act quickly. Jefferson had criticized Federalists for loosely interpreting the Constitution, but now he shared their expansive view of national powers. He put aside his doubts and bought Louisiana, nearly doubling the nation's territory. Jefferson's flexible leadership earned the respect of many who had doubted him. His Republicans even temporarily united Americans across sectional boundaries, obscuring the significant differences between North and South.

Although Jefferson's presidency was not a revolution, his election in 1800 was revolutionary. In economics and diplomacy he followed the path established by Washington and Adams. Historians correctly highlight the significant continuities between Jefferson and his predecessors. However, Jefferson accurately labeled the 1800 election a "revolution." The peaceful transition of power between rival parties was a revolution in modern world history. In addition, Jefferson's victory in 1800 marked a fundamental shift in the prevailing vision of who ought to rule in America. A cultural and political revolution occurred when the elitist Federalists collapsed in favor of the more inclusive Republicans. Not only did that shift take place, but Federalists accepted and grudgingly ratified it. Jefferson's ideal of political equality among white men would become an American ideal during the next decades.

Still, this revolution was not without irony. Jeffersonians, after all, were strongest in the South, the home of slavery in the United States. The Republicans preached equality while strongly favoring slavery. Indeed, the additional Electoral College votes the South gained from the Constitution's Three-Fifths Compromise permitted Jefferson to win in 1800. The democratic revolution of 1800 could not have occurred without slavery. Jeffersonians may have been revolutionary for their time, but 1800 was a distinctly limited revolution.

SELECTED BIBLIOGRAPHY

Appleby, Joyce. *Capitalism and a New Social Order: The Republican Vision of the 1790s*. New York: New York University Press, 1984. Emphasizes the cultural and economic ideals of the Jeffersonians.

Banning, Lance. *The Jeffersonian Persuasion: Evolution of a Party Ideology*. Ithaca, NY: Cornell University Press, 1978. Crucial for understanding Jeffersonian thought in the 1790s.

Brown, Ralph Adams. *The Presidency of John Adams*. Lawrence: University Press of Kansas, 1975. A useful study of Adams's presidential administration.

Buel, Richard, Jr. *Securing the Revolution: Ideology in American Politics, 1789–1815*. Ithaca, NY: Cornell University Press, 1972. Emphasizes the influence of public opinion on politics.

Cunningham, Noble E., Jr. *In Pursuit of Reason: The Life of Thomas Jefferson*. Baton Rouge: Louisiana State University Press, 1987. A thorough, thoughtful, and relatively brief biography.

———, ed. *The Making of the American Party System, 1789–1809*. Englewood Cliffs, NJ: Prentice-Hall, 1965. A useful collection of primary source documents.

Elkins, Stanley, and Eric McKitrick. *The Age of Federalism: The Early American Republic, 1788–1800*. New York: Oxford University Press, 1993. A massive and important synthesis by two highly respected historians of the period.

Ferling, John. *John Adams: A Life*. Knoxville: University of Tennessee Press, 1992. An important biography that is sympathetic to Adams.

Fischer, David Hackett. *The Revolution of American Conservatism: The Federalist Party in the Era of Jeffersonian Democracy*. New York: Harper & Row, 1965. An influential profile of the Federalists.

Hoadley, John F. *Origins of American Political Parties, 1789–1803*. Lexington: University Press of Kentucky, 1986. Employs statistical analysis to conclude that by the 1790s parties existed in national politics.

Hofstadter, Richard. *The Idea of a Party System: The Rise of Legitimate Opposition in the United States*. Berkeley: University of California Press, 1970. An important study by a distinguished historian of American politics.

Johnstone, Robert M., Jr. *Jefferson and the Presidency: Leadership in the Young Republic*. Ithaca, NY: Cornell University Press, 1978. Uses political science methodology to demonstrate Jefferson's significance as president.

Kerber, Linda K. *Federalists in Dissent: Imagery and Ideology in Jeffersonian America*. Ithaca, NY: Cornell University Press, 1970. Contrasts Federalist and Republican cultural ideals.

Malone, Dumas. *Jefferson and the Order of Liberty*. Boston: Little, Brown, 1962. The most detailed exploration of Jefferson during the 1800 election.

McCoy, Drew R. *The Elusive Republic: Political Economy in Jeffersonian America*. Chapel Hill: University of North Carolina Press, 1980. Analysis of the ideas and public policies of the contending parties.

McDonald, Forrest. *Alexander Hamilton: A Biography*. New York: W. W. Norton, 1979. A sympathetic but fair biography.

Randall, Willard Sterne. *Thomas Jefferson: A Life*. New York: HarperPerennial, 1994. A solid examination of Jefferson's public and private life.

Sharp, James Roger. *American Politics in the Early Republic: The New Nation in Crisis*. New Haven, CT: Yale University Press, 1993. Emphasizes sectional and partisan conflict.

Sisson, Daniel. *The American Revolution of 1800*. New York: Alfred A. Knopf, 1974. Argues strongly that a revolution did occur with Jefferson's election.

Tucker, Robert W., and David C. Hendrickson. *Empire of Liberty: The Statecraft of Thomas Jefferson*. New York: Oxford University Press, 1990. The best analysis connecting Jefferson's diplomacy and politics.

Appendix A

Glossary

Austrian Succession, War of (1740–1748). A war pitting Austria, Great Britain, and Holland against Prussia, France, and Spain over who should claim the throne of the Holy Roman Empire after the death of Charles VI in 1740. Generally, British land and naval forces prevailed and the war ended with the Treaty of Aix-la-Chapelle in 1748, confirming the accession of Charles's daughter, Maria Theresa.

Bank of the United States (1791–1811). Located in Philadelphia, this bank was established following a proposal of Alexander Hamilton. It had an initial capital of $10 million and was a commercial bank, forbidden to deal in real estate or commodity trading, or to charge more than 6 percent interest on loans. The bank worked well for twenty years as a federal government bank and as a stabilizing influence on state banks. Its charter was not renewed in 1811 because of questions about its constitutionality.

Barré, Isaac (1722–1802). The son of a French refugee living in Ireland, Barré graduated from Trinity College, Dublin, in 1745, joined the army, fought, and was wounded in the French and Indian War. He entered Parliament in 1761 and opposed the Stamp Act, making him a hero in America and an enemy of George III.

Checkerberry. The name of any of several red berries but most commonly applied to the spicy red berry-like fruit of the wintergreen.

Emerson, Ralph Waldo (1803–1882). A writer, lecturer, and philosopher, Emerson was the chief architect of the transcendentalist movement in the 1830s. As such, he spoke and wrote that social reform must come from the hearts of individuals rather than from organized political efforts.

Frelinghuysen, Theodorus (1691–c. 1748). A Reformed Dutch minister, Frelinghuysen came to America in 1719 and lived and preached in New Jersey. The popularity of his revivals did much to bring the spirit of the Great Awakening to New Jersey and the surrounding area.

Fries, John (1750–1818). Born in Pennsylvania, Fries was a militia captain and auctioneer who gained notoriety by leading a group of Pennsylvania Germans in opposition to a federal property tax. Arrested and convicted of treason, Fries was sentenced to death but pardoned by President John Adams.

Hanoverian succession. This term refers to the royal family from the German principality of Hanover which assumed the British crown in 1714, after Queen Anne died, leaving no children. During the eighteenth century, the Hanoverian kings were George I (1714–1727), his son George II (1727–1760), and George II's grandson, George III (1760–1820).

Henry, Patrick (1736–1799). A lawyer, Henry was elected to the Virginia House of Burgesses in 1766. He helped organize the Committee of Correspondence in Virginia in 1773, served in both Continental Congresses, and was governor of Virginia from 1776 to 1779 and again from 1784 to 1786. He was a delegate at the Virginia ratification convention, where he opposed ratification of the Constitution because it did not contain a bill of rights.

Indentured servant. During colonial times, indentured servants were adult whites who were under contract (called an indenture) that obliged them to work for at least three years. Some were willing to do this in return for their passage to America, some were virtually kidnapped, and some were convicts. The practice was regulated by colonial governments and ended after the American Revolution.

Jacobite. This term refers to one who supported the royal house of Stuart after its exile from England in the Glorious Revolution of 1688–1689. Jacobites included Scottish Highlanders, who rose against the English in 1689, 1715, and 1745.

Jay's Treaty (1794). Negotiated by John Jay of New York, this treaty with Great Britain settled a number of issues left over from the American Revolution and its aftermath. It was prompted by problems arising from Britain's refusal to leave forts in the Old Northwest and barring

American ships from West Indian ports. In the treaty, the British agreed to evacuate the forts, while the Americans guaranteed payment of old debts left over from the Revolution. Nothing was done about maritime issues. The treaty was narrowly ratified in the Senate after stubborn Republican opposition.

King George's War (1742–1748). This was the American phase of the War of the Austrian Succession. The French tried to recapture Port Royal (called by the English Annapolis Royal) but failed, while the British captured Louisbourg, Nova Scotia, in 1745. The French and their Indian allies raided towns in what is now Maine, and the Iroquois Indians fought with the British against the French. The war ended with the Treaty of Aix-la-Chapelle, which returned Louisbourg to the French and restored America to the *status quo ante bellum.*

King Philip's War (1675–1676). This was a war between Indians living in New England, led by "King" Philip, and colonists of the region. The Indians frightened the colonists with their strategy of swiftly executed raids on Massachusetts towns, and the colonist counterattack failed because the Indians were too mobile. After a year and further losses, the colonists gained the advantage and killed Philip in August 1676. A peace treaty, providing for a prisoner-of-war exchange, was signed in April 1678.

King William's War (1689–1697). This was the American phase of the War of the League of Augsburg. It was fought between English and French forces on Hudson Bay and between the Iroquois and the French in the region of the St. Lawrence River. The French attacked the northern border in present-day New Hampshire, while the English captured Port Royal in 1690, only to lose it back to the French a year later. The war ended with the Treaty of Ryswick (1697), which restored the *status quo ante bellum* in North America.

Laissez faire. In economics, the theory of laissez faire postulates that the economy will perform most effectively when the state refrains from interfering in economic life.

Locke, John (1632–1704). An English political philosopher, Locke is best known for his work, *An Essay Concerning Human Understanding* (1690), dealing with what questions individuals were and were not capable of understanding. His work remained highly influential throughout the eighteenth and much of the nineteenth centuries.

Loudon, Lord John Campbell (1705–1782). A career army officer, Loudon was named commander-in-chief of British forces in America in 1756. He alienated the colonists by the illegal practice of billeting officers and by forcing an embargo on colonial trade. Militarily, his strategy failed to defeat the French despite an advantage in troop strength. After his failure to capture Louisbourg, he was recalled by William Pitt and reassigned to Portugal in 1762.

North, Lord Frederick (1732–1792). North entered Parliament in 1754 and served until his death. He rose in Tory circles, becoming chancellor of the exchequer in 1767 and prime minister in 1770. He was prime minister throughout the American Revolution era, resigning only after the British surrender at Yorktown.

Owen, Robert Dale (1801–1877). Born in Scotland, Owen came to the United States in the 1820s and was among the group that founded the Utopian community of New Harmony, Indiana. He was involved in various social reform movements and was a strong supporter of the emancipation of slaves.

Paine, Thomas (1737–1809). Born in England, Paine came to America in 1774, bearing letters of introduction from Benjamin Franklin. He became a free-lance journalist, and wrote *Common Sense* at the suggestion of Dr. Benjamin Rush, a colonial leader. Paine fought in the American Revolution until 1777, and then took a job with the Second Continental Congress. Later, he spent time in Europe promoting the design of an iron bridge he had invented and became a defender of the French Revolution. His criticism of George Washington ruined his reputation in the United States after his return in 1794.

Pinckney, Charles Cotesworth (1746–1825). Pinckney graduated from Christ Church College in 1764 and was admitted to the South Carolina bar in 1770. He was an aide to George Washington in the American Revolution until the British took him prisoner. He was exchanged in 1782, represented South Carolina at the Constitutional Convention in 1787, and was a delegate at the South Carolina ratification convention in 1788. Appointed minister to France in 1794, he was not recognized by the French government and became involved in the XYZ Affair. He was John Adams's vice-presidential running mate in 1800.

Pinckney, Thomas (1750–1828). The brother of Charles Cotesworth Pinckney and a graduate of Oxford University, Pinckney was admitted to the South Carolina bar in 1774. He fought in the American Revolution, serving under Lafayette at the battle of Yorktown. He was governor of South Carolina (1787–1788), president of the South Carolina ratification convention (1788), and a member of the state legislature (1791–1795). He negotiated Pinckney's Treaty with Spain in 1795; this treaty clarified the U.S.-Spanish border and gave the United States navigation rights on the Mississippi River. He was a vice-presidential candidate in 1796 and a member of the U.S. House of Representatives (1797–1801) and fought in the War of 1812.

Queen Anne's War (1702–1713). The American phase of the War of Spanish Succession, this conflict saw England and France fighting in North America only sporadically and inconclusively. An English expedition attacked the Spanish Florida town of St. Augustine in 1702, causing much damage, and other English forces captured Port Royal in 1710. The Treaty of Utrecht ended the war; the English received Newfoundland, Acadia, and Hudson Bay, while the French retained Cape Breton and the islands of the St. Lawrence River.

Rockingham, Marquis of [Charles Watson-Wentworth] (1730–1782). Rockingham became a member of the British House of Lords upon his father's death in 1750. He rose in Whig circles and generally opposed the policies of George III. He succeeded George Grenville as prime minister in 1765 and brought about the repeal of the Stamp Act. In 1782, he returned as prime minister following the resignation of Lord North, and worked on peace negotiations with the United States until his sudden death in July of that year.

Seward, William Henry (1801–1872). Governor of New York (1839–1843) and senator from the same state (1848–1861), Seward is best known as Secretary of State under Presidents Abraham Lincoln and Andrew Johnson (1861–1869), where he successfully prevented foreign intervention on the side of the Confederacy during the American Civil War and, in 1867, negotiated the purchase of Alaska from Russia.

Sons of Liberty. The Sons of Liberty were organizations founded in many colonies after the news of the Stamp Act reached America in 1765. Members drew up petitions, intimidated colonial agents, committed occasional acts of violence, and propagandized the issue, contributing to the repeal of the Stamp Act in 1766.

Stanton, Elizabeth Cady (1815–1902). A leading figure in the woman suffrage movement, Stanton attended the Seneca Falls convention (1848) that launched the drive for suffrage and worked toward that goal with Susan B. Anthony for many years as an organizer, lecturer, and writer.

Tennent, Gilbert (1703–1764). The son of William Tennent, Gilbert Tennent was a Presbyterian minister, ordained in 1726, who attracted a large following with his evangelism and dramatic preaching style. He was closely associated with George Whitefield and the Great Awakening.

Tennent, William (1673–1746). Born in Ireland, William Tennent came to America around 1717 and became an evangelical minister who helped prepare the way for the Great Awakening. His son, Gilbert, was a prominent figure in that movement.

Thoreau, Henry David (1817–1862). A New England writer and poet, Thoreau was important in the transcendentalist movement, dealing with those aspects of one's nature that do not relate to actual experience. Thoreau is best known for his essay *Walden*, on his experiment of living alone and being completely self-reliant.

Tory. The name given to a British political party (or one of its members) between 1630 and 1830. The Tory party is the forerunner of the present-day Conservative Party and was usually supported by the landed gentry and the Church of England. Pro-monarchy in its views, the Tory party was opposed by the *Whig* party of commercial interests and religious dissenters.

Westminster Confession. This was a statement of Calvinist faith written by the Westminster Assembly of Divines in the 1640s. With modifications, it is still the doctrinal basis of the Presbyterian Church in the United States.

Appendix B

Timeline

1701	Yale College founded
1704	Indians attack Deerfield, MA. Forty killed, 100 carried off
	Boston News Letter, first regular newspaper, started by John Campbell
1709	British and colonial troops capture Port Royal from the French
1712	Slave revolt in New York. Six committed suicide and twenty-one were executed
1716	First theater opens in Williamsburg
1732	Benjamin Franklin's *Poor Richard's Almanac* first published
1735	Peter Zenger's acquittal on libel establishes the right of freedom of the press
1740–41	Vitus Bering reaches Alaska
1741	Second slave revolt in New York. Thirteen hanged, 13 burned, and 71 deported
1744	British and colonial troops capture Louisbourg
1752	Benjamin Franklin establishes that lightning is electricity by flying kite in storm

1754	French and Indian War begins. French occupy Fort Duquesne (Pittsburgh)
1755	British move Acadian French from Nova Scotia to Louisiana
1759	British capture Quebec
1763	French and Indian War ends
1764	Sugar Act places duties on lumber, foodstuffs, molasses, and rum
1765	Stamp Act requires revenue stamps to help defray costs associated with French and Indian War
	Declaration of Rights passed by nine colonies opposing taxation without representation
1766	Stamp Act repealed
1767	Townshend Acts levy taxes on paper, glass, and tea
1770	Boston Massacre
	Townshend Acts repealed on all items except tea
1773	East India Company tea ships turned back in Boston, New York, and Philadelphia
	Boston Tea Party
1774	Intolerable Acts of Parliament curtail Massachusetts self-rule until tea dumped at tea party paid for
	First Continental Congress meets in Philadelphia
	Rhode Island abolishes slavery
1775	Patrick Henry delivers "give me liberty or give me death" speech
	Paul Revere's ride
	Minutemen fight British at Lexington
	Ethan Allen captures Fort Ticonderoga
	Battle of Bunker Hill
	George Washington named commander-in-chief
1776	France and Spain provide arms to Americans
	Declaration of Independence adopted
	Nathan Hale executed as spy
	Washington crosses Delaware River and defeats Hessians at Trenton
1777	Battle of Saratoga
	Articles of Confederation adopted
	France recognizes American independence

1778	France signs treaty of alliance with United States and sends fleet to aid Americans
1779	John Paul Jones defeats *Serapis*
1780	Charleston falls to the British
	Battle of Kings Mountain
	Benedict Arnold discovered to be a traitor
1781	Bank of North America founded in Philadelphia
	Cornwallis surrenders at Yorktown
1782	Preliminary peace treaty signed in Paris
1783	Massachusetts Supreme Court outlaws slavery
	Britain and United States sign Treaty of Paris
	Washington orders army disbanded
	Noah Webster publishes *American Spelling Book*
1784	Jefferson's proposal to ban slavery in new territories defeated
1787	Debt-ridden farmers stage Shays' Rebellion
	Northwest Ordinance adopted, setting up government for Northwest territories
	Constitutional Convention opens in Philadelphia
1788	Ratification of Constitution complete
1789	George Washington chosen first president
	First Congress meets in New York City
	Congress submits Bill of Rights to states for ratification
1790	Capital moved to Philadelphia
1791	Bill of Rights goes into effect
1792	U.S. Mint established in Philadelphia
	White House cornerstone laid
1793	Eli Whitney invents cotton gin
1794	Whiskey Rebellion in Pennsylvania
1795	United States pays tribute to Barbary pirates to ransom seamen
	North Carolina establishes first state university
1796	Washington's farewell address
1797	First two frigates built for navy
1798	Alien and Sedition Acts passed
	War with France threatened over raids on U.S. shipping

Appendix C

Population of Colonies and Selected Colonial Towns (in thousands)

Population of American Colonies, 1700–1790

	1700	1720	1740	1750	1770	1790
Connecticut	26.0	58.8	89.6	111.3	183.9	238.0
Delaware	2.5	5.4	19.9	28.7	35.5	59.0
Georgia	n/a	n/a	2.0	5.2	23.4	83.0
Maryland	29.6	66.1	116.1	141.1	202.6	320.0
Massachusetts	55.9	91.0	151.6	188.0	235.3	379.0
New Hampshire	5.0	9.4	23.3	27.5	62.4	142.0
New Jersey	14.0	29.8	51.4	71.4	117.4	184.0
New York	19.1	36.9	63.7	76.7	162.9	340.0
North Carolina	10.7	21.3	51.8	73.0	197.2	394.0
Pennsylvania	18.0	31.0	85.6	119.7	240.1	434.0
Rhode Island	5.9	11.7	25.3	33.2	58.2	69.0
South Carolina	5.7	17.0	45.0	64.0	124.2	249.0
Virginia	58.6	87.8	180.4	231.4	447.0	747.6
All colonies	250.9	466.2	905.6	1,170.8	2,148.1	3,929.2

Population of Selected Colonial Towns, 1700–1790

	1700	1720	1742	1760	1775	1790
Boston	6,700	12,000	16,382	15,631	16,000	18,300
Charleston	2,000	3,500	6,800	8,000	12,000	16,300
Newport	2,600	3,800	6,200	7,500	11,000	6,700
New York	5,000	7,000	11,000	18,000	25,000	33,100
Philadelphia	5,000	10,000	13,000	23,750	25,000	42,444

Source: U.S. Department of Commerce, *Historical Statistics of the United States: Colonial Times to 1970*. Washington, D.C.: Government Printing Office, 1975

Index

About the Editors and Contributors

THOMAS CLARKIN is a graduate student in American history at the University of Texas at Austin. His research interests include the Civil Rights Act of 1968 and federal Indian policy during the Kennedy and Johnson administrations.

PETER G. FELTEN is chair of Liberal Arts at Tulsa Community College. He received a Ph.D. in history from the University of Texas. He has authored a book on the 1965–1966 U.S. intervention in the Dominican Republic and has published widely on topics in Caribbean and U.S. history. His current research analyzes the connections between political and religious activism in U.S. history.

JOHN E. FINDLING is professor of history at Indiana University Southeast. He earned his Ph.D. at the University of Texas and is the author of *Dictionary of American Diplomatic History* (1980, 1989); *Close Neighbors, Distant Friends: United States–Central American Relations* (1987); and *Chicago's Great World's Fairs* (1995). With Kimberly D. Pelle, he edited *Historical Dictionary of World's Fairs and Expositions, 1851–1988* (1990) and *Historical Dictionary of the Modern Olympic Movement* (1996), and with Frank W. Thackeray, he edited *Statesmen Who Changed the World* (1993) and the other volumes in the *Events That Changed the World* and *Events That Changed America* series.

RICK KENNEDY is associate professor of history at Point Loma Naza-rene College in San Diego. He received his Ph.D. from the University of California at Santa Barbara and is the author of *Aristotelian and Cartesian Logic at Harvard* (1995). His current research deals with the history of logic from Aristotle to modern times.

CARL E. KRAMER is vice president of Kramer Associates, Inc., a public historical consulting firm, and adjunct lecturer in history at Indiana University Southeast. He received his Ph.D. from the University of Toledo and is the author of *Capital on the Kentucky: A 200-Year History of Frankfort and Franklin County* (1986) and *Pride in the Past, Faith in the Future: A History of the Michigan Livestock Exchange* (1997). A former president of the Kentuckiana Association of the United Church of Christ, he has a special interest in that denomination's history.

THOMAS C. MACKEY divides his time between Louisville, Kentucky, where he is an associate professor of history and an adjunct instructor in law at the University of Louisville, and Long Island, New York. He completed his undergraduate studies at Beloit College and his doctoral studies at Rice University. Constitutional, legal, and political issues are his specialties.

HENRY E. MATTOX retired from the U.S. Foreign Service in 1980 after twenty-four years of service, most of it abroad. Since that time, he has earned a doctorate in U.S. history from the University of North Carolina at Chapel Hill and has engaged in teaching and writing. Among his publications are *Twilight of Amateur Diplomacy* (1989) and *Army Football in 1945* (1990). Currently he teaches at North Carolina State University in Raleigh and edits the Internet journal *American Diplomacy*.

THOMAS A. PRASCH is assistant professor of history at Washburn College. He received his Ph.D. in British history from Indiana University, where he was the film review editor for the *American Historical Review*. He has done extensive research and writing on the history of British photography and on British world's fairs.

DONALD A. RAKESTRAW is associate professor of history at Georgia Southern University. Specializing in U.S. diplomatic history, he is the author of a number of works, including *For Honor or Destiny: The Anglo-American Crisis Over the Oregon Territory* (1995), and, with Howard Jones, *Prologue to Manifest Destiny: Anglo-American Relations in the 1840s* (1997).

STEVEN E. SIRY is associate professor of history at Baldwin–Wallace College. He received his Ph.D. from the University of Cincinnati. His publications include articles in the *Journal of the Early Republic, Locus, Statesmen Who Changed the World* (1993), and *Events That Changed America in the Nineteenth Century* (1997).

FRANK W. THACKERAY is professor of history at Indiana University Southeast. He received his Ph.D. from Temple University. He is the author of *Antecedents of Revolution: Alexander I and the Polish Congress Kingdom* (1980) as well as articles on Russian–Polish relations in the nineteenth century and Polish–American relations in the twentieth century. With John E. Findling, he edited *Statesmen Who Changed the World* (1993) and the other volumes in the *Events That Changed the World* and *Events That Changed America* series. He is a former Fulbright scholar in Poland.

JULIA A. WOODS is a Ph.D. candidate in history at the University of Texas at Austin. She has an M.A. in history from the University of Texas and a law degree from the University of North Carolina at Chapel Hill. She is currently researching her dissertation, tentatively titled, "Not Yet Sharks: Antebellum Southern Lawyers."